D1551684

# Managed Care Contracting

*A Guide for Health Care Professionals*

**Wendy Knight**
President
Knight Communications
and Consulting
Vergennes, Vermont

AN ASPEN PUBLICATION®
Aspen Publishers, Inc.
Gaithersburg, Maryland
1997

Library of Congress Cataloging-in-Publication Data

Knight, Wendy.
Managed care contracting : a guide for health care professionals / Wendy Knight.
p. cm.
Includes bibliographical references.
ISBN 0-8342-0883-0 (hardbound)
1. Managed care plans (Medical care)—United States.
2. Medical care—Contracting out—United States.   I. Title.
RA413.5.U55K65   1997
362.1'01258–dc21
97-12838
CIP

Orders: (800) 638-8437
Customer Service: (800) 234-1660

**About Aspen Publishers** • For more than 35 years, Aspen has been a leading professional publisher in a variety of disciplines. Aspen's vast information resources are available in both print and electronic formats. We are committed to providing the highest quality information available in the most appropriate format for our customers. Visit Aspen's Internet site for more information resources, directories, articles, and a searchable version of Aspen's full catalog, including the most recent publications: **http://www.aspenpub.com**
**Aspen Publishers, Inc.** • The hallmark of quality in publishing
Member of the worldwide Wolters Kluwer group.

Editorial Resources: Ruth Bloom

Library of Congress Catalog Card Number: 97-12838
ISBN: 0-8342-0883-0

Printed in the United States of America
1  2  3  4  5

*To my beautiful daughter, Alexandra,*
*whose intelligence, determination,*
*and spirit I admire greatly.*

# Table of Contents_____

# Contributors

**Michael J. Alper**
President
Meridian Health Care
   Management, LP
Thousand Oaks, California

**Kim Bellard**
Executive Director
Prudential Health Care
Cincinnati, Ohio

**Michael J. Benenson**
President
Benenson & Associates
Woodland Hills, California

**Dolores M. Blanco**
Executive Vice President
Meridian Health Care
   Management, LP
Thousand Oaks, California

**Raymond R. Girouard,
   MHA, FACMPE**
Managed Care Director
MedPartners of Virginia
Alexandria, Virginia

**Alan Gnessin, Esq.**
Partner
Gnessin & Waldman
Washington, D.C.

**Richard A. Gold**
Consultant
Towers Perrin Integrated
   HealthSystems Consulting
San Francisco, California

**Steve Gutman**
Senior Consultant
Advanced Health Corporation
Tarrytown, New York

**John S. Hoff, Esq.**
Washington, D.C.

**Donald H. Hutton, FACHE**
Founder and President
Morgan Consulting Group
Atlanta, Georgia

**John L. McDonald, MS, MPH**
President
McDonald & Company
Avon, Connecticut

**Kathi S. Patterson, FSA, MAAA**
Actuary
Milliman & Robertson, Inc.
Seattle, Washington

**Edward P. Potanka, Esq.**
Assistant General Counsel
CIGNA Corporation
Bloomfield, Connecticut

**Nancy L. Reaven**
Principal Consultant
Reaven Consulting Group
La Canada, California

**Richard B. Ryan**
President
Dental Management Decisions
Lake Forest, California

**Lisa A. Sansone**
President
Nutmeg Consulting
Wethersfield, Connecticut

**Kenneth W. Schafermeyer, PhD**
Associate Professor
St. Louis College of Pharmacy
St. Louis, Missouri

**Philip A. Shelton, MD, JD, FACS, FCLM**
Partner
Shelton & Shelton
West Hartford, Connecticut

**Eric Sorkin, RPh**
Vice President, Provider Relations
Express Scripts, Inc.
Maryland Heights, Missouri

**C. Joël Van Over, Esq.**
Counsel
Swidler & Berlin
Washington, D.C.

**Peggy M. Vargas**
Director, Administrative Services
Dental Management Decisions
Lake Forest, California

**M. Toni Waldman, Esq.**
Partner
Gnessin & Waldman
Washington, D.C.

**Vance J. Weber, MD, FACC**
President, Mid-Atlantic Cardiology, PA
President, Cardiology First of New Jersey, PA
Springfield, New Jersey

**Richard M. Weinberg, MD**
President and Chief Executive Officer
Morristown Memorial Physician Hospital Organization, Inc.
Morristown, New Jersey

**Ross Wetsel, DDS**
President and Chief Executive Officer
Grant/Moana Dental Offices
Reno, Nevada

**Beth Winter**
Senior Director, Provider
  Relations
NYLCare Health Plans of the
  Mid-Atlantic, Inc.
Greenbelt, Maryland

**Ruth Zachary, MSW, CSW**
Executive Director
West Park Medical Group, PC
New York, New York

# Foreword

There was a time when the only contract a health professional made was with a patient. It was a simple contract; a service was provided, and payment in some form was made directly by the patient. In the early part of this century, health services, particularly those provided by physicians, were not accessible to everyone. For many, they were available only in times of severe illness or injury and then often only through public facilities. Sometime after the great Depression, new mechanisms of "social insurance" were introduced to provide secure financing for health care. This added a third party to the professional-patient relationship. Two different approaches emerged to stabilize the economic certainty for both clinician and patient. One, indemnity insurance, paid most of the fee that was charged for each service rendered. The other, prepaid group insurance, now known as managed care, paid a fixed total amount in advance to a group or foundation for all services. Each approach had pluses and minuses, proponents and opponents, and evolved a separate set of rules to complicate the professional-patient relationship.

We are now somewhere in the middle of a convulsive transition in health services delivery and financing and must deal simultaneously with the strengths and weaknesses of both traditional insurance and managed care. Over the years, each approach has evolved into a spectrum of contractual relationships between purchasers, insurers, professionals, and patients. At every point on that spectrum, physicians and other professionals must deal with a different set of obligations, rules, and payment methods. Since most of the funding for health services flows through these multiple financing channels, few practitioners can afford the luxury of working with only one source; therefore, we must master many for economic success. That is one reason why this book is a practical guide to professional survival in this period of practice in transition.

So, what are we transitioning to? As practitioners, we are still searching for the ideal payer-professional relationship: a fair, simple, efficient financing mechanism that supports the integrity of the professional-patient relationship, as well as the cost and quality outcome expected by the purchaser and the patient. Managed care gets us closer to this ideal but with a new set of side effects and unintended complications. While we might be tempted to condemn and abandon managed care, we recognize the familiarity of the situation. Clinically, continued symptoms and complications must be endured, managed, and mitigated until the next improvement in treatment is found. Physicians must not expect one breakthrough penicillin-like solution to redefine how we finance and contract for professional services.

But fatalistic acceptance of managed care's complexity by professionals and health plan contractors is not an option either. Managed care has changed forever how we finance and organize health care, and how we compensate health professionals. At its best, managed care has maintained or improved the quality of care while significantly reducing cost. It will not and should not go away, but it cannot remain as it is.

The health system and professional contracting will evolve incrementally, not by dramatic breakthrough, however. This realization presents both a challenge and an opportunity for health professionals. How can health plans help clinicians reduce cost while supporting improvements in clinical quality without intruding too much in the relationship with the patient? Can we find a method to align physician incentives without creating fear that under-utilization of service is done to create profits? Can we effectively educate health plan members to support evidence-based practice and contracting? If we intend to better define the payer-professional-patient relationship, it may be only after things get more complicated and frustrating. Thoughtful and constructive critique by health plans, health care professionals, and patients is necessary. Knowledge and understanding of the current managed care contracting realities is a baseline for pursuing this continuous evaluation and search for improvement.

*Managed Care Contracting* provides an essential technical guide to professional survival in an increasing competitive environment. It is a comprehensive summary of the complex world of professional contracting in managed care and contributes greatly to the practitioner's understanding and knowledge.

*Patrick H. Mattingly, MD*
*Senior Vice President*
*Harvard Pilgrim Health Care*
*Brookline, Massachusetts*

# Preface _____

I vividly remember the first managed care contract I negotiated. Just two months after graduating from college and one week after starting my new job, I was sent by my health plan employer to contract with a pharmacy in East Los Angeles—armed only with a standard pharmacy contract, some sample plan designs, and a vague understanding of managed care. I briefly explained how the program worked and gave the pharmacist the reimbursement rate; he asked what a member's I.D. card looked like and where to send his claims. Then he signed the contract. No proposal, counter-offer, or negotiation, not even a question about the contract terms, just an exchange of basic—and clearly incomplete—information between two individuals not well prepared and remarkably ignorant of the implications of the transaction we had just completed.

Several years and markets later, I have seen minor changes in the way some health plans and providers approach contract negotiations. Managed care plans create network development or physician recruitment strategies infrequently and they seldom train their contracting staff adequately. Although many physicians and other health care providers negotiate contracts with managed care companies, either themselves or through an administrative agent, few approach contract negotiations with a complete understanding of the process or a strategic purpose or approach to participation in managed care networks.

*Managed Care Contracting* intends to better prepare individuals for contract negotiations by: (1) examining the processes and deliberations involved in developing a provider network, (2) offering strategic considerations for contract negotiations, and (3) providing tools to evaluate contracts and their financial and operational impact. Because the book offers this information in a detailed, organized, and readable manner, it is equally useful to those new to managed care contracting and those with a fair amount of experience.

*Managed Care Contracting* is designed as a valuable reference guide for physicians, dentists, pharmacists, ancillary care providers, ambulatory care facilities, home health care companies, medical group administrators, IPA executives, health plan managers, and other health care professionals involved in developing and negotiating managed care contracts. It does not address contract negotiations between managed care plans and hospitals, rehabilitation centers, and other facilities, except to the extent these entities are part of integrated delivery systems or other provider organizations discussed in the book. Although *Managed Care Contracting* discusses the fundamental steps involved in contract negotiations, it is not an introductory book on managed care. It assumes the reader has a basic knowledge of managed care.

The chapters are authored by consultants and attorneys with significant experience in managed care, and in particular, provider network development and contract negotiations. Each chapter is followed by a separate, shorter piece written by a health care professional representing a provider organization or health plan. The "Comments from the Field" sections give the reader an individual's unique perspective of some aspect of managed care contracting and a sense of how other provider groups or health plans approach this complex and often contentious process.

The first four chapters of *Managed Care Contracting* address the basic elements of contracting, from understanding how the process works to negotiating the contract and reviewing contract language and financial terms. These chapters offer a thorough discussion of all aspects of the contracting process and provide detailed information on how to establish and evaluate such arrangements. The next five chapters discuss contracting issues pertaining to specific providers: provider groups, specialists, ambulatory and ancillary care providers, pharmacists, and dentists. These chapters focus on the unique considerations of these providers as they negotiate with managed care plans. The final two chapters review the regulatory and antitrust aspects of managed care contracting. Although a summary of the law can seem tedious for non-lawyers, Chapters 10 and 11 present concise and engaging discussions of the important legal considerations of contract negotiations.

A contract is the basis for a health care professional's participation in a managed care plan. As managed care becomes the dominant way to deliver health care across the country, more physicians and other health care providers will continue to join managed care plans. Consequently, it is crucial for those involved to acquire a thorough knowledge of the contracting process and pursue a thoughtful approach to contract negotiations.

# Acknowledgments_____

First and foremost, I thank my colleagues who contributed to this volume. Their experience in managed care contracting is unsurpassed and I am fortunate that they found time in their busy schedules to impart their vast knowledge. I am particularly grateful to John McDonald whose continual assistance enabled me to complete the manuscript on time.

Steve LaRose, Jack Bruggeman, and Bob Howard at Aspen Publishers were instrumental in the development and publication of the book. I have benefited from their wisdom and helpfulness throughout the long bookmaking process. I thank Sam Havens for offering useful suggestions about the content and structure of the book.

Various colleagues and mentors have offered me abundant opportunities to learn continually about managed care contracting, especially Roberta Holtzman, Amy Knapp, Sharon Dunn, Mike Stocker, and Chan Wheeler. I have been very fortunate to work with these individuals. My first editor, Ligeia Fontaine, taught me the essentials of writing and editing and I will always be grateful to her for that.

Cindy Ringer was reliable, diligent, and enduring—essential traits for an administrative assistant, particularly on a project of this nature. Her assistance in preparing this book was invaluable and I am indebted to her as a result. Finally, I thank Ken for his editorial comments and steadfast patience and encouragement.

# 1

# Understanding Managed Care Contracting

*Wendy Knight*

## CHANGES IN THE MARKETPLACE

Without question, today's health care marketplace is vastly different than the marketplace of ten, or even two, years ago. Traditional providers, payers, and purchasers of care are being replaced by consortiums, alliances, and newly merged entities that scarcely resemble their earlier configurations. The integration and consolidation in the health care marketplace are blurring conventional notions of managed care plans and products. Indeed, in fully integrated markets there are no discernible distinctions between providers and managed care organizations (MCOs). The following four recent developments have most impacted the shape of the contemporary health care maketplace.

### Product Diversification

To remain competitive or gain market dominance, MCOs diversify their health benefit offerings. Designing new products enables MCOs to appeal to broader markets and satisfy the mercurial demands of the market. As health maintenance organizations (HMOs) offer point-of-service (POS) plans and administrative services only (ASO) products, and preferred provider organizations (PPOs) develop gatekeeper PPOs, the traditional organizational types erode.

### Merger and Acquisition

With escalating pace, health insurance companies are merging with HMOs, HMOs are purchasing PPOs, physician practice management companies are acquiring large medical group practices, and hospital

1

systems are attempting to buy all types of MCOs, further eliminating the differentiations between providers and payers.

## Medical Practice Integration

The rapid growth of managed care has fostered the integration of physicians, hospitals, and other health care providers. There are innumerable combinations of provider networks and alliances today. They include specialists who are creating specialty contracting organizations and joining physician-hospital organizations (PHOs), PHOs that are forming PHO alliances, and primary care physicians (PCPs) who are joining staff-model HMOs. Such provider integration often shifts the balance of power in favor of providers and forces MCOs to modify their contracting strategies and expectations.

## Employer Ascension

In the past decade, many employers have become dissatisfied with the ability of MCOs to stem rising health care costs, account for expenditures, define or measure quality care, or prove their value. Consequently, many employers have developed their own plans by contracting with physician and hospital networks directly or through consortiums of employers.

The present integration of the market makes it difficult to categorize the primary participants in managed care contracting; however, it is useful to understand the definitions and distinctions of MCOs, as vague as they may be, to develop a reference point from which to comprehend the market changes and how they alter the managed care contracting process.

## DEFINING A MANAGED CARE ORGANIZATION

MCOs combine the financing and delivery of health care services and are characterized by the following:

- arrangements with physicians, hospitals, and other health care professionals to provide a defined set of health care services to members;

- criteria and processes for selecting and monitoring health care providers;
- programs and systems to gather, monitor, and measure data on health services utilization, physician referral patterns, and other quality and performance measures;
- incentives or requirements for members to use providers and procedures associated with the plan;
- activities aimed at improving the health status of members; and
- incentives for providers to encourage the appropriate use of health care resources.[1]

MCOs market and sell their health benefit products to purchasers—employers, employer coalitions, associations, government agencies, labor unions, individuals, and other entities that are financially responsible for offering health benefit coverage to a select group of people. A purchaser becomes a client of the MCO and, when enrolled in the plan, the purchaser's employees, retirees, and dependents become the MCO's "members." The MCO is legally obligated to provide a set of benefits to these members at specific dollar or percentage levels.

## ORGANIZATIONAL FORMS

Changing distinctions of MCOs aside, a discussion of the types of organizations that sponsor market managed care programs is useful in understanding the diverse contracting relationships that MCOs and providers construct. To negotiate successful contracts, it is imperative for physicians and physician organizations to be familiar with the divergent contractual arrangements and processes that exist.

### Health Insurance Companies

Within recent years, traditional health insurance companies have entered the managed care market by forming subsidiaries or separate business units to develop and market managed care products. For example, several of the independent Blue Cross and Blue Shield plans have created separate managed care divisions or for-profit subsidiaries in the hope of converting their huge indemnity market share into managed care enrollees.

Many health insurance companies continue to maintain their sizable indemnity business and consider managed care divisions as a way to offer a continuum of health care products. Others have undergone major corporate reengineering in every aspect of their business—operations, systems, personnel, products, philosophy—to become MCOs. Health insurance companies may operate an HMO as a separate product line (or "lines" for those with Medicare-risk and Medicaid products) or sell managed care products, such as PPOs, POS plans, or other hybrid arrangements, through an existing insurance license. Many health insurance companies pursue multiple strategies depending on the particular market conditions.

## Health Maintenance Organizations

HMOs are most commonly associated with managed care. HMOs are organizations that offer the integration of financing and delivery of health care service to members. As with other MCOs, the distinctions among HMO models are fading. A recent report showed that 55 percent of the HMOs identified as staff and group models used a variety of arrangements with providers (thus, actually mixed models).[2]

*Staff Model*

In a staff-model HMO, physicians are salaried employees and provide care primarily to members enrolled in the HMO. However, in response to competitive pressures for low administrative costs, some staff-model HMOs are contracting with PPOs and other MCOs (though usually not with other HMOs) in selected markets to function as participating providers in competitor networks. Only 44 percent of group and staff models surveyed stated that their members accounted for most of the patient base of their physicians' practices.[3] Group Health of Puget Sound is an example of a staff-model HMO.

*Group Model*

Traditionally, this model consisted of a large physician practice that contracted on an exclusive basis with the HMO to provide comprehensive benefits to the HMO's enrollees. (Because of the exclusive nature of the group model arrangement, group and staff models are often confused.) Both group and staff-model HMOs are beginning to augment their staff (or principal) physicians with contracted community physicians. Kaiser is the most well known group model.

### *Independent Practice Association Model*

Independent practice association (IPA) model HMOs contract with individual physicians or associations of physicians (referred to as IPAs) who practice in their own offices, either as solo practitioners or small group practices. Some IPA-based HMOs that contract with individual physicians directly (rather than IPAs) are called direct contracting models. Because of the rapid integration and consolidation of medical practices, IPA models are becoming network (or mixed) models by default. United HealthCare of Texas and Oxford Health Plans are primarily IPA-model HMOs.

### *Network Model*

Network models often refer to HMOs that use a variety of contractual arrangements with providers or that contract with several multispecialty groups or IPAs. Contrary to the IPA model, the network model often structures relationships with larger medical groups, not individual physicians or small practices. Pacificare and Humana Medical Plan of South Florida are network models.

These represent traditional definitions of HMO models. In reality, the rapid changes and demands of the marketplace are blurring the distinctions among HMO types. To remain competitive and responsive, HMOs are adapting organizational structures and plan characteristics, including contractual arrangements with providers, based on local market requirements. For example, in some markets, a national or regional HMO may operate a group-model HMO, whereas in another, the market dynamics may tolerate only an IPA model. Moreover, the changing physician marketplace alters the characteristics of HMO models. As physicians abandon solo practice in favor of large group practice, and staff-model HMOs contract with community physicians, the differences among HMO models become even less obvious and relevant.

## Preferred Provider Organizations

PPOs are broad networks of hospitals, physicians, and other health care providers. Members have health care coverage when they access care from network or non-network providers. When seeking care from the network, members are responsible for a co-payment and are not required to select a PCP or obtain authorization to receive specialty care.

Among other entities, PPOs are owned and operated by employers, health insurance companies, hospitals, and independent investors. In contrast with many HMOs, PPOs are enlarging their provider panels. In 1994, PPOs contracted with an average of approximately 6,000 physicians; this is an increase from an average of 4,900 physicians in 1993.[4] The predominant form of payment for physicians in a PPO is fee-for-service, although some PPOs are beginning to negotiate risk-sharing arrangements with providers.

### Integrated Delivery Systems

Integrated delivery systems (IDSs) are groups of hospitals, physicians, and other health care professionals and facilities that provide the full spectrum of health care services under one legal structure.

More recently, the term has been identified with newly formed entities of physicians and hospitals developed largely in response to the growing dominance of MCOs. Some integrated systems employ physicians, hospitals, and other health care professionals. Employment relationships often characterize IDSs formed by academic medical centers or larger hospital systems. IDSs also can be joint ventures or other legal arrangements created to gain greater leverage in highly penetrated managed care markets.

### Self-Insured Employers or Coalitions

Employers who self-insure for their health benefit costs assume the financial risk of paying for employee medical claims. Some of these self-insured employers (or groups of employers) develop their own managed care programs. Rather than purchase a managed care product from an existing MCO, they elect to create their own plan based on fundamental managed care features, such as a network of physicians and utilization management controls. These employers or coalitions may retain a benefits consulting firm or create an in-house unit to establish and manage the plan.

## PRODUCTS AND SERVICES

To meet the challenges of today's health care purchaser and to stay competitive in today's changing environment, MCOs are offering an array of managed care products. Often, managed care programs developed for different populations are called "product lines" or "products." This diversification can be challenging for the physicians and provider organizations participating in the managed care networks.

## Closed Panel Plans

The traditional HMO is a closed panel product, that is, members do not have health coverage when using non-panel providers. The exclusive provider organization (EPO) is another closed panel product. It combines elements of HMOs and PPOs. Under an EPO health benefit option, a member has access to a network of physicians and health care providers. As with a PPO, the member does not select a primary care physician (PCP) upon enrollment in the plan or an authorization from a PCP to see physicians for non-primary care services. Similar to an HMO, the member does not have coverage if he or she elects to see a health professional outside the network. The majority of EPOs are developed and managed by independently-owned PPOs.

## Open-Access PPOs

An open-access PPO is the conventional benefit design of a PPO. The member has health coverage when using network and non-network providers. They usually are responsible for a co-payment when obtaining care from a participating provider, and a deductible and coinsurance if seeing providers outside the network. Under an open-access PPO, members do not need to see or receive authorization from a PCP before seeking specialty care (hence, the term open access). However, they may need to contact the MCO for prior authorization of hospitalization and certain diagnostic treatment.

## Gatekeeper PPOs

Like HMOs, gatekeeper PPOs require members to select a PCP who manages the member's care and refers him or her to contracted specialists. Some product designs contain an out-of-network feature, where members have coverage when using non-network providers. In these instances, gatekeeper PPOs are similar to POS plans. Usually, a gatekeeper PPO has fewer utilization management requirements than an HMO, although its credentialing and quality assurance standards tend to mirror those of it sponsor; that is, if the sponsor is a PPO, the gatekeeper PPO will have less rigorous credentialing requirements than if the sponsor is an HMO.

## Point-of-Service Plans

Many allude to POS plans as organizational structures. Actually, POS plans are benefit designs that can be offered by self-insured employers, health insurance plans, PPOs, or HMOs. Similar to gatekeeper PPOs, POS plans (often called open-ended HMOs or POS HMOs) provide coverage for services obtained from network and non-network providers (also referred to as "in" and "out" of network). One approach in structuring a POS plan is for the HMO to offer it as a distinct product. Another is for the MCO to operate the in-network portion of the POS plan through an existing HMO license and the out-of-network component under the indemnity plan.[5] The in-network portion of the plan functions like an HMO—the member must select a PCP and abide by the utilization management and prior authorization procedures of the MCO.

## Other Products and Services

There are an abundance of "specialty" managed care programs that provide specific health care services, such as prescription drugs, dental care, mental health and substance abuse services, and vision care. These are commonly developed and marketed as separate programs, or "stand alone" products, that compete with or supplement broader managed care plans. Managed care concepts are also being integrated into other insurance programs such as workers' compensation and auto liability.

## PRIMARY CONTRACTING ARRANGEMENTS

To fulfill contractual obligations to provide health care services for members, MCOs must structure contractual relationships with providers. Although there is an expanding range of contracting options, there are five principal types of contractual arrangements between MCOs and non-hospital providers. Typically, an MCO will have separate standard contracts for each type.

## Primary Care Physicians

The PCP, or family physician, is the hallmark of many managed care programs. MCOs will contract with a physician trained and certified in internal medicine, family practice, general practice, or general pediatrics to serve as the member's principal point of contact. To meet the demands of employers, some MCOs permit female members to select an obstetrician or gynecologist as a PCP. Others permit mid-level practitioners (physician assistants and nurse practitioners) to serve as PCPs, especially in areas where there are insufficient numbers of physicians trained in primary care disciplines.

Many MCOs, predominantly HMOs, contract with PCPs on a capitated basis, that is, a fixed pre-payment per member per month for a defined set of health care services. Although only 10 percent of PPOs pay primary care physicians capitation, 84 percent of HMOs identifying themselves as network or IPA models capitate PCPs.[6]

## Specialty Care Providers

Contractual arrangements with physicians who provide specialty care services to members can be in the form of individual contracts with physicians or small group practices or with same-specialty physicians organized in networks, called single-specialty networks or specialty care organizations. MCOs prefer to contract with specialists who are board certified in a particular specialty and generally do not like specialists to function as PCPs (obstetricians and gynecologists are an exception) or vice versa. However, some MCOs will designate internists as PCPs and also recognize them as specialists in their respective subspecialty, for example, gastroenterology.

## Multispecialty Providers

Several MCOs contract with medical groups, IPAs, or other multispecialty provider organizations to provide the majority of professional (non-hospital) services to designated members. Usually these contracts arrange for the provision of all physician (and sometimes ancillary) services, including primary and specialty care. Contractual arrangements for institutional services are made with hospitals and other facilities directly. As more physicians organize into larger practices, provider groups are becoming the dominant contracting vehicle for many MCOs.

## Integrated Delivery System

IDSs encompass the variety of integrated provider organizations that currently are evolving, such as the PHO. An IDS offers the MCO a single contracting entity for most or all health care services. Most PHOs have been formed by hospitals with the intent to improve the managed care contracting outcomes for physicians and hospitals.[7] Typically, PHOs are legal entities owned jointly by physicians and one or more hospitals. The hospital and physicians continue to operate separately in most non-managed care activities, but delegate managed care contracting and administrative responsibilities to the PHO. Although PHO boards comprise both hospital and physician representatives, most are dominated by specialists and hospital personnel.

## Ancillary Care Providers

To provide the full complement of services to members, MCOs will contract with assorted ancillary care providers and facilities. These include the following:

- home health care agencies;
- hospices;
- ambulance companies;
- physical, occupational, and speech therapists;
- laboratories;
- surgical centers;
- durable medical equipment suppliers;
- sub-acute care facilities;
- rehabilitation centers; and
- diagnostic imaging centers.

Traditional hospital-based physicians, such as pathologists, radiologists, anesthesiologists, and emergency medicine physicians, are often considered ancillary providers because they support primary and tertiary physician and hospital services. As physicians and hospitals integrate and physicians define their specialties more expansively, many of these ancillary services are incorporated into broader contractual relationships between MCOs and provider organizations.

## EVALUATING THE MANAGED CARE ORGANIZATIONS

It is prudent for a provider organization contemplating participation in an MCO to become familiar with the MCO first. Beyond verifying that the MCO is indeed licensed to sell health care coverage in relevant markets, the provider organization should review a series of questions related to other issues that will impact its contract negotiation and ongoing operational relationship with the MCO.

### Solvency

As a condition of maintaining its license, an MCO is required to maintain monetary reserves to cover unexpected costs, such as higher-than-expected utilization or a disease outbreak. Insurance plans are required to maintain higher levels of reserves than HMOs. What are the solvency requirements for the MCO? Does it meet those requirements?

### Organizational Structure

What is the central organizational form of the MCO—PPO? Insurance company? Staff model HMO? IPA model HMO? Where is the corporate headquarters? Is the MCO owned by a parent corporation or by local physicians or institutional investors? Is its tax status for-profit or not-for-profit? Are its service areas national, regional, or local?

### Management

What types of people constitute the senior management of the organization? Are they experienced in managed care? Have they worked in a provider organization, hospital, or insurance company previously? Does the MCO have clinicians in executive positions? If a national organization, does the MCO have a local management team? Who makes the contracting and other decisions on behalf of the MCO? Who has responsibility for the profit and loss of the plan?

## Corporate Philosophy

Most MCOs have a predominant philosophy of delivering health care and conducting business. This encompasses internal conceptions of the organization, general business strategies, and approach to vendors and customers. Is the organization intent on becoming a market leader? Do they gain market share through acquisition or creation? Are they service-oriented? Historically, are they conservative and slow to respond to market pressures or do they nurture an entrepreneurial spirit?

## Care Management

The basic care management approach of the organization is critical to the provider. Does the MCO maintain strong control over utilization management and physician referral decisions or does it delegate responsibility for these functions to providers? What guidelines does it use in determining appropriate care management? Is it focused solely on reducing unnecessary care or does it pursue activities that seek to improve overall patient care? For example, does it conduct outcomes research studies, develop clinical protocols, and implement disease management programs?

## Provider Relations

Because the provider's principal communication with the MCO is through the provider relations department, the staffing, experience, responsibilities, and attitude of the MCO's provider relations representatives are of utmost importance. What is the MCO's principal contracting strategy with physicians? Is it adversarial, collaborative, or permissive? Is it flexible in creating alternatives to standard contracting arrangements or terms or does it present a "take it or leave it" or "can't do" attitude? Does it work with physicians to educate them about managed care and the particular policies of the plan? How does it respond to physicians' concerns? Does it respond in a timely manner?

## Marketing and Sales

The ability of the MCO to deliver members to providers is paramount to the success of the managed care relationship. Who are the MCO's existing and prospective clients? Is its enrollment declining or growing? What is its enrollment growth rate? Is it aggressive in obtaining new business? What is its retention rate? Does it pursue or avoid particular market segments, such as employers with fewer than 25 employees? It is competitively priced?

## ASSESSING THE MARKET

Before the MCO enters a new service area or expands its existing provider network, it will (or should) conduct an assessment of the market. The elements for assessing a market for a new entrance or expansion are similar. Obviously, with a network expansion, the MCO is likely to have at its disposal more complete information because of its existing relationship with providers and its experience in the market.

An MCO may desire to expand or reconfigure its existing provider network because of the following:

- a decision to expand into a new service area;
- a contract termination with a large medical group;
- a change in contracting strategy; and
- actual or expected enrollment growth.

Key components of a market assessment include the following five items:

## Market Overview

The overview will outline the general characteristics of the market, including total population and population distributions by age, sex, and race; expected population growth or decline; total health care expenditures; and percentage of population uninsured or insured through various health benefit programs. In addition, the MCO may want to know if there are geographic or socioeconomic considerations that influence patterns of care, such as dense populations, remote areas, major highways, mountains, high-crime areas, and poverty.

## Economic Profile

An economic profile will outline the unemployment rates, employment growth rates, a per capita income, and general economic conditions of the market. The MCO will gather and analyze information on the characteristics of area businesses, which may be sorted by industry, number of employees, and annual revenues. What percentage of the businesses are small businesses, self-insured businesses, home-based businesses? Are companies laying off workers? Does the market have dominant industries, such as computer technology or manufacturing?

## Competitive Analysis

In preparing a competitive analysis, the MCO will first ascertain the stage of the managed market: infancy? adolescence? maturity? And the managed care penetration? Of particular interest to MCOs is how their competitors conduct business in the market. Who are the other MCOs? Their clients? Providers? What is their marketing strategy? Are their networks broad or narrow? How do they contract with providers: risk arrangements? fee-for-service? direct contracts with physicians? through PHOs?

## Provider Community Assessment

As part of its overall market assessment, the MCO will assess its existing network if it is considering a market expansion or the availability of providers if it is entering a new market. Elements the MCO will review include the number of providers, managed care contracting experience or receptivity, relationships with other providers and MCOs, referral patterns, and level of integration.

## Legislative and Regulatory Analysis

As many state legislatures intensify their scrutiny of MCOs, they are proposing and passing anti-managed care laws, such as any willing provider (AWP) laws and mandating coverage for certain health care services. In addition to reviewing state and federal legislative activity, the MCO will assess the requirements to obtain appropriate licenses and meet other regulatory obligations.

## PROVIDER NETWORK ANALYSIS

Before developing or expanding a provider network, the MCO analyzes the existing network or available providers and identifies prospective providers to target for participation in the network. Upon entering a new market, the MCO will identify available providers, compare the availability of providers with the marketing needs of the plan, and develop a network development or recruitment plan accordingly. The MCO will do a similar analysis with its existing provider for a network expansion. Identification of providers can come from a variety of sources. Often, feedback from existing or prospective clients is useful in targeting providers with satisfied patients and stellar reputations.

### Network Composition

While developing or expanding a network, the MCO will identify the kinds of health care providers needed to provide services for which it has contracted with purchasers. For a comprehensive plan, this generally includes a full spectrum of health care services including primary, specialty, ancillary, and hospital care. Most MCOs will develop an extensive primary care panel and hospital network first and then build a specialty network based on PCP referral patterns or hospital admitting privileges. Essential specialty disciplines include the following:

- allergy;
- cardiology;
- neurology;
- gastroenterology;
- general surgery;
- orthopedics;
- dermatology;
- ENT;
- ophthalmology;

- cardiovascular surgery;
- obstetrics and gynecology;
- urology;
- pulmonary;
- nephrology;
- hematology and oncology;
- neurosurgery;
- plastic surgery;
- infectious disease;
- rheumatology; and
- endocrinology.

After the MCO has contracted to ensure coverage in these disciplines, it will arrange relationships with subspecialists and specially trained physicians, such as pediatric cardiologists, pediatric surgeons, hand surgeons, and physicians specializing in the treatment of HIV-positive patients. An MCO must balance the market need to have as comprehensive a network as possible with the operational obligation to maintain sufficient membership levels per physician or provider organization and the competitive imperative to keep administrative costs low.

Depending on the MCO's contracting strategy, it will pursue these contracts directly or work with existing provider organizations to ensure coverage in all required disciplines. Provider organizations receiving capitation payments for most or all services will often be given the "right of first refusal" when contracting for additional specialty services. As part of its agreement with the MCO, the group may be given the option to expand access to specialty care as needed by the MCO either through sub-contractual arrangements with providers outside the group or by developing the service internally.

## Network Adequacy

Using member-to-physician ratios (that is, "X" amount of members for every physician), the MCO will ensure that the network includes a sufficient number of physicians in each specialty. By identifying an acceptable ratio (number of members each physician can serve sufficiently), the MCO can determine the optimal quantity of physicians it needs in each specialty, develop targeted recruitment strategies, and allocate resources accordingly. MCOs apply different ratios for primary and specialty care providers. For example, acceptable ratios for

PCPs range from 1:250 to 1:500, that is, one PCP can serve 250 to 500 members from one MCO. Depending on the specialty and the market, ratios for specialists can be 1:2,500 or more.

The marketing department of an MCO can be instrumental in gathering data to assist the MCO in its development and expansion activities. A ZIP code analysis of clients can target current deficiencies or future needs of the provider network. The MCO obtains a listing of employees from the client organized by ZIP codes of employee residences and matches this employee data against similar physician data by ZIP codes. This produces specific member-to-physician ratios by client and by ZIP code, which is useful to the MCO in expanding a network to accommodate client-specific membership growth.

Many MCOs establish network access standards that stipulate geographic availability of participating physicians to members. For example, an MCO may guarantee purchasers that every member will have access to at least one PCP within 15 miles of his or her residence or job site.

## PROVIDER NETWORK DEVELOPMENT

Depending on the MCO's network development strategy, it may build its network by recruiting physicians or entering into contract negotiations with larger provider entities. When MCOs contract with individual physicians, as do many PPOs and IPA-model HMOs, there is limited negotiation of the contracts. A negotiation usually takes place when an MCO contracts with larger organizations or multiple parties (such as integrated medical groups or PHOs) delegates financial risk or administrative functions to the provider organization, or requires a key specialist in a market where there is a shortage.

### Recruitment

If the MCO builds its network through contracts with individual physicians, the network development will involve recruiting physicians. The terms for physicians participating are well-established, identical for all physicians, and not negotiable. Generally, the provider contracts for PCPs will include standard contract language and the same fee-for-service or capitation schedule for all physicians. Because there is little deviation from the standard arrangement, MCOs and physicians do not generally "negotiate" the contract. The

MCO representative will explain the terms of the arrangements and answer questions about the physician's responsibilities as a participating physician.

The MCO will send a prospective physician a recruitment packet that includes information on the MCO such as policies and procedures, sample benefit plans, a physician application, a provider directory, and a credentialing checklist. In the physician application, the MCO will request basic information on the physician and his or her practice such as specialty, degree, location of office(s), office hours, hospital affiliations, training, and board certification status to ascertain the physician's qualifications and accessibility.

When reviewing completed applications, the MCO will check to determine if all questions are answered and requested materials are submitted. Generally, a site visit from a provider relations or health services representative will occur before the contract is executed. After receiving and reviewing all the materials, the provider relations representative will submit the physician's packet to a medical director or recruiting committee for final approval.

**Contract Negotiation**

Depending on the scope of the intended relationship, a provider relations coordinator, contract manager, or network development director will assume the lead in negotiating the contract with the provider organization. The contract negotiations will consist of a series of proposals, counterproposals, and exchanges of other information until the parties agree upon a final version of the provider contract. These negotiations are like a well-choreographed dance: the contracting parties seldom react spontaneously or perform well without extensive rehearsal.

Exhibit 1–1 illustrates a sample contracting checklist used by an MCO representative. The contracting checklist is useful in guiding MCO representatives, even seasoned negotiators, through the detail-oriented work of provider contracting. It is also an important tool in documenting important contracting steps for purposes of receiving accreditation by the National Committee for Quality Assurance (NCQA).

Throughout this process, the MCO and provider organization representatives may seek approval to modify proposals and contract terms from various internal sources including lawyers, chief financial officers (CFOs), medical directors, information systems experts, and

**Exhibit 1–1** Sample MCO Contracting Checklist

---

PR/Contracts Coordinator: _____
Provider Organization: _____

|                  Contract Step                  | Date |
|---|---|

1. Send or present initial proposal to provider organization. Proposal should include overview of MCO, summary of products, sample benefit design, provider directory, sample contract, rate proposal (if appropriate), and application.    _____
2. Obtain list of providers and completed questionnaire from provider organization.    _____
3. Arrange pre-contractual audit. Provider relations and medical management (health services) representatives visit site to review physical location, administrative procedures, and clinical protocols of the group.    _____
4. Review results of pre-contractual audit and completed questionnaire with appropriate management.    _____
5. Engage in contract negotiations. This includes reaching conclusion on all financial, administrative, and contract language issues.    _____
6. Prepare final contract for review by appropriate management. All language changes and deviations from the initial proposal must be approved in writing by management before sending to provider for signature.    _____
7. Send provider two clean copies of the agreement for signature.    _____
8. Receive both signed copies of the agreement from provider and submit to management for counter-signature.    _____
9. Bring the group to operational status. This includes assigning provider codes, entering physician information in the database, creating a provider file, notifying appropriate departments of new provider (marketing, claims, health services), and scheduling a provider orientation.    _____
10. Send one copy of executed agreement to provider and file the other one in provider file.    _____

---

senior management. To avoid unworkable or detrimental contractual terms and unnecessary delays in the contracting process, the MCO will often establish contracting guidelines for the provider relations representative.

Other MCOs require a formal approval process for all provider contracts. In these cases, the provider organization and MCO representatives may need to renegotiate verbal agreements based on the concerns of senior management. It is important that the provider organization understand the particular contracting procedures and processes of each MCO with which it is negotiating to avoid the frustration and delay that may occur from a protracted approval process.

## Credentialing

Verifying the credentials of prospective participating providers is an essential part of the network development and recruitment process. The NCQA has established guidelines that plans must meet or exceed to receive accreditation from the private accrediting body. These guidelines require primary source verification, that is, contacting the source directly to verify information submitted on the application, such as medical schools and state medical boards. Exhibit 1–2 is an example of a credentialing checklist an MCO will use in the network development process.

The MCO may consider delegating a portion of its credentialing responsibilities to an outside vendor or provider organization. A provider group that contracts on a capitated basis with several MCOs is likely to have developed a physician database with detailed and updated credentialing information. In this case, it is often more efficient for the MCO to delegate the responsibility for verifying physician credentials to that provider organization. However, the MCO must retain and use proper oversight of these activities, particularly considering the rigorous standards to obtain accreditation from the NCQA. The extent to which an MCO delegates its credentialing responsibilities can have a negative impact on its accreditation status from the NCQA, as it did recently for one Maryland HMO.

## Contract Execution

Frequently, the person negotiating the contract on behalf of the MCO will not be the one who executes it, but will be a general manager, vice president, executive director, medical director, or other corporate officer. If the MCO representative has sought approval throughout the contracting process, it is likely that the negotiated contract will reflect an agreeable arrangement to the MCO, and the signature process will be a formality. However, a lengthy signature process with various levels of management personnel reviewing and approving the negotiated contract may be involved before the contract can be executed. It is important for the physician group to know who will be executing the contract on behalf of the MCO and the

**Exhibit 1-2** Credentialing Checklist

| Please verify that you are returning the following materials: | |
|---|---|
| 1. Completed Application | _____ |
| 2. Signed Contract | _____ |
| 3. Copy of State Medical License | _____ |
| 4. Copy of Board Certification Diploma | _____ |
| 5. Copy of Certificate of Malpractice Insurance | _____ |
| 6. Copy of DEA Registration Certificate | _____ |
| 7. Curriculum Vitae | _____ |

contract negotiation parameters established for the contracting representative before negotiating the contract.

## CONCLUSION

The process by which MCOs develop provider networks can be lengthy and laborious or expedient and effortless depending on many factors, including the market, type of contractual arrangement, approach to contracting, management structure, and internal network development procedures. By acquiring a clearer understanding of the MCO's contracting process, providers will strengthen their competence in developing contracting strategies and methods to negotiate workable and profitable managed care contracts.

## NOTES

1. Adapted from the HIAA definition of managed care published in *The Fundamentals of Managed Care*. 1991. Washington, DC: Health Insurance Association of America.
2. Gold, M. et al. 1995. A national survey of the arrangements managed care plans make with physicians. *The New England Journal of Medicine* 333, no. 25: 1678–1683.
3. Gold, M. et al. 1995. A national survey of the arrangements managed care plans make with physicians. *The New England Journal of Medicine* 333, no. 25: 1678–1683.
4. *HMO-PPO Digest*. 1995. First Edition Managed Care Digest Series, NJ: Hoechst Marion Roussel, Inc., 68.
5. Wagner, E. 1996. Types of managed care organizations. In *The Managed Care Health Care Handbook*. 3d ed. Gaithersburg, MD: Aspen Publishers, Inc., 33–45.
6. Gold, M. et al. 1995. A national survey of the arrangements managed care plans make with physicians. *The New England Journal of Medicine* 333, no. 25: 1678–1683.
7. Abbey, F., and K. Treash. 1995. *Reasons providers form PHOs*. Westchester, IL: Healthcare Financial Management Association, 38–46.

# Understanding Managed Care Contracting— Comments from the Field

*Kim Bellard*

---

The preceding chapter does a thorough job of explaining many of the entities involved in managed care contracting and the processes they use. Many observers of the health care industry (and more than a few insiders as well) may view the entire arrangement between managed care organizations (MCOs) and health care providers as needlessly complicated. These relationships can be as complex, confusing, and stereotypical as romantic relationships. Both sides keep wondering, "What does the other want?"

## WHAT DO MCOs WANT?

Let's go back to the basics. MCOs want to satisfy their customers. While this sounds easy enough, it is often a difficult task because it involves two central but sometimes contradictory driving forces: cost versus access. In a perfect world, customers would review detailed information about MCOs, including their networks, programs, and the effect of these on the quality of patient care. Some of this information is available now and organizations like the National Committee for Quality Assurance (NCQA) are committed to assuring that more information becomes available as quality measures improve. Although the current information available remains less than ideal, some customers, particularly large employers, already use this kind of systematic approach to choosing MCOs.

Customers, however, have their own ideas about what to look for. The two most common questions the retail purchaser (e.g., an individual employee) or wholesale purchaser (e.g., an employer) will ask about a prospective MCO are similar. For the retail customers, the two key questions are: "Is my doctor in the network?" (access) and "How much will it cost me?" (cost). For the wholesale purchaser, the questions are: "Are my employees' doctors in the network?" (access) and "What will this cost my organization?" (cost).

## COST VERSUS ACCESS

Some MCOs simply take the strategy of signing up virtually every provider in an area. That way, customers are rarely dissatisfied with the available provider choices. If the MCO can do this while charging competitive prices, this can be a very effective strategy. The fact that most MCOs do not adopt this strategy suggests the adverse effect that such an inclusive network strategy has on costs.

This should not be a surprise. An important method that MCOs use to control or reduce costs is negotiating favorable pricing arrangements with providers. A common issue involved in such negotiations is how much volume the MCO can potentially deliver to the provider. The provider believes the discounted unit prices granted to the MCO will be offset by increased volume, so that overall revenues stay the same or grow. The increased volume comes from the MCO steering more members to that provider. Because it is often easier to simply restrict members' choices, most MCOs limit how many competing providers are in their network, trading some degree of access for more control over cost.

Some providers may be consciously left out of or removed from networks because their costs are believed to be too high, either due to higher unit prices or higher utilization of services. Others may simply be left out because there already is a sufficient number of providers in the network. Of course, MCOs could carry the exclusive network strategy to its extreme, paring networks down to the bare minimum with the very lowest cost providers. If the effect on cost is great enough, the strategy may work; it is more likely, however, that there will be a negative customer perception of access, and sales will suffer. The trade-offs involved in access versus cost are at the root of an MCO's contracting strategy.

## BUILDING A NETWORK

In creating or modifying their networks, MCOs start by determining which providers are most important to customers, that is, which doctors or hospitals are imperative to include in the network. Although there are many ways to discover this, one of the most effective is to talk directly with consumers such as in one-on-one conversations, focus groups, or telephone surveys.

Alternatively, brokers and consultants usually have a good sense of provider "hot points" for clients. As a result, MCOs do their best to stay in touch with these middle-men. Another way is to obtain copies of competitors' directories and see which providers are in the network. An MCO could choose to have its networks mirror those of competitors, or to create a more distinct network in the hope of serving a niche market (e.g., the population who like the excluded providers). To accommodate changes in the marketplace this process must be continuous. Customer preferences change, competitors modify their networks, and providers themselves change through consolidations and mergers.

## HOSPITALS VERSUS PHYSICIANS: WHO ARE THE DRIVERS?

Hospitals and physicians have a symbiotic relationship. Generally, physicians have definite hospital preferences. It is not useful for an MCO to have a hospital in a network without its affiliated physicians, and vice versa. Historically, MCOs have tended to build networks around hospitals. After securing a contract with the desirable hospitals, they contract one by one with the physicians who admit to those hospitals. This has worked reasonably well in areas where physicians are solo practitioners or belong to small practices and there are a limited number of hospitals. That environment, however, is changing rapidly.

Increasingly, MCOs are building networks around physician organizations (i.e., group practices, independent practice associations [IPAs], or other entities). These physician organizations may offer an immediate number of physicians and, potentially, a tighter medical management process. They may be willing to accept capitation or other risk arrangements that are attractive to MCOs. Physician organizations can be tied to certain hospitals for historical or convenience reasons or may treat hospitals as vendors, shopping for hospitals that will help assure the lowest costs and the best service. The physician organizations, then, drive the hospital choices for the MCO. Moreover, diverse structures that incorporate hospitals and physicians, such as physician-hospital organizations (PHOs), integrated delivery systems, and hospital-owned physician groups, are approaching MCOs or employers directly.

The "correct approach" may vary by market, depending on the level of sophistication of both the marketplace and the medical community. MCOs in the same marketplace may have different views on the "correct" approach, depending on their philosophies concerning provider structures. For example, some MCOs dislike PHOs, usually due to a perception of overly strong hospital control, while others see them as quick ways to assemble a network and transfer risk. Most MCOs agree that strong physician leadership is crucial to the success of a contracting relationship.

Clearly, the trend is to offer clients greater provider choices at the least expense. Provider organizational structures that offer MCOs more access points (number of providers and/or locations), at minimal organizational time, and help assure lower costs (through strong medical management processes or risk arrangements) will be attractive.

## TO TRANSFER RISK OR NOT?

In many markets, MCOs are beset with a variety of provider organizations seeking contracts of some sort of risk basis. Some are specialized carve-out networks organized by diagnosis (e.g., mental health) or type of service (e.g., laboratory), while others are more global (e.g., multispecialty physician organizations). Choosing between the multitude of choices can be difficult. The following are considerations in contracting with provider groups.

- *Exclusivity.* Will the provider organization require some degree of exclusivity? If so, how will this exclusivity affect market perception of the network? Will it be too small? Do the exclusive providers have a positive reputation? If not exclusive, how will the providers receive a sufficient volume of patients?
- *Degree of influence.* Does a contract with the provider group give them an uncomfortable degree of control over the MCO? Would their termination leave the MCO with a critical hole in its network?
- *Ability to control costs and accept risk.* Does the provider organization have the medical management and other types of infrastructure necessary to control costs? Does the provider organization have the capital to assume possible losses under a risk management? A provider organization that suffers big losses is likely either to fall apart leaving network problems or request more money from the MCO which the plan may not have anticipated in its initial contracted rates.

- *Conflict with other providers.* Does the scope of services overlap with services already contracted for? For example, a cardiac group may seek a global capitated arrangement for cardiac services that are covered in the MCO's contract with a multispecialty group.

## CONCLUSION

This is not a war that either MCOs or providers can "win" against the other. The best products are not going to be those with the highest benefits, those whose claims are paid the fastest, those with the largest provider networks, or even those with the lowest prices. The best products will be those that provide services consumers think will help them stay healthier or receive better care. Both "sides" need to buy into the concept of improving health care for consumers.

# 2

# The Contract Negotiations

*John L. McDonald*

When fee-for-service medicine was prevalent, the interaction between physicians and health insurance companies was limited to disputes over reasonable and customary fees. Providers set their fees and managed care organizations (MCOs) paid them. Because managed care represents a greater source of income for most practices, providers are now finding themselves in the unfamiliar position of negotiating their reimbursement and other practice issues with MCOs and other health plans.

Until recently, the negotiations between providers and MCOs have been a mismatch. Inexperienced providers muddle through complex contractual issues, whereas managed care administrators usually are well-versed in the business aspects of medicine. Fortunately, providers are becoming more sophisticated, learning the language and protocol of contract negotiation, sometimes through difficult experience. In this chapter, we will examine the contract negotiation process from the development of a negotiating position to the contract negotiation itself.

## ASSESSING ONE'S MARKET POSITION

Chapter 1 discussed the need for providers to assess the capabilities and value of the MCOs operating in their particular market. In addition to knowing the MCO before entering into a contract negotiation, provider groups must be willing to examine their own position in the marketplace. Self-analysis may be an uncomfortable process, particularly for providers unfamiliar with traditional ways businesses measure their strengths and weaknesses relative to their competitors and markets. The self-assessment process serves as an important source of baseline information for the business plan. Key components of the self-assessment include addressing credentialing deficiencies and examining the strengths and weaknesses of the practice.

## Preparing A Business Plan

A comprehensive evaluation of one's market position serves as the foundation for the development of a business plan for the practice. A business plan is an excellent tool for practices to understand their current market position, establish growth goals, and design workable strategies for achieving these goals. Although many providers find this to be a worthwhile and educational exercise, the task can be managed effectively by many office managers, practice administrators, or consultants. Depending on the size of the practice, a functional business plan can cost $5,000 to $25,000. Most practices, even some fairly large multispecialty groups, do not develop an annual business plan, yet this should be standard procedure for any business with more than one million dollars in annual revenue. The business plan need not be elaborate or exceptionally verbose. After all, most provider groups are not searching for outside sources of capital. The business plan should serve as a planning document that establishes annual goals for the practice and provides benchmarks for measuring progress against these goals during the course of the year. A typical business plan for a practice consists of the following components:

- an environmental or situational assessment that describes the market forces that will impact the practice over the coming year. This section provides a context for market strategy and financial projections;
- financial pro formas that establish financial targets based on the marketing and operating plans;
- a marketing plan that covers projected sources of patients and revenues, including those generated through new products, and outlines expected competitive threats; and
- an operating plan that identifies practice management issues and presents a plan for addressing these issues over the next year.

## Addressing Credentialing Deficiencies

An assessment of credentials has both objective and subjective elements and is a straightforward initial step in the process. Most

MCOs have received, or are actively seeking, accreditation by the National Committee on Quality Assurance (NCQA). The NCQA sets strict standards for credentialing, which MCOs desiring accreditation must meet. The NCQA is rapidly becoming a "Good Housekeeping Seal of Approval" for MCOs, without which large employers and others are not likely to offer them as health benefit options. Practices with updated credentialing information, letters of reference on file, and current and adequate malpractice, and that are willing to help simplify this admittedly onerous process will be well received by the MCOs.

Problems with the credentials of any physician should be identified and addressed up front. Issues that may jeopardize credentialing include the following:

*Large Number of Malpractice Claims*

Most managed care applications require the provider to give details on any adverse findings (judgments or settlements). It is advisable for the physician to prepare this document before the request and include any mitigating circumstances, as well as corrective actions that have been taken subsequently. This information is also useful for the risk management and quality improvement activities of the practice.

*History of Impairment*

This is a controversial issue. If this history or episode of impairment has been addressed through a peer review procedure or hospital sanctions, then it is likely the information has been communicated to the National Practitioner Data Bank (NPDB). The provider should be truthful about the issue in the application process. A detailed description of the issue can be prepared in advance for this purpose. This description should indicate the duration of the impairment, when the problem was resolved, and any past or ongoing corrective actions taken by the provider. Within reason, the provider should agree to submit to any oversight program that the MCO deems appropriate.

*Medicare or Medicaid Sanctions*

As more MCOs provide coverage to Medicaid and Medicare populations, past sanctions in these programs can be a significant barrier to participation in a managed care network. Assuming the physician has been reinstated, he or she should prepare an explanation of the situation, including any mitigating circumstances, remedial actions taken, and current status. Such sanctions are often billing disputes settled without court action. As long as the sanctions have been lifted, MCOs may be willing to overlook past problems, particularly when capitation is involved.

## Board Certification

Board certification status impacts some physicians more than others, particularly specialists and urban rather than rural physicians. Although most physicians dispute the value of board certification as a barometer of quality, the fact is that as specialty panels are pared down, this is often a key reason for de-selection. If a physician is still eligible, then it is strongly recommended that he or she prepares and sits for his or her boards. Physicians who are no longer eligible to sit for their boards have to conduct a careful assessment of their market and financial situation. A specialist who is well-respected by his or her peers in the community, who is part of a key referral group, and who has strong primary care relationships may be able to overcome the concern of most MCOs relative to insufficient board status. Continued post-graduate training can help. A physician who is not in a strong market position may elect to complete a fellowship to reinstate his or her board eligibility.

## Hospital Privileges Status

A change in hospital privileges may result from an impairment or other serious situation. The best defense is a carefully phrased description including a presentation of extenuating circumstances and resolution of the situation, prepared in advance and included as part of the application. Hospitals are required to report significant changes in the privileges of physicians to the NPDB. MCOs are required to check the NPDB database for all potential participating providers.

Credentialing problems like those described previously are the most obvious and difficult to overcome in the case of solo or small group practices. Larger groups offer some protection in these areas to individual physicians because MCOs generally contract with the group as a whole. Most physicians will not face any significant credentialing issues in their encounters with MCOs. Simplifying the process enhances physicians' value by lowering the administrative burden for the MCO and indicates a willingness to help the MCO meet its own external accreditation requirements.

## Determining Strengths and Weaknesses of the Practice

Determining market position involves a thorough analysis of the strengths and weaknesses of the practice. The analytical parameters include geographic coverage, the range of services provided, market share, and key affiliations of your practice. In addition, providers should understand their immediate competitive environment as well as potential competition from outside their service area. Managed care experience and administrative capabilities are also important factors.

*Geographic Coverage*

This can be measured in various ways. The simplest approach is to draw a travel time circle around each practice location. In urban or suburban areas, this circle should represent a fifteen-minute travel time for primary care physicians and a thirty-minute travel time for specialists. This circle can be increased, often substantially, in rural areas. Subspecialists can have service areas that encompass a wide area. Beyond this simple distance calculation, practices will find it useful to track patients by ZIP code. This approach will enable providers to define their current market and will also provide them with valuable insight into potential expansion areas.

*Range of Services*

The range of services provided by a given practice is defined at the highest level of the given specialty. Within the specialty, providers may subspecialize in particular areas. A gastroenterology group will often have members who specialize in upper and lower gastroenterology problems, and physical therapists will specialize in a particular aspect of rehabilitation, for example, sports medicine or stroke.

*Special Services*

The practice should evaluate its ability to offer special equipment or other marketable services. For example, a cardiology group may have an in-house diagnostic lab that includes echo and other equipment. Multilingual capabilities enable practices to attract patients from new markets.

*Quality and Cost Effectiveness*

Many practitioners do not have a good sense of where they stand on the quality and cost effectiveness continuum. Sources of this information include hospital and MCO utilization and quality statistics. Although this information is inevitably flawed at some level, providers should recognize the deficiencies, but use the information to understand their current position and as a benchmark for improvement.

*Market Share*

Market share is an admittedly unfamiliar concept for many providers. Unfortunately, accurate denominators for provider market share are difficult to come by. A rough estimate can be developed by dividing the number of providers with a particular specialty into the total number of specialists of the same type within a defined geographic area. This estimate should be tempered by an estimate of leakage outside the areas. Hospital-based specialties may also be able to extrapolate their market share from competitive statistics collected by the hospital.

*Patient Mix*

As demand for certain specialty services declines, untraditional markets like Medicaid or workers' compensation may become more attractive. Each practice should track patient flow and revenues from all payer sources. MCO patient flow and revenues in particular should be monitored carefully as this will serve as a foundation for the practice's contracting strategy.

*Administrative Capabilities*

This category is primarily a measurement of how well a practice is able to administer its relationships with the MCO; however, overall quality of service to patients should be factored into the equation as well. Accuracy and timeliness of claims submission, average wait times for patients, telephone responsiveness, and the time required to schedule appointments are several factors that should be considered as part of this analysis.

*Managed Care Expertise*

These days, nearly all providers have had some experience with managed care, thus expertise must be measured on a continuum. Practices that have successfully managed capitated arrangements for more than a year represent the upper end of the continuum. Conversely, providers whose experience is limited to preferred provider organizations (PPO) relationships are not likely to be as well prepared for more demanding managed care relationships.

*Affiliations*

As the health care market becomes more complex, alliances and affiliations become more important. Traditional hospital affiliations still carry some weight in the market, but these affiliations are being supplanted by participation in physician-hospital organizations (PHOs) and independent practice associations (IPAs) or associations with primary care and multispecialty groups. The value of these relationships is defined by the number of covered lives delivered and the ability to manage those lives effectively.

*Competition*

Competition among providers was only tacitly acknowledged in the past. In certain specialties in many urban and suburban markets, competition is becoming very real. Providers in this transitional marketplace must identify their competitors and assess their strengths and weaknesses vis à vis these competitors.

The following profiles of three different practices illustrate this analytical process:

**Profile I:** Three-person ophthalmology group located in a mid-size city in Illinois.

- *Geographic Coverage*—one satellite office in neighboring town. Service area covers approximately a thirty-mile radius around the city and a similar radius around the satellite office.
- *Range of Services*—general medical and surgical ophthalmology, corneal subspecialty care, and optometric and dispensing services.
- *Special Services*—laser surgery on site, optical shop on site, Saturday office hours, Spanish spoken.

- *Quality and Cost Effectiveness*—average based on reports from existing managed care MCOs.
- *Market Share*—approximately one third of all ophthalmology services in service area; small share of optometry and optical market.
- *Patient Mix*—Medicare-eligibles critical part of mix; some Medicaid; mix of commercial MCOs.
- *Administrative Capabilities*—computerized operations, able to track physician productivity; somewhat heavy on overhead expense.
- *Managed Care Expertise*—participate with three MCOs, optical shop, and optometrist; participate in VSP (a vision carve-out plan); Medicare HMOs are only beginning to appear in the market.
- *Affiliations*—optical shop is viewed as competitive by some referring optometrists; part of PHO in local hospital.
- *Competition*—one five-man group and four solo practitioners.

*Prognosis.* The group is reasonably well positioned in the market, although with an estimated 25 percent oversupply of ophthalmologists, complacency is not advisable. In a capitated environment, competition from the other group in town could be intense. The group should solidify its base by affiliating with or incorporating one or two of the solo practitioners into the group to expand their geographic coverage and leverage their fixed equipment costs. An informal network of optometrists should be cultivated in anticipation of exclusive agreement with MCOs. Medicare risk plans are in their infancy in the market, and capitated eye care is not far behind. Preparations for this shift (including rate development and internal utilization management) should begin immediately, and when adequately prepared, the group can launch a preemptive strike with the MCOs (described in detail later in this chapter). Pressure on revenues in the market is likely to increase as reimbursement seeks to reach Medicare levels. To maintain profitability, the group needs to reduce overhead by 10 to 20 percent over the next two years.

**Profile II:** Sixty-person, multispecialty group in a major metropolitan area of the Southwest.

- *Geographic Coverage*—several satellite offices located in the city and suburbs; primary central city location with most specialists; service area covers approximately a sixty-mile radius around city.
- *Range of Service*—good primary care base including pediatrics and obstetrics and gynecology. Most common specialties represented.
- *Special Services*—on-site laboratory and imaging center.

- *Quality and Cost Effectiveness*—past billing disagreement with Medicare (settled); perceived as above average quality and somewhat high cost.
- *Market Share*—well-established group; certain satellites are under capacity.
- *Patient Mix*—full range including Medicare and Medicaid.
- *Administrative Capabilities*—sophisticated group practice management system; recently hired clinic administrator with managed care experience.
- *Managed Care Expertise*—mixed bag of fee-for-service contracts; recently negotiated first capitation contract.
- *Affiliations*—primary relationship with major tertiary hospital.
- *Competition*—one other comparably sized group practice in the market; various PHOs and IPAs either formed or in the process of forming.

*Prognosis.* Given the soild primary care base, broad range of services, and administrative support systems, the group is well positioned for managed care. Contracts with MCOs will enable the group to fill available capacity in satellite clinics, however, a market strategy based on current and future potential will be required for each satellite.

This analysis should incorporate sources of patients, clinical staffing needs, and a realistic assessment of the location(s) and operations. To be fully prepared, the group must place more importance on their primary care component. Part of this process is reducing the disparity between the compensation of specialists and primary care physicians. Also, the group should convert the compensation system from one based solely on productivity to one that rewards efficiency and recognizes the special contribution of primary care in attracting patients to the group.

The group has taken a step in the direction of risk contracting, but must monitor its performance carefully. Substantive changes in practice patterns will be necessary to succeed under capitated arrangements. In particular, internal referrals must be minimized to reduce the demands on specialty services. The capabilities of the internal reporting system need to be exploited to track the efficiency of individual providers in the group. Formal alliances need to be established with key referral providers in anticipation of full-risk capitation contracts.

**Profile III:** Five-person cardiovascular surgery group associated with a major teaching hospital in Boston.

- *Geographic Coverage*—unknown; with proper packaging, service area could extend 100 to 150 miles for procedures such as cardiac bypasses.
- *Range of Services*—full range of cardiovascular surgery procedures including complex cases (no heart transplants).
- *Special Services*—none of note.
- *Quality and Cost Effectiveness*—considered high quality; cost is above average, but in mid-range for academic medical centers.
- *Market Share*—above expected share; draw from wide service area based on reputation.
- *Patient Mix*—balanced.
- *Administrative Capabilities*—average.
- *Managed Care Expertise*—participate on a fee-for-service basis with four managed care plans.
- *Affiliations*—participate in hospital PHO; connections with key primary care groups are limited.
- *Competition*—several other cardiovascular groups; primary competition from group associated with other teaching hospital in system; cardiovascular surgery programs in less expensive community hospitals taking some patients; managed care plans directing patients to providers with whom they have global fee contracts.

*Prognosis.* This is perhaps the premier cardiac surgery group in the city, but, unfortunately, many patients follow the direction of their primary care physician or health plan. Most managed care plans reimburse physicians for surgical services on a discounted fee-for-service basis in the Boston area. With the advent of the Medicare Resource-Based Relative Value Scale (RBRVS) system, most surgeons, including this group, experienced a gradual decline in revenues as commercial fees declined to the Medicare level.

A more aggressive marketing posture is the prescription for this group. To stem the loss of market share to other providers, they need to work with the hospital to develop competitive global rates for bypass and other services. The hospital should have staff capable of aggressively marketing these products to managed care plans and to IPAs, PHOs, and other risk-bearing provider organizations that do not have cardiac surgery programs within their medical community. Effective service areas can be extensive for cardiac bypass and other high-tech procedures. Alliances with other provider organizations and MCOs outside the traditional service area should be actively pursued to expand service area boundaries. Quality will become an important differentiation for high-tech services. A system (in collaboration with the hospital) for collecting severity-adjusted outcomes data will need to be developed to create a profile that supports the group's subjective quality image.

The preceding examples provide a glimpse of the criteria that providers must use to define their market position. In markets like southern California, Florida, and Washington, D.C., physicians have experienced dramatic reductions in revenues over short periods, as little as 18 months in some instances. Physicians must understand the existing source of their patient base (that is, health plan participation and primary care referrals) and from where patients are likely to come in the future. Barriers to market penetration must be mitigated or eliminated.

## PREPARING FOR NEGOTIATIONS

Preparation is the key to a successful negotiation. Providers need to research the MCO and the market before entering into substantive discussions with any MCO.

### Document Collection

The initial step in the research process before negotiations is collecting as much information as possible from the MCO. MCOs usually send the application, associated credentialing criteria, and a copy of the proposed contract to the provider. In many cases, the proposed reimbursement schedule is provided as well. Some MCOs prefer that the provider offers an initial reimbursement proposal. The following information should be requested if it is not provided by the MCO initially.

*Utilization Management and Quality Assurance Policies and Procedures*

In most contracts, providers are bound to an MCO's utilization management program. The utilization management polices and procedures of an MCO will give the provider insight into the modus operandi of the plan.

Providers are also bound contractually to follow the quality assurance policies of the MCO. Utilization management and quality assurance programs are good indicators of the way that the MCO relates to providers, as well as the balance between quality and cost containment. MCOs who are heavy-handed and proscriptive in their approach to providers give themselves away in the design of these programs.

*Historical Utilization and Cost Data*

The provider should request data on utilization of services for the plan overall and for those specific services to be covered under the proposed contract. Detailed cost and utilization data are often propri-etary; however, the MCO should furnish utilization data assumed in capitated contracts. Although the data are often surprisingly weak, they do serve as a comparison point for independent actuarial or market benchmarks, as well as a way to set corridors for the capitation arrangement should utilization exceed MCO projections.

*Historical Utilization and Costs for Your Particular Provider Group*

MCO data specific to the provider group provide a useful, if not entirely reliable, barometer of the group's performance in comparison with their peers. In capitation arrangements, the utilization data can help to develop an appropriate rate and determine the likelihood of success under a capitated arrangement.

*Stop Loss Policy*

The issue of stop loss (or provider excess) is important in capitated contracts, particularly global capitation agreements when a substan-tial portion of the medical expense budget is at risk. Stop loss is advisable in any capitation agreement that covers hospital services; it is less critical in arrangements covering professional services only. Recently promulgated Medicare guidelines require provider excess coverage for groups accepting risk for services they do not provide directly. MCOs may require capitated groups to purchase excess coverage. This is a negotiable item (see Chapter 9).

*Covered Services*

Any provider entering into a contract with an MCO should know what services are covered. MCOs should share with the provider the benefit-plan designs it sells to clients. For capitation contracts, the services covered under the capitation rate should be clearly identified. The exclusion of specific services (for example, angioplasty in a cardiology capitation agreement) will dramatically reduce the overall capitation rate.

*Administrative Procedures*

Participating providers are required to follow the administrative procedures established by the MCO. Therefore, providers should fully understand these procedures and assess their ability to comply before electing to proceed with any MCO. Many MCOs are delegating administrative responsibilities along with financial risk. Credentialing, utilization management, and reporting responsibilities included in many capitation contracts may have substantial associated costs. These should be factored into the negotiated rate. Also, the MCO must be able to provide current enrollment data in an electronic format to any contracted group.

A thorough understanding of the proposal is one of the fundamental tenets of any negotiation. The documents outlined previously are a necessary prelude to the negotiation process. For example, a description of the covered services and the stop loss policy are necessary for the group to calculate, develop, and/or respond to a rate proposal.

## Comparing Managed Care Organizations

The speed with which the marketplace is changing is intimidating to the point of paralysis for many providers. Providers can take more control over their destiny by developing a strategy to guide their dealings with MCOs over the near and long term. The foundation of any strategic plan is information. More specifically, a provider must understand the position that different MCOs occupy in the market presently, and how that position is likely to change over the next two or three years. They also need to know in detail how much impact MCOs have on the revenue of the practice. The fundamental questions that must be considered in crafting this strategy include the following:

- Where do your patients come from?
- How much revenue does each MCO represent for your practice?
- How fast is each MCO's market share increasing (or decreasing)?
- Which MCOs are growing fastest in the market? Who will be the market leaders over the next three years?

- Which MCOs have the most favorable reimbursement arrangements?
- Which MCOs work most collaboratively with providers?

These are the fundamental questions that need to be answered before entering into any negotiations. Although providers typically do not have this information in hand, many have the tools to develop a database to monitor and analyze the information. These include a practice management system, publicly available market research, and the experience with MCOs that physicians have accumulated.

The best way to approach this process is to create a comparison chart as illustrated in Table 2–1. A financial spreadsheet program like Excel or Lotus, or the table functions in word processing programs such as Word or WordPerfect work well for this type of exercise. The comparison chart divides MCOs into the following two broad categories: major and minor. Major MCOs include health maintenance organizations (HMOs) with substantial covered lives in the provider's service area. Minor MCOs are those without the ability to direct substantial numbers of members to the provider. PPOs, most smaller HMOs, and large staff-model HMOs generally fall within this designation.

Completing Table 2–1 will take some work and research; however, most providers have access to this information. The following areas should be reviewed:

*Patients*

MCO assignments are generally determined through a review of active patient charts. Primary care physicians (PCPs) or capitated groups also receive enrollment lists or electronic files from the MCO. Patients covered by MCOs with multiple products should be distinguished by HMO/point-of-service (POS), PPO, and indemnity product lines.

*Revenues*

Many practices have billing systems that are able to aggregate revenues by MCO. Although this is likely to be a problem for many practices, three years of collecting data is ideal to determine trends. If current systems do not enable the practice to track revenues, an approximate revenue may be generated by reviewing revenues for two to three months and extrapolating for the balance of the year.

**Table 2–1** Comparing Managed Care Organizations

|  | Major MCOs | | | Minor MCOs | | |
|---|---|---|---|---|---|---|
| Patients | | | | | | |
| Revenues (last year) | | | | | | |
| Claims turnaround | | | | | | |
| Fee ranking | | | | | | |
| Contract type | | | | | | |
| Covered lives | | | | | | |
| Change over 3 years | | | | | | |
| Support index | | | | | | |
| Hassle factor | | | | | | |

*Claims Turnaround*

Essentially, this is a measurement of your accounts receivable by payer. MCO administrative capabilities are more refined than in the past and most should be able to process a clean (accurate with no coordination of benefits [COB] or subrogation implications) claim within 14 days of receipt. Claims paid beyond 30 days are not within acceptable industry practice. Turnaround time is determined from past experience and an analysis of accounts receivable.

*Fee Schedule Ranking*

The practice should develop a table comparing fees by MCO for the top 20 Current Procedural Terminology (CPT) codes. Capitation payments are difficult to compare to fee-for-service arrangements (see Chapter 4); however, reimbursement per relative value unit (RVU) can be determined by careful tracking of the utilization during the term of the contract. (This is something that should be done in preparation for contract renegotiation anyway.) MCOs are ranked as above average, average, and below average. Over time, the practice may wish to develop a more precise ranking system based on frequency and cost, but this simplified system will suffice initially.

### Contract Type

This category defines the nature of the contract, for example, HMO/POS or PPO, capitated or fee-for-service (FFS), and exclusive, semi-exclusive, or nonexclusive.

### Covered Lives

Covered lives is a key measure of market strength. A three-year trend analysis provides insight into future market potential. Data are available through a variety of sources including local business journals, HMO and medical association trade publications, and state regulatory filings.

### Support Index

This is a subjective measure of an MCO's responsiveness to provider concerns, ability to provide utilization and cost data, and willingness to be flexible in contractual arrangements. MCOs should be ranked as above average, average, and below average.

### Hassle Factor

This part of the analysis measures the intrusiveness and inflexibility of MCO utilization and quality management programs. MCOs with collaborative or unassertive utilization management (UM) programs should be ranked above average. More intrusive programs should be ranked as average or below average. Information can be derived from various sources including the procedure manual furnished by the MCO and the experience of colleagues familiar with the MCO.

In a time of diminishing revenues, information such as this is essential for effective business planning and the development of contracting strategy. The process enables providers to step back from the day-to-day issues and objectively assess the present and potential value of an MCO to their practice. For example, the analysis is likely to show that certain MCOs generate few patients and significant operational problems. Developing a negotiation strategy for this type of MCO is relatively simple—bargain for higher reimbursement levels and less hassle. After all, the cost of walking away is nominal. On the other hand, MCOs that represent a substantial part of your practice must be approached more carefully.

## DEFINING A CONTRACTING STRATEGY

Developing a negotiation strategy is an important step in the negotiation process. A provider should have a clear idea of what he or she wants in a contractual relationship. A negotiation strategy is developed on the foundation provided by the group's analysis and MCO assessments discussed previously. Key elements include the following:

- the MCO's market position;
- the provider group's market position;
- the projected role the MCO will play in the practice's market strategy over the next three years; and
- an understanding of the MCO's flexibility and willingness to be creative in contractual arrangements with providers.

The negotiation strategy should be in writing and prepared in advance. This will help the group clarify the issues before engaging in negotiation, which can become heated and long drawn-out. An outline should include the following components:

- *Contractual Issues*—identification of all problems and the development of realistic business and contractual language alternatives.
- *Covered Services*—definition of services to be covered or excluded under the proposed contract.
- *Service Area*—determination of whether the contract will be exclusive or semi-exclusive for a defined service area.
- *Reimbursement Options*—identification of the minimum acceptable reimbursement thresholds for the practice and the definition of reimbursement options to be offered during negotiations.
- *Risk Management*—development of stop loss and risk corridor protections based on covered services and utilization projections.
- *Administrative Issues*—specification of claims turnaround, utilization, and cost reporting expectations of the MCO.

- *Medical Management*—identification of any concerns regarding precertification, concurrent review, and credentialing requirements.
- *Other Issues*—projection of potential MCO issues with the provider group and definition of volume guarantees in exchange for favorable pricing.
- *Cost of Walking Away*—projection of current and future losses should the practice decide not to contract with the MCO.

Although the preparation to this point has been extensive, expressing the strategy in writing will help define the issues and enable the practice to rank each issue in terms of importance. Before entering into negotiations, providers should know which issues are deal breakers and which can be traded.

## THE NEGOTIATING TEAMS

An essential part of the negotiation process is determining who will be conducting the negotiations on behalf of the MCO. Providers must identify a team of negotiators and supporting resources that will enable them to match up effectively with the MCO. The following section discusses how providers can determine the composition of the MCO negotiating team, what implication this has for the selection of their own team, and what specific role each member of the team will play.

### Knowing the Other Side

One of the first things the practice needs to know is who will be negotiating on behalf of the MCO. The experience and composition of the provider group's negotiating team depends in large part on the provider group's importance in the market. The larger, more strategically positioned groups will command more attention and have a higher level negotiating team. Less well-placed groups or solo practitioners often negotiate, at best, with an entry level contracting person and, at worst, are forced to communicate by mail and telephone. Providers, regardless of their strategic importance, need not accept contractual terms by mail. An audience with a live contracting person is nearly always possible and advisable, although flexibility in terms of place and time may be required.

The provider should find out the name and title of the person who will be conducting negotiations on behalf of the MCO. This will help the provider group to determine the level of preparation necessary and whom it should designate as his or her representative in the negotiations. In particular, if the MCO wishes to include legal counsel throughout the process, the provider then must decide whether to bring their own legal representatives to the meeting as well. This tends to result in a more protracted and expensive negotiation process and is not the preferred use of expert support. This will be discussed in greater detail subsequently.

## Designating A Lead Negotiator

Provider groups often make decisions by consensus. This is not an efficient or particularly effective way to conduct MCO negotiations. In the current environment, provider groups that are nimble and responsive (whether during contract negotiations or in response to some other opportunity in the market) have a much greater chance of success. Provider groups should designate a single member of the group as its chief negotiator. Alternatively, an external consultant can assume these responsibilities. It is also useful to include one additional associate as back-up and the practice administrator to assist with follow up and to provide business support. The lead negotiator and supporting team can report to (or consult with) a steering committee, but should be granted wide latitude to make decisions on behalf of the group.

The ground rules for this approach include the following:

- The chief negotiator should be accepted by the group as capable of speaking on the group's behalf. Negotiating parameters should be determined in advance as much as possible.
- The candidate should be selected based on his or her temperament ("cool under fire"), broad understanding of the market, and negotiating skills.
- The practice administrator should play a key role as strategist and organizer, but should not conduct the negotiations without substantial physician support.
- Expert support (for example, legal and actuarial) is advisable, but these individuals should remain in the background with certain notable exceptions.
- The lead negotiator should not be unduly second-guessed by other members of the group, especially in public.

- When the deal is made, the group should live up to its side of the agreement.

## Legal Counsel

Providers, even solo practitioners, should have legal support. The selection of a law firm is key. Generally, the firm that handles wills and property transactions is not the one that should be reviewing contract terms from MCOs. This is a technical business that requires experts in the field. Experienced health and insurance counsel can be identified through the local medical society or through colleagues. Once the group has identified two or more firms, they should interview the partners. Some questions to ask include the following:

- What is the firm's experience with MCO negotiations on behalf of providers?
- Describe some of the firm's cases and the outcomes.
- Has the firm had experience with the following MCOs? (Fill in the blanks with target MCOs.)
- Who will the firm assign to our practice and what are his or her rates? (If associates will be involved, as they often are, ask about their experience and the firm's procedures for supervising their work.)

Providers should select a law firm with the appropriate experience and a willingness to work with the group as a strategic advisor in the process. In most negotiations, legal representatives play a support role, providing expert guidance on key contractual issues. The counsel will review the contract and provide negotiation guidance initially and before concluding the agreement. During the course of the negotiations, legal counsel will develop alternative language to address issues that arise. Legal counsel should be included as part of the direct negotiating team under the following circumstances:

- The MCO includes counsel as part of its negotiating team.
- There is a question of breach of contract on either side.
- The contract requires extensive revision before an agreement can be concluded.
- The contract is of such complexity that involving legal counsel streamlines the process.

The latter two cases apply primarily to large provider groups negotiating comprehensive, global capitation agreements with MCOs. In most instances, the contract negotiations are not complex. The MCO provides a boilerplate contract for review by the provider and their attorney. Although there is some opportunity for negotiation on specific contractual issues, experienced MCOs have moderated or eliminated many of the one-sided components of the provider agreements. A detailed discussion of contractual language issues is found in Chapter 3; the legal aspects of provider contracts are addressed in Chapter 9.

## Actuarial Support

Another key support member of the negotiating team is an actuarial consultant. Actuaries are the "high priests" of risk in the managed care and insurance business. They are specially trained to develop and understand provider reimbursement arrangements, particularly those involving capitation. Unless you are negotiating a capitated agreement, actuarial support is probably not required. If you are entering into a risk arrangement, particularly for the first time, an actuary can guide you through the process of rate development and can verify the adequacy of a rate proposed by an MCO.

Although a capitation formula appears simple, it can be complex. Utilization rates can be difficult to predict accurately, and can vary dramatically from community to community.[1] MCO utilization data are often weak. An actuarial consultant can compare a rate proposed by an MCO with his or her own internal database of utilization and fees to determine its adequacy. It is important for the physician to select an actuarial firm and an actuary experienced in the development and analysis of capitated rates.

Before selecting a firm, check with the local medical society or national specialty association for recommendations. The practice should follow the interview guidelines previously described under "Legal Counsel." References should be checked whenever possible. It is important to be specific about the scope of the analysis and to agree on either a firm price or an hourly rate with a "not to exceed" ceiling. A well-defined analysis may cost between $5,000 and $20,000 depending upon its complexity. Exploring multiple "what if" scenarios can generate actuarial billings substantially above this range.

Actuarial support is less critical for providers who have experience with capitated arrangements. Assuming, of course, the practice has been tracking its experience with these contracts, historical data should be sufficient to develop a rate for a similar contract. Alternatively, national medical associations such as the American College of Cardiology and the American Academy of Ophthalmology have developed guides to help their members respond to capitated proposals.

## Consultants

Providers may also enlist the aid of experienced managed care consultants to assist in negotiations with MCOs. Although these consultants will not supplant the need for legal or actuarial support entirely, they can help the provider efficiently manage the use of these resources. An experienced consultant will understand the marketplace factors that will shape the negotiation, such as prevailing reimbursement rates, contract models, and utilization management policies. Often, a local consultant will have direct knowledge of the MCO's negotiating team and contracting strategy. He or she should know some of the contractual issues in advance and may have experience with similar capitated arrangements that will help to keep actuarial expenses in check. Billing rates for experienced managed care consultants vary, but are generally comparable to the mid-range or below those of legal and actuarial resources. Solo managed care consultants or "boutique" firms can be difficult to locate. Recommendations from fellow providers, conferences, and trade associations are useful sources of information.

## THE NEGOTIATIONS

Contract negotiations consist of meetings, written and telephone correspondence between the parties, and various levels of legal and financial review. The intensity and length of the negotiation process are usually proportional to the complexity and comprehensiveness of the relationship under consideration. The following section discusses the preparation and conduct of the initial and follow-up meetings and describes the overall process from the initial meeting to the successful conclusion of the agreement.

### Initial Meeting

The first meeting with an MCO serves as an opportunity to understand the goals and objectives of both parties and to establish personal relationships that hopefully will smooth the negotiation process. The meeting should be structured around an agenda and conducted within a specified time frame.

The agenda can be either formal or informal, but a formal agenda (agreed upon in advance) is advisable if the negotiations are likely to be long and complex. A typical agenda consists of the following components (in approximately this chronological order):

### Introduction of the Participants

Let the MCO know who will be on your negotiating team and which roles each will play. Make sure the MCO knows who will be the prime contact person and understands how decisions will be made by the group. By the same token, providers need to understand who is representing the MCO, their level in the organization, and their ability to make decisions on behalf of the organization.

### Establishing Objectives

Both parties should establish objectives for this meeting and for the negotiation process in general. Typically, the objectives for the initial meeting should be to understand the contracting options, identify any business issues, and explore potential financial terms.

### Review Contracting Options

This is an opportunity for the provider to understand how the MCO views its relationship to providers, what types of arrangements have been negotiated in the past, and which alternatives may be considered in the future. The provider should begin to focus on a contracting model based on the MCO's presentation.

### Defining the Business Issues

Business issues fall into two categories—responsibilities of the parties and financial terms—both of which are ultimately spelled out in the contract. These issues should be outlined in general terms during the initial meeting.

### Reviewing the Contract

A detailed discussion of contractual issues is often premature in the first meeting. It is generally preferable to outline contractual issues in general terms at the initial meeting. Detailed written comments on the contracts should be provided to the MCO, with specific contractual language negotiated in the second meeting.

## Establishing Next Steps

The initial meeting will have established a basis for further discussions, including outlining the responsibilities of both parties, establishing areas of agreement and disagreement over the business issues, and setting the stage for follow-up meetings to cover specific contractual and financial issues. The first meeting should conclude with a clear path to the second meeting. Specific issues to be addressed include the following:

- the date and time for the next meeting (Set up the next meeting when everyone is present and you will save significant administrative time and effort.);
- identification of information to be supplied by each party, who will be responsible for furnishing the information, and a deadline for its submission; and
- a preliminary agenda for the next meeting.

Before the initial meeting with the MCO, the provider will have selected their negotiating team, defined their negotiation strategy, and prepared all the appropriate documentation in advance. Preparation for the initial meeting is summarized in Exhibit 2–1.

So, when and where does this initial meeting take place? The answer depends upon whether the negotiation is for a contract renewal with a clear expiration date or for an entirely new agreement.

In the case of contract renewals, many MCO agreements have evergreen clauses, which automatically renew the agreement each year unless either party serves notice of termination. It is usually

---

**Exhibit 2–1** Preparing for the Initial Meeting

**What to Bring to the First Meeting**
- Background on the group—summary of credentials, service area, utilization, and quality differentiation.
- A marked-up copy of the contract.
- Suggested contract language changes.
- Questions for the MCO.
- Comments and questions on the rate proposal.

sufficient to notify the MCO in writing (or by telephone) that you wish to renegotiate the contract. The notification should be neutral in tone and suggest possible meeting times and places.

A dramatic, but somewhat dangerous, strategy is to serve the MCO with a notice of termination. Usually, termination requires a sixty- to ninety-day notification period. A frontal assault is not advisable unless you have outstanding issues or can risk losing the contract. Even if the group does occupy a favored position in the market, it is likely that the MCO will react negatively and the tenor of the negotiations may be adversely affected by such a move.

Initial negotiations with an MCO present a different situation. Both parties have no history to provide a context. The timing of the meeting depends, in part, on the market position of the provider and the importance of the MCO in the provider's near- and long-term strategy. A provider who is in a strong market position (for example, a large pediatric group in a key part of the service area) can afford to "sit back" and wait for the MCO to approach the group. Conversely, a solo dermatologist in a large urban area may have to market his or her services actively to generate interest on the part of the MCO. If the MCO has been identified as a key part of the provider's overall strategy, it is advisable to work collaboratively to establish a mutually convenient meeting time and place.

The location of the meeting should not be a big issue. Traditional strategies like "meeting on your home turf" are generally over-rated. Most MCOs are willing to meet with providers at their offices and work around their patient care schedule. At some point during the negotiations, providers may find it educational to meet with the MCO at the MCO's office. This meeting should take place during business hours so that the provider can view the plan's operations. A visit to the MCO offers the provider an opportunity to assess the internal workings of the plan and meet with utilization management and provider relations staff before concluding an agreement.

## A Preemptive Strike

There are two circumstances when providers should aggressively pursue contracting with an MCO. Providers who are in a relatively weak market position should be willing to meet with the MCO at the MCO's convenience. Ego should be sublimated to practical market considerations. Also, providers who are in a strong market position and want to expand their market share through an innovative relationship with an MCO should present a detailed proposal to the MCO.

Providers with a strong market position can be too complacent. Although waiting to hear from an MCO can be a satisfactory strategy, it may or may not increase the group's patient flow and market share. Based on the self-analysis process, a provider group should have important knowledge necessary to develop a proposal designed to capture additional market share. For example, the provider group should consider the following questions: (1) Who are the group's competitors? and (2) What is the group's effective service area?

The answers to these questions will enable a provider group to target a particular area for additional market share. To expand market share, a group may have to negotiate with the MCO to be the exclusive provider within a given service area. Unless this is a medically underserved area, this usually means that the group gains patients at the expense of other providers.

A preemptive strike proposal should include the following elements:

- a description of the proposed service area;
- service(s) to be provided;
- a list of providers and their credentials; and
- a financial proposal.

Providers should be prepared to negotiate more than the financial terms, including the definition of exclusivity, the size of the service area, and services to be provided. Exclusivity is usually defined by geography, but some MCOs link specialty groups to primary care physicians for purposes of capitating specialists. Providers may want to ensure they are the sole contracting entity for a proposed service area. Additional providers may be added through subcontracting arrangements to meet the requirements of the MCO.

Until recently, exclusive arrangements have been restricted to multispecialty groups and IPAs. Providers across the country are forming alternative groups capable of pursuing exclusive MCO contracts. As a result, large, loosely formed IPAs are being replaced by organized and tightly managed single and multispecialty IPAs and PHOs.

The initial meeting sets the framework for all subsequent meetings. The components of this framework include the MCO's view of its relationships with providers, its current contracting models, and where the MCO stands on the general business terms. Providers must use what they know already, incorporate any new information, and craft a strategy leading to an acceptable agreement with the MCO.

Subsequent meetings are focused on the details of the business and financial issues.

## The Follow-Up Meetings

Before beginning the second meeting, the provider should have a good understanding of the areas of concurrence and disagreement. Formally review these issues and develop a position (for example, where you can give, what the deal breakers are, what you can trade) for each issue using a T-chart or matrix as illustrated in Table 2–2.

Table 2–2 indicates the range of acceptable options across several key components of the prospective agreement between the provider group and the MCO. For example, the group in this case wants to assume more control over the medical management of its patients or, more specifically, to manage pre-certification and concurrent review internally. Ideally, the group is proposing to be exempted from the MCO's pre-certification processes. Should the MCO resist this option for administrative or other reasons, the group's back-up proposal is to develop a transition plan over the first six months of the contract that would lead to an exemption from the MCO's traditional pre-certification program. In addition to the business case issues outlined in the chart, providers should come to the second meeting prepared to discuss specific modifications to the provider contract. Legal counsel will have already conducted a thorough review of the agreement with suggested additions, deletions, and alternative language.

The agenda for the follow-up meeting should be formal and focused. The components include the following:

**Table 2–2** Understanding the Alternatives

| Issue | Alternative I | Alternative II |
|---|---|---|
| Service area | Subcontract with additional providers | Accept smaller service area definition |
| Credentialing | Managed by group with oversight by MCO | Managed by MCO—transitioned to group within 2 years |
| Medical management | Group exempted from MCO pre-certification | Develop transition plan with MCO |
| Financial terms | Capitation rate upper range | Capitation rate lower range with exclusions |

- *Establishing Objectives*—Many negotiations can be concluded during the second meeting if the appropriate foundation is laid in the first meeting and both parties come fully prepared.
- *Defining the Business Relationship*—The responsibilities of both parties should be negotiated early on in the second meeting. The provider and MCO need to come to terms on issues like the contracting model, for example, exclusive, semi-exclusive, or simple participating provider and capitation or FFS. Agreement needs to be reached on basic issues like the medical management and credentialing processes, reporting responsibilities of each party, and so forth.
- *Coming To Financial Terms*—Once agreement has been reached on the business relationship, the emphasis switches to the specific financial proposal. Ideally, the MCO will have made a proposal to the provider before the meeting that has already been reviewed by the provider's business advisors. Providers should be prepared with either an initial proposal or a counterproposal at the second meeting.
- *Contract Negotiations*—Legal counsel should have reviewed the contract in advance, and the group should know what its options are. The MCO should receive the group's comments before the meeting. The discussion should focus on contract language, with the goal of coming to agreement on specific terms, if possible.

The meeting should conclude with a discussion of the necessary follow-up steps such as the preparation and signing of the agreement, and the approval process; the timelines for administrative issues like identifying a contact person for implementation of the agreement, method for communicating information for both parties, and the process for problem resolution during term of the contract should also be determined.

## CONCLUSION

The situations and concepts outlined in this chapter will be familiar to many providers. At the risk of overstating the obvious, the world is changing at a breakneck pace for health care providers. The comfortable fee-for-service world, which dominated the landscape from the advent of Medicare, is disappearing in most metropolitan markets; even rural markets are not insulated from these sweeping changes. As variations on Medicare RBRVS reimbursement and the diminished financial return that they represent become the norm, many providers are taking another look at risk arrangements. If properly structured, these arrangements offer better reimbursement along with the potential for greater control over the management of patients.

At the same time, MCOs are also recognizing that their traditional, heavy-handed approach to managing care and controlling costs is not suitable to an environment where substantial risk has been transferred to providers. Providers (at least those who have developed a certain level of sophistication) understand that with financial risk come the right and responsibility to reassume control over the management of their patients. Providers who acquire contract negotiation and managed care expertise will be able to reassume control of their patients and their practice without sacrificing their income stream.

---

**NOTE**

1.  Wennberg, J. 1973. Small-area variations in health care. *Science* 182:1102.

# The Contract Negotiations— Comments from the Field

*Ruth Zachary*

---

There is no question that managed care poses formidable challenges to physicians, who must make significant changes in their practices. Frequently, they must move from independent to organizational practice, and from fee-for-service to risk compensation models such as capitation and package pricing. This often requires them to learn new skills and ways of handling new or difficult situations. Managed care can also be an opportunity for those physicians who engage in the activities and changes required by the evolving health care environment.

There are essential elements to successful managed care contracting for provider groups. They include physician commitment, organizational functionality, risk contracting expertise, and legal and financial advice. These elements are essential because managed care contracting, particularly negotiations involving risk contracts, can be a long and complicated process.

Physician commitment and organizational functionality are required to maintain the drive and tenacity needed during the contract negotiation process. Experience in risk contracting is often useful in negotiating contract terms that are fair and appropriate for the group's needs. By obtaining a legal review of proposed contracts, the provider group can ensure that the contract language reflects the agreements of the parties and the contract meets the requirements of applicable laws. Finally, a thorough financial analysis may protect the group from accepting financial terms that are too low or involve excessive risk.

The unwary provider group that moves into managed care contracting without these fundamental elements is likely to negotiate an inferior contract and may place itself at undue financial risk.

## PHYSICIAN COMMITMENT

Providers must commit to a process of change. Even a provider group with an appropriate organizational structure, large membership, significant financial resources, and favorable risk arrangements will not succeed without the commitment of its member physicians. Without consistent physician commitment to the group's managed care activities and goals, the viability of the group may be jeopardized.

Success in managed care contracting does not happen overnight. It takes an investment of time and work to understand the managed care marketplace, contractual terms, and effective negotiation strategies. It also requires the fortitude and patience to withstand initial failed contracting attempts. The reasons for such failures may include lack of interest on the part of managed care organizations (MCOs), the state of the managed care marketplace, or the inability to agree on contractual or financial terms. Provider groups can learn from these failed attempts and reposition themselves better for their next contracting venture.

## ORGANIZATIONAL FUNCTIONALITY

Functionality is more important than specific organizational form. Can the group get things done? This is a critical factor in the ability of a provider group to negotiate a managed care contract successfully. The size and structure of a provider organization may vary based on legal requirements, market variances, and physician culture. They are not determinants of the group's success exclusively. The ability to negotiate successful contracts will hinge more on how committed the member physicians are, if the group is focused on the right activities and objectives, and if the group can make decisions readily and intelligently.

Successful provider organizations are those with a realistic and goal-oriented approach, hardworking leadership, an ability to make decisions, and appropriate managed care expertise. A well-functioning organization keeps its eye on the marketplace and can change its organizational form and size, if necessary, to meet evolving legal or business circumstances.

## EXPERIENCE IN RISK CONTRACTING

Risk contracting can provide significant opportunities for physicians. It is crucial for the provider organization to negotiate fair contract terms in a risk contract. An experienced managed care consultant or practice administrator can be valuable in negotiating contracts.

Because it is usually the MCO that prepares and proposes the contracts, the contracts tend to be complicated and more favorable to the MCO. A knowledgeable and experienced advocate for the provider will translate the contract into understandable terms, help prioritize contractual issues, and bring experience from negotiating other deals to the table. In addition, an experienced consultant or practice administrator should be cognizant of the priorities of the MCO and be able to move the parties toward a fair contract without unnecessary delays.

Although there is an initial cost associated with hiring experienced consultative assistance, it can be a valuable investment because these seasoned negotiators regularly negotiate provisions that save the group money or increase revenues substantially. Experienced consultants can also be instrumental in imparting their managed care knowledge and negotiation skills to physicians. A consultant with practice management experience can assist the provider group in anticipating and handling operational changes required for the group to perform successfully in a risk arrangement. Once a provider group has become more experienced in risk contracting, it may be able to use consultants more selectively.

Another important aspect to risk contracting is the level of risk taken by the provider group. Groups new to risk contracting should consider shared or limited risk arrangements initially. Such arrangements limit the group's downside risk, which is helpful until the group has some experience with the agreement and gains confidence in its ability to perform under such terms. Also, shared risk arrangements are more likely to foster cooperation between the provider group and the MCO. As the provider group improves its ability to manage care appropriately, it may consider negotiating a gradual increase in the level of risk it assumes over a period of years.

## LEGAL AND ACTUARIAL ASSISTANCE

Both legal and actuarial assistance are valuable resources when negotiating a contract, if only to provide a quick review of contract terms and financial proposals. The identification of even one overlooked contract "pitfall" can be worth the cost of the review.

In their enthusiasm to achieve a risk contract, provider groups sometimes neglect to perform the necessary financial reviews to determine whether the risk contract is sufficiently funded. This important step should not be skipped. The financial analysis should assure the provider group that the reimbursement terms are reasonable and will not generate a fiscal loss for the group. Without such a review, a provider group may unknowingly place itself in financial jeopardy.

## CONCLUSION

The transition to managed care may seem daunting and confusing, especially as the provider group begins the process. Many provider groups are succeeding in shifting to a managed care environment that involves substantial risk to the provider. Such groups have positioned themselves for success in managed care contracting by retaining committed physicians and building a functional organization. In addition, they use managed care, legal, and financial expertise to obtain fair and appropriate risk contracts.

# 3

# Reviewing the Provider Contract

*M. Toni Waldman*
*Alan Gnessin*

A provider contract entered into by a managed care organization (MCO) and one or more providers has one major purpose—to describe the relationship between the parties. All of the business considerations negotiated by the parties, such as the division of responsibilities, compensation arrangements, and product lines to be serviced should be clearly articulated in the contract. Furthermore, post-contract termination responsibilities, if any, should also be set forth to ensure that individuals enrolled in the managed care organization will continue to receive care if the relationship between the parties ends.

## CLARITY AND TONE

Clarity is the most important quality of the provider contract and perhaps the most difficult to achieve. Each provision should be reviewed to ensure that a reader who has no prior knowledge of the relationship between the parties can understand the exact terms of the obligations of each. Simplifying the contract's terms may increase clarity; the same terms should be used consistently throughout the contract. For example, using one term to describe the MCO's procedures, protocols, policies, and rules will eliminate confusion and disputes when the MCO seeks to enforce certain requirements. Furthermore, the term used should be the one the MCO uses in its everyday communications with providers. Clarity will also be enhanced if the contract is well organized.

However, clarity should not be mistaken for brevity. Each word of the contract should add to the contract. Significant concepts should be described in as much detail as necessary to illustrate the pertinent points. Repetition of key concepts does not always simplify them, and several restatements of a single concept, each in a slightly different manner, may yield an internally inconsistent document. Rarely will such restatements clarify the concept; therefore, one provision should be devoted to each topic.

Another means of ensuring clarity is to define often-used terms in the beginning of the contract. Excessive use of defined terms, however, especially those that are not subject to differing interpretations, may interfere with the readability of the agreement. A definition section should not be a laundry list of terms that are rarely used in the agreement, but a section that defines key terms and concepts that are crucial to understanding the contract's provisions.

If the contract covers a variety of product lines, the contract will need to be clear to ensure differentiation among the various products and the associated contractual responsibilities. For example, provisions regarding referrals may apply only to certain products and the contract must clearly establish under what circumstances and to which products such provisions apply. As the need for clarity increases, the contract's tone will become more businesslike to address the greater number of material issues as well as the complexity of the various products.

The tone of the provider contract can be a positive influence on the contract negotiation and an aid in establishing a collaborative relationship between the MCO and the contracting provider. When the contract is with a provider organization, for example, the MCO may want to acknowledge the importance of the independent practice association (IPA) or physician-hospital organization (PHO) by contractually requiring consultation with the group when certain administrative decisions are made. When establishing the MCO's ability to make certain determinations, the use of such terms as "reasonable" and "good faith" will reinforce the collaborative spirit even though good faith and reasonableness are incorporated into all contracts as a matter of contract law. How "provider-friendly" an agreement is will depend largely on how aggressively an MCO intends to manage its providers.

## ORGANIZATION

Regardless of the number of the sections, the provider contract should address each aspect of the relationship between the parties.

Concepts that are related should be organized together. The greater the specificity of each provision, the less likely that the parties will dispute a provision's meaning. However, specificity about each concept covered by the contract may result in a long, unwieldy document. Therefore, the two will need to be balanced.

There is no right or wrong way to set forth the terms of the provider contract, so long as all significant points are covered. One agreement can be drafted for all providers of medical (as opposed to hospital) services, or an MCO can elect to draft a primary care physician and a specialist physician agreement. Variation of the physician agreement will be necessary for providers of hospital services and ancillary services. The following discussion summarizes the provisions common to all types of provider contracts.

Most provider contracts follow a set pattern of introducing the parties and purpose of the contract through an introductory paragraph and "WHEREAS" clauses. A paragraph reciting the consideration exchanged by the parties should follow with the body of the contract next. In the body, the various obligations of the parties should be set forth in detail with reliance on attachments and other materials as necessary. In the last section of the provider contract, boilerplate provisions should be included with signature lines at the end of the agreement.

Many jurisdictions have imposed requirements on the content of provider contracts by statute or regulation (see Chapter 9). The requirements may be general or specific in nature and, therefore, obtaining a copy of such requirements is essential to the provider contract drafting process. Sometimes, the statute or regulation actually sets forth the language to be included in the provider contract. Such a statute and/or regulation may also require that a form of a provider contract be approved before its use in a particular jurisdiction. Such review should not be problematic if the required provisions are included from the outset.

## Purpose

At the front of the provider contract, the parties that will perform the contract services should be clearly identified. If the provider is a group consisting of more than one provider, then the terms and conditions of the contract, as applicable, should be made to apply to each member of the group in some provision of the provider agreement.

The "WHEREAS" clauses may further identify and recite the general purpose(s) of the agreement. Although these provisions are generally not enforceable, they further explain the parties' intent in entering into the provider agreement and, in the event of a dispute, could be used to support a certain interpretation of the agreement. Consequently, important terms and conditions should be set forth in the body of the contract rather than in the introductory clauses.

## Definitions

Certain key terms should be defined in the beginning of the contract. The definitions of such terms should mirror those used in the underlying coverage documents to avoid inconsistencies. It is important to note that defined terms should be used in the context of their meanings and the name of the provider should not be a defined term. Examples of defined terms include the following:

- consulting (specialist) physician;
- covered services;
- emergency;
- enrollee;
- evidence of coverage or certificate;
- medical director;
- medically necessary;
- participating provider;
- primary care physician; and
- utilization management.

## Parties' Rights and Responsibilities

An explanation of the parties' rights and responsibilities follows the definition section. How these are divided and organized is a matter of preference. Regardless of their order, certain provisions should be found in all provider contracts and an explanation of these follows, beginning with those of the MCO, then the provider, and finally miscellaneous provisions.

## STANDARD CONTRACT TERMS

### MCO Obligations

The MCO's major obligation is to ensure that the provider is compliant with the MCO's utilization management, quality assur-

ance, credentialing, administrative practices, and procedures necessary for the MCO to fulfill its contractual obligations to its clients.

## Administrative Procedures

This section permits the MCO to establish reasonable policies and
protocols with which the provider must comply. Incorporating such
policies and protocols into the agreement itself will severely limit the
MCO from revising those policies and protocols to respond to changing operational and competitive needs. If the MCO chooses to incorporate such policies and protocols, then specific language permitting
the MCO to bypass the contract amendment process for changes to
such policies and procedures may be included.

## Enrollee List

This provision is important to establish a mechanism for the
provider to verify the eligibility of an individual presenting for services before rendering such services. The MCO is obligated to give the
primary care physician and any other capitated provider periodic
listings of individuals enrolled in the MCO. Regular supplements to
such listings should be furnished by a certain date. This section may
also outline alternative eligibility verification techniques of the MCO
and how retroactive enrollment and disenrollment will be handled
and will affect compensation.

## Compensation

The MCO's obligation to compensate the provider should be included in the explanation of the MCO's obligations. This should be a
general provision that sets forth the compensation methodology for
the provider and distinguishes between the respective payment obligations if this is a multi-party agreement. The compensation attachment should give a detailed explanation of the compensation arrangement, whether fee-for-service or risk sharing, including the date
by which the provider is to be paid, and whether any claim for
payment under a fee-for-service system will be deemed waived if the
claim is not filed by a certain date. In addition, the compensation
attachment may contain provisions regarding automatic increases or
decreases in compensation rates or a formula by which any increases
or decreases will be calculated.

*Reports*

A section requiring the MCO to give the provider timely reports regarding patient utilization, referral patterns, and provider financials should be included. Providers who are not at financial risk may not need such reports, but if the parties contemplate moving on to a financial "risk" relationship, then this provision may become more critical for the parties to have accurate data with which to negotiate the terms of a "risk" relationship.

*Other Obligations*

Other obligations of the MCO should also be included as appropriate. If the parties have agreed that the MCO will have an exclusive arrangement with this provider for its services, then a provision outlining the exclusive arrangement may be included. If the MCO will provide marketing services for the provider, then a provision to this effect should be included. All of the obligations that the MCO has agreed to fulfill should be set forth as the parties have agreed.

## Provider Responsibilities

*Provision of Health Care Services*

The provider's obligation to provide health care services to individuals enrolled in the MCO should be stated in the first provision of the provider responsibility section of the contract. The services to be provided should be identified by Current Procedural Terminology (CPT) codes or other descriptive means, preferably in an attachment to the contract. If the provider is providing primary care services, then its obligations will include the provision of services as well as its responsibility to arrange and coordinate the individual enrollees' overall health care. An attachment outlining the provider's services should be included to ensure that no gaps in service coverage will occur for which the provider will be at risk to provide. Identification of these services in a meaningful manner may avoid future disputes in that the parties will have a document on which to rely should a disagreement arise. For a capitated relationship, the parties may always agree to rely on the actuarial formula used to calculate the compensation rate when a dispute arises.

If there are multiple products or multiple parties involved in the agreement, it may be necessary to use alternative attachments. In addition, this section should state any administrative responsibilities related to the provision of services. Finally, this provision can be expanded to establish protocols for the provider to follow in the event that it provides non-covered services to an individual enrolled in the MCO.

## Referrals

An explanation of the procedures pertaining to the primary care physician's referral of the member to specialists and ancillary providers should be outlined in this provision. Such requirements might include the use of a referral authorization form or the need to consult with the MCO's medical director on specific medical treatment plans or an obligation to comply with the MCO's utilization management and quality assurance program. This provision should also identify the differences in procedures when physicians refer within or outside of the provider network, and any financial disincentives associated with the provider failing to make a referral in a manner consistent with the agreement or MCO policies and protocols. In the event that a primary care physician is allowed to provide specialty services to his or her enrollee panel, this section should also establish appropriate guidelines for such "self referrals" and refer to applicable provisions in the attachment covering compensation for such services.

## Hospital Admissions

This section should state or reference the procedures for admitting members to the hospital on an emergency and non-emergency basis. It should include specific reference to pre-authorization protocols, compliance with length-of-stay certifications, and the use of "preferential" facilities, if applicable. Again, any financial disincentives for failure to follow the MCO's established procedures for pre-admission or length-of-stay certifications should be included in this provision, or at the least, cross-referenced to the stated penalty provisions for inappropriate referrals.

## Accepting Enrollees

This section will outline the provider's responsibility to accept as patients any MCO member who selects him or her, regardless of such individual's race, sex, age, or health status. Although this section serves to satisfy a state mandate of non-discrimination, the MCO may expand it to address the ability of the provider or MCO to limit the provider's panel size, or restrict future members from enrolling in the practice, also referred to as "closing a practice," and administrative requirements related to the closing and reopening of the provider's enrolled panel. In addition, this section should prohibit disparate treatment of MCO patients relative to the provider's other patients.

*Billing Enrollees*

This section should state the circumstances and manner under which the provider may collect payments from members of the MCO, including co-payments, deductibles, and charges for non-covered services. In addition, it should discuss whether the provider's obligation to collect co-payments and/or deductibles is mandatory or permissive. This section should also inform the provider that the MCO will not be financially responsible for any amount not collected, whether voluntarily or not, by the provider and that the provider is required to notify his or her enrolled MCO patients when non-covered services are being rendered.

*Enrollee Non-Liability*

The provider contract should comply with any state requirement regarding the billing of individuals enrolled in a health maintenance organization (HMO). In standard hold harmless provisions, the provider agrees not to bill enrollees or other practices, except the MCO, for covered services, except co-payments and/or deductibles and charges for non-covered services. Many state statutes or regulations require the inclusion of specific language; hence, the text will duplicate the statutory or regulatory section verbatim. This section must also state that it survives expiration of the agreement (if it is not automatically renewable) or termination for whatever reason.

Although hold harmless statutes may not be applicable to all members in a multi-party agreement, many payers, both insurers and self-insurers, want this protection for individuals enrolled in their health benefit programs and include hold harmless language for all various product lines and payers.

*Records and Reports*

If the provider is required to submit encounter data and/or reports to the MCO, then this provision should address these requirements.

This section should also discuss the exchange of such other medical, financial, and administrative records and information because the MCO may require inclusion of information that is necessary for HEDIS reporting, or the MCO may be required to submit information to any governmental agency with which it contracts. In addition, this section should also stipulate what information needs to be included in the medical record or the standards to be met and it should provide for direct MCO and regulatory agency access to such records, including medical records, and the right of the MCO to copy those records or the obligation of the provider to provide copies and at what cost, if any. It is also important for the MCO to establish its right to use general medical record releases that may be included in its enrollment applications to obtain copies of these records.

*Professional Requirements*

The section dealing with the provider's adherence to certain professional requirements and other provisions regarding the rendering of services must address a number of issues. It should state the provider's obligations to make services available to members, including twenty-four–hour availability, establishment of a minimum number of appointment hours, and coverage arrangements when the provider is not available, if this is appropriate to the type of services being rendered by the provider. Regarding such covering arrangements, this provision may be expanded to establish the method by which covering physicians are compensated.

This same section should address the provider's adherence with standards of practice in the community, continuing education requirements, and compliance with the MCO's credentialing requirements. The provider should be required to notify the MCO in the event of any restriction of its licenses to practice and/or prescribe controlled substances, as applicable; the imposition or threat of imposition of any malpractice action by an enrollee; the suspension or disqualification from any governmental program; and any other matter that may affect the provider's ability to be included in the MCO's provider panel. The following items may also be addressed in the same section: the provider's assistance in accessing the National Practitioner Data Bank (NPDB), and in cooperating with the MCO's accreditation efforts, and the provider's compliance with the Clinical Laboratory Improvement Act and the Patient Self-Determination Act requirements.

*Insurance*

A subsection requiring the provider to obtain malpractice and general liability insurance for itself and employees as well as establishment of the levels of such coverage should be included in a section outlining the provider's obligations. For providers who have the financial wherewithal to pay a large award, self-insurance may replace the need for conventional insurance. Regardless of whether insurance or self-insurance is chosen, the MCO should have the right at any time to ask for proof of such insurance coverage and the provider should be required to comply in a timely fashion. Conversely, detailed provisions requiring "indemnification" of the MCO should be stricken unless the provider can obtain assurances from its malpractice carrier that such liability is insured. If the indemnification is mutual, the MCO's obligation should also be deleted in such a case. Alternatively, general reference to the parties' compliance with common law principles of contribution and indemnification may be different.

*Administration*

The provider must agree to cooperate and comply with all utilization, quality assurance, audit, coordination of benefits (COB), and grievance procedures established by the MCO, and a separate section of the provider agreement should address this subject. Although these procedures should not be incorporated into the agreement by reference to preserve the MCO's operational flexibility as stated previously, this section should provide for the advance notice of any changes to such procedures before their implementation to give providers an opportunity to comply with the changes. The provider should also be required to cooperate with the MCO in its efforts to implement such procedures and to abide by any of the MCO's decisions made pursuant to these procedures.

Another provision of this section should require the provider's cooperation in providing information to be used in the MCO's membership and marketing materials. Finally, this section should also state whether the primary care physician, the MCO, or both retain the right to coordinate benefits and retain subrogation recoveries.

## Other Provisions

Several miscellaneous provisions must be included in the agreement that defines the business relationship of the parties. Because these provisions are not specific obligations of either party, they should be separate from the recitation of the provider's and MCO's obligations. These requirements may merit their own sections of the agreement.

### Modification of the Provider Contract

The first miscellaneous provision dealing with amendments to the contract should provide for a method by which the agreement can be modified. Typically, modification is by mutual consent but the provision can also provide for automatic modification upon thirty days notice by the MCO to the provider. If the provider fails to object to the proposed modification during the notice period, then the modification will take effect on the date established in the amendment. If the provider objects to such modification or amendment, the MCO can reserve the right to terminate this agreement upon written notice. Such right does not mean that the MCO has to exercise it; rather, the MCO could elect to negotiate with the provider to avoid termination. Inclusion of this automatic amendment provision has the advantage of providing operational flexibility to the MCO. This section should also provide for automatic amendment to comply with changes in applicable state and/or federal law.

### Relationship of the Parties

Another miscellaneous provision that could merit its own section is a provision establishing that the provider and MCO are independent contractors and that, notwithstanding a coverage determination by the MCO, the provider has the obligation to advise the enrollee regarding his or her medical treatment based upon its medical judgment. This section should also obligate the provider to inform the enrollee of his or her rights to appeal an adverse coverage determination by the MCO.

### Proprietary Information

A subsection protecting the MCO from the misappropriation of its proprietary materials should be included in a separate section of the contract. It must require that all materials provided to the provider are the proprietary materials of the health plan and that they may not be disclosed or used for any purpose other than the purpose intended by the agreement. This section may further provide that the provider will not solicit enrollees to enroll in another benefit program. Finally, this section should have the provider acknowledge that upon its breach, the health plan is entitled to an injunction. To the extent requested by the provider, the proprietary materials language can be mutual.

*Term and Termination*

The last miscellaneous provision that could have its own section would set forth the term of the agreement and circumstances under which it may be terminated. The term will be for a certain period or may renew from year to year unless affirmatively terminated; for example, an evergreen contract. This provision should also provide flexibility to terminate the agreement on short notice and immediately for a specified cause. The MCO may want to have the opportunity to terminate the contract without cause and, in most cases, providers will insist that this is a reciprocal right; therefore, the MCO may wish to tie termination without cause only to the renewal date or on no less than 90 days notice. There should be a further obligation that (1) regarding patients receiving care at the time of termination, the terms of the agreement will remain in full force and in effect until completion of treatment or until other arrangements can be made by the MCO, and/or (2) regardless of the status of the course of care, the provider will continue to care for his or her enrollee-patients until the anniversary date of the then outstanding group or individual agreements. This section should also permit the immediate transfer of a provider's patients upon notification of termination and obligate the provider to cooperate with such transfer including the transfer of medical records.

Other boilerplate provisions include a choice of law and venue provision, a provision prohibiting assignment of the contract by the provider without the MCO's permission, a waiver of enforcement provision, a severability provision, a provision stating how the parties will notify each other of certain events, and a provision deeming the contract and its attachments as the entire agreement. These provisions are standard in most agreements.

## MULTIPLE PRODUCT AND PAYER AGREEMENTS

### Multiple Product Agreements

To the extent that different services will be provided, or different compensation rates will be paid, separate attachments to the main contract need to exist. Each product should have its own attachment listing the covered services to be rendered by the particular provider and an analogous compensation attachment. If the products differ because one permits enrollees to self-refer to specialists or to go out of network, then the various requirements stated in the body of the agreement will have to be qualified to indicate that the enrollee's health benefit plan may permit referrals that are normally prohibited. In addition, if the product has any unique characteristics that impact upon the manner in which care may be rendered, a separate attachment may need to be appended to the main agreement denoting such features.

## Multiple Payer Agreements

More than one MCO can be a party to an agreement with a provider. In these cases, the agreement must identify each MCO and state that the relationship between the provider and each MCO is independent of the others. If the provider services and the compensation rates differ from payer to payer, then attachments corresponding to each payer may be appropriate. In addition, certain modifications may be required if the MCO is not financially at risk for services rendered to enrollees of a self-insured plan that the MCO administers. In other situations, self-insured plans will remit compensation through the MCO directly and the provider would still seek compensation from the MCO. These types of distinctions must be clearly articulated in the agreement to avoid confusion and disputes.

In addition, multi-payer agreements must contain other provisions that reflect the multi-party nature of the agreement. If the MCO permits the provider to choose to "opt out" of rendering services for certain payers, then the agreement needs to state so. Also, the agreement needs to discuss how the parties will communicate with each other about such matters. Providers should acknowledge that the MCO has the right to negotiate with a variety of payers and to enter into agreements with such payers, which may include different compensation arrangements than those described in the agreement, and that the provider will agree to the terms that the MCO negotiates. The termination provision should explicitly state that termination of the agreement regarding one payer has no effect on the agreement regarding other payers.

In addition, the MCO may want to add a more general provision, permitting it to decide whether a provider will be included in the provider panel offered to the various payers. This will maximize the MCO's operational flexibility. Furthermore, the MCO may include a provision expressly disavowing the creation of joint liability or the cross guarantees for the various payers. In this way, the MCO can be sure that it will not become the payer of "last resort."

## EXECUTION OF THE PROVIDER CONTRACT

The provider contract should be executed by the provider or, if the provider is an entity, an officer or other person who has authority to bind the provider. If the agreement permits, it may be executed in counterparts (for example, on two different originals). Although the execution of the contract usually occurs before the provider begins to render care to enrollees, the parties may agree to commence the relationship before executing the agreement (subject to applicable law) and can elect to make the contract effective retroactive to the date on which the provider began to render services.

## CONCLUSION

Provider contracts should reflect the business arrangements between MCOs and providers. When drafting the provider agreement, the MCOs should strive to draft a document to be used with a variety of products and payers and to reserve operational flexibility to ensure that the provider agreement will govern the many different relationships an MCO may negotiate with providers. Most importantly, the provider agreement should be clear, concise, and internally consistent to establish a collaborative relationship with the provider.

# Reviewing the Provider Contract—
# Comments from the Field

*Raymond R. Girouard*

---

While it is important to be cognizant of the various segments and key passages of a provider agreement, it is ultimately as important to look at the overall relationship between the provider and the managed care organization (MCO) and how this relationship impacts the provider's practice and its patients.

There are various steps involved in contracting with an MCO and it is practical for providers to attend to some of these before reviewing the contract. First, it is important to review all components of an information packet to develop a sense of the MCO. For example, is the material well prepared and presented in a professional manner? Are all the product offerings clearly stated? Is reimbursement methodology explained? If so, is it specific to the practice? Are both credentialing applications and agreements included in the packet? Is a check-off sheet included in the material? Is an approximate timetable included that meets the practice's expectations for completion?

Combining the materials from the MCO and the group's internal data is the next step in contract preparation. Regardless of whether the contract is initiated by a patient, employer group, or MCO, the practice administrator needs to accumulate pertinent practice information and demographic data from the MCO. This includes a minimum of 12 months of practice utilization data, a breakdown of patients by age and sex, the number of annual physician visits (i.e., encounters) computed to the revenue and cost per encounter, and data comparing the Resource-Based Relative Value Scale (RBRVS) fee schedule to capitation payment rates. As more data become available and can be analyzed in a concise and useable method, the negotiating position with the MCO will improve.

With this information, the administrator can perform a reimbursement analysis based on value-driven estimates of past performance. To determine whether the practice is receiving adequate fee-for-service reimbursement, the group should base its analysis on those services that are provided most frequently and cause the most impact. In a capitated environment the practice should work with the MCO to determine what its revenue per encounter would be under the proposed agreement. Moreover, the practice should assess the impact co-payments and withholds have on reimbursement levels and the practice's profitability.

## INITIAL REVIEW OF THE AGREEMENT

Reviewing the overall layout and content of the agreement can range from a quick visual scan to an in-depth review and rewriting of the sections. The initial review of the agreement can often tell the practice whether the intended relationship between provider and MCO is collaborative or adversarial.

As one begins to review the agreement, it is essential to understand the organizational structure of the MCO. For example, is it clear that the MCO is a health maintenance organization (HMO) offering both fee-for-service reimbursement and capitation payments? Does the agreement encompass a preferred provider organization (PPO) product? Does the MCO have a contracting relationship with another entity (i.e., third party) that will reimburse the practice? It is essential that the physician group has a clear understanding of the entity with which it intends to contract.

## CONTRACT SECTIONS

Terms in the definition section should be included to avert future disputes, add clarity, and enhance brevity. They should be included only if they are referenced in the body of the agreement.

Sometimes the onerousnous of the agreement can be clearly identified in the section outlining the responsibilities of the parties. By scanning the respective sizes of the provider and MCO responsibilities, the practice can ascertain if there appears to be equality in the terms. For example, how often is the provider required to provide utilization data to the MCO? In what form? Is the provider required to submit such data for both capitated and carve-out (or "bill above") services?

More importantly, does the MCO reciprocate the data requirements? Certainly, in today's era of utilization and cost management, provisions should be required for the MCO to forward performance data to the physician group, at least on an annual basis. Included in such performance information should be comparisons of all physicians within a particular specialty and within a specific geographic region. This information keeps providers abreast of their practice and referring patterns. In the future, providers should expect physician profiling to be a significant tool for the MCO to reduce provider panels.

The provider should be aware that the administrative section of the agreement often contains reference to policies and procedures that are not usually part of the initial proposal packet. Some agreements include specific reference to the MCO's policies and procedures, corporate documents, or state or federal statutes. Providers should ask for copies of these documents as they work through the negotiating process.

The administrative section also addresses the timely filing and prompt payment of claims. Whether placed in this section or the reimbursement section, provisions for timely filing, prompt payments, refunds, coordination of benefits (COB), and annual increases must be included. For capitated contracts, the practice can include a provision for an annual increase. Providers should exercise caution when using the Consumer Price Index (CPI) to determine the level of increase as this may not enhance capitation payments that are already inadequate. The practice may need to renegotiate the compensation section of the agreement instead.

The agreement should make clear how the referral management and utilization review will be performed. Specifically, the provider should know the MCO's response time for utilization review requests, how the appeals process works, and the extent of his or her accessibility to the medical director.

## HOT POINTS

Often, MCOs provide little flexibility on the term, termination, amendment, and assignment sections of the agreement. However, negotiating these provisions can protect both the MCO and provider from unilaterally changing the agreement. When founded on the principle of open communication, these sections can avert the fulfillment of hidden agendas.

The term of the agreement is generally for one year, renewed annually on the anniversary date. Agreements with provisions that prohibit the provider from canceling the agreement prior to the end of the initial term negate the fact that termination provisions exist for this eventuality.

Termination clauses can take many forms and can be quite one-sided. "Without cause" termination notices should have similar time periods as those outlined in the amendment section. It is not acceptable for the MCO to request a 90 day termination notice from the provider, while the MCO only needs 60 days to amend the contract. This section should also include provisions for continuing care management upon termination. In most instances this can be negotiated. Provisions that obligate a provider to continue care for greater than 90 days after termination place too much onus on the provider.

With the negotiation of more risk contracts, it is advisable to implement term and termination provisions that coincide with the time frames established for the calculation and distribution of risk pools. For example, if utilization data are reviewed and performance measured on a calendar basis, the initial term of the agreement should be through December 31 and renew automatically each January 1.

Amendments provide the opportunity to keep the document current. However, few agreements allow providers to amend the document. Moreover, many contracts contain inflexible and one-sided language that offers the provider the option to terminate if it does not accept the proposed amendment. We prefer to include more palatable language such as, "This agreement may be amended from time to time by either party with a 60 day notice. The provider or MCO will have 45 days during which to respond. If no such response is received the provisions will go into effect on the date noted."

Fairness and moderation temper the ability of the MCO to assign the agreement, as well. Providers should recognize that the assignment sections are very explicit. Agreements that allow the MCO to assign the agreement without notice to the provider are not advisable in our opinion. Usually, the amendment provisions allow the parties to assign the agreement.

## CONCLUSION

The current trend of MCOs offering multiple products (i.e., HMOs, PPOs, point-of-service (POS) plans, and indemnity plans) makes it worthwhile for the practice to consider implementing an "all-products" strategy. Regulatory efforts supporting self-referral, benefit design, and reimbursement variations make this strategy attractive both administratively and clinically. Because each product requires different contract arrangements the agreements should be reviewed as a singular umbrella document with differing terms and conditions, reimbursement guidelines, and appeal procedures as appropriate.

It is unfortunate that some MCOs do not offer group contracts to providers. The singular physician agreement is outdated, time consuming, and wasteful. When possible, providers should pursue group agreements.

Providers should approach contract negotiation with new MCOs who are recruiting a new panel of providers differently than with established MCOs. While new MCOs are eager to demonstrate to insurance commissioners that they offer their members a sufficient provider panel, providers should not feel compelled to sign agreements without a thorough examination of the provider contract and an assessment of the impact it will have on the practice.

Lastly, when the practice has concluded a contract, it should be sure to obtain a fully executed agreement to keep on file. Frequently, practices do not receive the executed contract with an effective date and appropriate reimbursement tables and attachments from the MCO. The practice should create a separate file for each MCO that houses a signed contract and all relevant contracting materials, including time-sensitive summary information.

# 4

# Analyzing Financial Arrangements

*Nancy L. Reaven*
*Kathi S. Patterson*

American medicine has been fundamentally transformed by the growth of the industry known as "managed health care." One of the most profound changes concerns the ways in which the "providers" of health care services are paid. Physician reimbursement has rapidly evolved from a system of direct payments from patients to doctors, through the inception and implementation of scheduled fees, to, in some cases, a system of prospective payments for services known as capitation, wherein payments for anticipated services are remitted before any actual services occur. This chapter will begin with a brief look at this evolution, before covering in detail the current technologies of payment.

## TRADITIONAL PAYMENT METHODOLOGIES

Before World War II, the vast majority of physicians were paid directly by the patients they served. After the war, as systems of third-party reimbursement were initiated, insurance companies began to underwrite the risks of health insurance, which was paid for through premiums charged to employers or to individuals. The federal government underwrote programs of health insurance for the elderly and the poor through the federal programs of Medicare and Medicaid.

During this period, physician reimbursement was based on physician charges, which were, in turn, based on what the market would bear, the market being local or regional. A reimbursement approach based on the notions of "usual and customary" evolved, so that only physician charges that were significantly above the local "usual and customary" definitions garnered any attention by third party payers.

81

By the early 1970s, it was generally agreed that health care costs were rising faster than the country could afford. Following the lead of the federal government, the market attempted a series of corrections to uncontrolled reimbursements to health care providers. Insurance carriers added a caveat to traditional physician reimbursement through the addition of the concept of "reasonableness" to "usual and customary" reimbursement policies. Insurers reviewed local physician billing patterns and established upper limits on reimbursement, based on the CPT-4 codes that define the services physicians provided. Reimbursement from insurers was limited to these maximums. Physician charges in excess of the usual, customary, and reasonable schedules became the responsibility of the patient.

New methodologies of physician reimbursement have developed along with cost-containment techniques. Figure 4-1 illustrates a continuum of reimbursement approaches that have been implemented by managed care organizations (MCOs) over the last two decades. They range from the methods representing the most flexibility for physicians to the least flexibility. The continuum also correlates the reimbursement methodologies with the level of cost containment they deliver as it tracks the evolution of risk transfer from MCO to provider. (See the following section titled "Reimbursement Arrangements" for a detailed discussion of each of these reimbursement methodologies.)

The primary goal behind the transfer of insurance risk to the providers of health care services is the modification of the traditional behavior patterns of physicians and other providers. Evidence suggests that the fee-for-service system of reimbursement promoted the use of technology and services without regard to the costs (or even the efficacy of such services in some cases.)[1] By shifting the financial risk for services to providers, MCOs rid themselves of insurance risk they cannot directly control. Providers, the argument goes, are in the optimal position to manage these risks. However, providers of care have an economic interest in managing care only if they are financially responsible for such care. Hence, evolving reimbursement meth-

---

(Most Flexible)                                                                    (Least Flexible)

Discount Fee-for-Service----------Fee Schedules----------Package Pricing-----------Capitation

(Least Cost Containment)                                            (Most Cost Containment)

**Figure 4-1** Reimbursement Continuum

odologies represent increasing risk transfer to providers of care, particularly physicians.

Under discounted fee-for-service (DFFS) and fee schedule–based pricing, the MCO still holds the insurance risk, which can be crudely estimated as the price of medical services multiplied by the utilization of services, compared against the premium received. Discounting provider fees impacts only one part of the equation, the price of services. The utilization of services is still uncontrolled. In addition, simple percentage discounts on services can be easily rendered ineffective by raising the charge basis upon which the discounts are calculated.

Fee schedule–based reimbursement programs are not as easily manipulated as simple percentage discount programs. However, the usage of services is often not well controlled under these systems. By increasing the level of service usage, physicians under fee schedule–based programs can generate revenue on the volume of services provided, which may compensate for any reductions negotiated in the price of services as reflected in the fee schedule.

Package pricing (and a variant known as case rate pricing) illustrates a first step toward the complete transfer of insurance risk to the providers of health services. The providers of care are "at risk" for the intensity of the services provided under the package price, for example, surgeries that are more complicated than anticipated, more medical consultant services, longer hospital stays, and more ancillary service usage. Although the provider takes some financial risk for the episode of care covered by the package price, he or she does not take risk for the population of members that constitute the base from which patients can be referred. In other words, the provider does not assume risk for the number of procedures that may be performed. The package price arrangement comes into play only when a patient has been referred for the specific procedure.

Capitation reimbursement represents fairly complete risk transfer to physicians. For a set monthly fee, the physician or group of physicians is responsible for a defined set of services covering a defined population of potential patients often known as "members." For the first time, the providers of health care services are responsible for an entire population of individuals who could become patients.


## POPULATION TYPES

The transfer of insurance risk to physicians requires physicians to understand a great deal more about the populations of patients they serve. Under most fee-for-service reimbursements, demographically linked variations in the services patients require are of little importance to physicians. However, under capitation programs, physicians cannot evaluate the adequacy of capitation payments, anticipate resource requirements, or manage the resulting insurance risks without understanding the differences in health services consumption characterized by the different populations of patients they are being asked to serve.

Insurers will typically offer separate provider contracts for different populations of patients. These populations are usually divided into the following three categories: commercial, Medicare, and Medicaid. At a minimum, the standard provider contract should contain exhibits that differentiate between these three population groupings and specify the contract and compensation features that are specific to each.

## Commercial Business

Commercial business is sometimes (and somewhat erroneously) referred to as group business. Commercial business refers generally to insurance contracts between insurers and employers or individuals who do not qualify for Medicare or Medicaid. Commercial business consists of insureds who are generally younger than sixty-five years and are employed or are dependents of an employed individual. (Note: for some employees older than sixty-five, Medicare can be a secondary payer to a commercial plan.) "Group" business is really a subset of commercial business and refers to insurance agreements that are generated through contracts with employers, covering groups of employees and their dependents.

Individuals who are self-employed or unemployed can purchase individual policies of health insurance; however, until recently, many MCOs shied away from this business, wary of the insurance risk posed by an insured individual or family. Presently, some health maintenance organizations (HMOs) offer coverage to individuals and families under provider contracts that reimburse providers at rates that can be significantly lower than for group business. The HMOs maintain that the medical underwriting performed on these covered individuals has eliminated all but the "best" risks. Although this may be accurate in the short term, over the long term even these individuals will become ill or injured and will use health services.

Commercial populations contain specific insurance risks, including pregnancy and childbirth, smoking-related diseases, and HIV infection.

## Senior Business

Senior business refers to insurance contracts that fall under the jurisdiction of the Health Care Financing Administration (HCFA) through the Medicare program. Physicians receive Medicare patients in one of two ways—through a direct relationship with HCFA by agreeing to accept Medicare assignment for payment for services, or through a contract with one or more of the HMOs that have contracted with HCFA for a Medicare risk contract. (There are also some pilot programs sponsored by HCFA, and some older "cost" contracts between HCFA and some HMOs, but these are relatively rare and will not be discussed in depth in this chapter.)

HCFA reimburses nonrisk business using a relative value schedule known as the Resource-Based Relative Value Scale, or RBRVS. This relatively new schedule was developed by the Harvard School of Public Health for HCFA and was designed to emphasize the value of patient evaluation and disease management services as opposed to Medicare or surgical procedures.

HCFA has also contracted with a number of HMOs under a risk contract methodology. According to a recent survey of the nation's HMOs, 21 percent had developed new Medicare risk contracts in 1995, and an addtional 34 percent planned to do so in 1996. As of January, 1995, 23 percent of the nation's HMOs had a Medicare risk contract.[2] These HMOs offer the comprehensive benefits typical of HMOs to Medicare beneficiaries with little or no additional premium payments, no deductibles, and low co-payments. HCFA pays the HMOs a prospective monthly fee for each Medicare member, similar to the premium paid by employers for coverage of their employees. The HCFA payment represents 95 percent of the area's historical fee-for-service Medicare costs, according to a schedule known as the adjusted average per capita cost, or AAPCC. The AAPCC attempts to reflect the wide geographic variation in physician and hospital fees stemming from the historical fee-for-service reimbursement system. (As an example, the 1996 AAPCC allocation for Part B Medicare in Palm Beach, Florida, was $267.70 per month, compared to Gosper, Nebraska, at $91.64 a month.[3])

The HMO negotiates reimbursement arrangements with the physicians and hospitals who are under contract to provide services to the HMO's Medicare enrollees. The HMO retains between 12 and 20 percent of the HCFA payment to fund its administrative expenses and profit, and may also retain additional amounts to cover services provided outside the HMO service area (commonly referred to as "out-of-area services") and other like "carve-outs." The balance is used to pay for physician and other health service costs. The reimbursement system for physicians can take several forms, but is typically based on a relative value schedule, like RBRVS, or a capitation methodology.

A population of senior citizens offers different challenges to the physician practices charged with managing their care. In general, seniors use overall health services at a rate approximately four times that of the commercial population (closer to two and a half to three times the rate of commercial populations for physician services). They see physicians more often, are admitted to hospitals more often, and stay in hospitals for longer periods. This is due to the chronic nature of the majority of the diseases affecting the elderly, their increasing frailty, and a variety of psychosocial factors that can leave them without adequate support systems.

## Medicaid

State governments have only recently joined the trend toward managed care in the federally mandated and state-administered programs of Medicaid. Medicaid covers the costs of care for the medically indigent and disabled. It is jointly funded by the federal government and by the state, and is operated by each state's Department of Health in accordance with federal mandates. Medicaid provides medical assistance to individuals who are eligible for cash assistance under such programs as Aid to Families with Dependent Children (AFDC) and Supplemental Security Income (SSI). Medicaid benefits may also be available to other people who have enough income for basic living expenses but cannot afford to pay for medical care.

Within the last five years, however, several state governments have implemented programs designed to move large numbers of Medicaid beneficiaries into HMOs. A Medicaid HMO functions much like a Medicare HMO, but is regulated at the individual state level. The state also develops its own policies regarding eligibility rules and requirements under a waiver process whereby HCFA authorizes state-proposed modifications to the federal program. For example, some states include only AFDC populations (representing approximately 70 percent of the overall Medicaid eligibles) in Medicaid HMO contracts. Other states include both AFDC and the SSI eligibles.

The state develops a premium payment, usually referred to as a capitation rate, which it pays to the HMO as compensation in full for treating the Medicaid beneficiary. Typically, the state will base its

HMO capitation on the projected Medicaid fee-for-service costs per capita in a specific geographic region, usually a county, and establishes a percentage reimbursement level, commonly between 90 and 100 percent of the projected fee-for-service costs. (HCFA regulations require that the payment to an HMO be no more than 100 percent of the fee-for-service costs.) Some states require a competitive bidding process for HMOs to win Medicaid contracts. The aggressiveness of an HMO in its bid will determine, in part, the monies available for physician reimbursement.

In general, the reimbursement levels offered to physicians by HMOs for Medicaid members are lower than those for commercial contracts (but may still be higher than traditional Medicaid fee-for-service reimbursement). This is due in part to the fact that the HMO capitation from the state is based on historical claims experience, and the states have not reimbursed Medicaid claims particularly generously in the past, averaging about 55 percent of billed charges. In addition, the HMO must also cover its own administration and profit, usually in the range of 12 to 20 percent.

The populations included under most state Medicaid programs have unique health characteristics. AFDC populations are primarily young women and children, with children accounting for approximately two thirds of the total. Expenditures associated with childbirth, premature delivery, and mental health are higher than comparatively aged commercial populations.[4] This segment of the Medicaid population also routinely seeks care from hospital emergency rooms. Therefore, these costs are also disproportionately high. SSI populations, however, often comprise patients with low income who are elderly and/or disabled. They are often afflicted with chronic diseases and complications resulting from their disabilities.

## REIMBURSEMENT ARRANGEMENTS

The following section describes the most common forms of provider reimbursement.

### Discounted Fee-for-Service

Discounted fee-for-service is a method of reimbursement that is based on the physician's normal schedule of charges. A physician executes a contract with an MCO to provide services at a percentage of this schedule of charges. The discount is usually a flat percentage applied to all procedures in the schedule. This form of negotiated reimbursement is the closest relative of the fee-for-service reimbursement used by indemnity carriers, and is commonly used by preferred provider organizations (PPOs) and sometimes by HMOs.

The MCO may include a clause in the contract that stipulates reimbursement maximums. These maximums are applied to the claim before the negotiated discount is taken and are similar to the usual, customary, and reasonable (UCR) maximum charge levels used by indemnity carriers. The discounted charge for a procedure is typically limited to a percentile of the community average charge for that procedure. The maximum is normally set somewhere between the fortieth and the eightieth percentile.

To receive payment for services rendered, the physician simply bills the MCO from the agreed upon schedule of charges. After adjudicating the claim, the MCO applies any applicable maximums to the billed charge and then applies the negotiated discount. The physician is then reimbursed this revised amount. The timing of payment will vary depending on the MCO, and is usually subject to state regulatory requirements, but a maximum time limit from the date of claim submission to payment should be included in the contract as an added protection. Physicians should also pay attention to the claims submission language included in provider agreements to ensure that their office procedures can accommodate these requirements.

*Evaluating Discounted Fee Schedules*

To evaluate the adequacy of a negotiated discount, the physician must have an understanding of his or her own charge base and its relationship to actual expenses. Physicians often set or adjust their schedule of charges based on informal or formal fee surveys. As a result, practice expenses associated with providing a particular service may not strictly coincide with the charge for that service. When a flat percentage discount is applied to all services, some procedures may now be in a loss position whereas others still maintain an adequate margin.

Expenses consist of the following two components: fixed costs and variable costs. Fixed costs exist regardless of the number of services provided, for example, rent, furniture, and salaries. Variable costs occur only when a service is rendered and refer to such factors as physician time, nurse time, and supplies. The margin for expenses and profit in each charge should contribute to covering fixed costs and profit, as well as the variable cost associated with providing that service.

Marginal costs decrease as patient volume increases, because fixed costs can be spread over a larger revenue base. If the contract under evaluation is intended to increase patient volume, then a discount might result in an increase in profit. However, if the contract is needed to retain existing patients, then a discount will simply reduce revenue by the discount on these patients. On the other hand, losing the patients may reduce revenue even more!

Another consideration is the mix of services provided. If the contract with the MCO will increase the physician's patient base, then it is likely that the mix of services will change. If it shifts toward services with lower margins, then lower-than-expected profits on this new business will be generated. For instance, if the contract in question will add a significant number of Medicare patients to a predominantly commercial patient base, those services rendered predominantly to this population will increase. If these services have smaller-than-average margins in the charge base, it is possible that this increased volume may actually produce losses for the practice.

Table 4–1 illustrates an "ideal" method for evaluating a discounted fee schedule. For this analysis, the physician must assign a variable cost to each procedure in the schedule of charges. An assumption for annual utilization by procedure is also needed for the appropriate population. This might be obtained from the MCO, an independent actuary, or if possible, the physician's existing patient information system if the anticipated population appears to be similar to the physician's existing patient base. The final element that must be determined is the amount of fixed expenses that are not already covered by the existing patient base. In a profitable practice, all fixed costs are already covered by the existing patient base. However, if the contract is needed to retain existing patients, this fixed expense analysis is more complicated. An actuary would be helpful in performing this type of analysis.

Column a in Table 4–1 lists the assumed utilization for the patients covered by the discounted fee-for-service contract for each procedure in the physician's schedule of charges, the fees of which are detailed in column b. Estimated revenue for each procedure, based on the assumed utilization and current fee for each procedure, is calculated in column c. Column d represents the discounted revenue, derived by applying the proposed discount to the estimated revenue (column c).

**Table 4-1** "Ideal" Discounted Fee-for-Service Evaluation

| CPT[1] | Procedure Description | (a) Assumed Utilization | (b) Fee | (c) Estimated Revenue (a) x (b) | (d) Estimated Discounted Revenue[2] (c) x 0.80 | (e) Estimated Variable Cost | Estimated Variable Expense (a) x (e) |
|---|---|---|---|---|---|---|---|
| 95819 | Electroencephalogram (EEG) | 15.64 | $196.00 | $3,065 | $2,452 | $105.00 | $1,642 |
| 96410 | Chemotherapy, infusion method | 27.54 | 109.00 | 3,002 | 2,401 | 68.00 | 1,873 |
| 99202 | Office/outpatient visit, new | 41.23 | 65.00 | 2,680 | 2,144 | 36.00 | 1,484 |
| 99212 | Office/outpatient visit, established | 140.58 | 40.00 | 5,623 | 4,499 | 24.00 | 3,374 |
|  |  | • • • | • • • | • • • | • • • | • • • | • • • |
| 99215 | Office/outpatient visit, established | 60.65 | 118.00 | 7,157 | 5,725 | 64.00 | 3,882 |
| 99222 | Initial hospital care | 125.40 | 151.00 | 18,935 | 15,148 | 88.00 | 11,035 |
| 99233 | Subsequent hospital care | 191.00 | 104.00 | 19,864 | 15,891 | 59.00 | 11,269 |
| 99385 | Preventive visit, new, 18–39 | 207.52 | 98.00 | 20,337 | 16,270 | 61.00 | 12,659 |
| 99386 | Preventive visit, new, 40–64 | 93.84 | 108.00 | 10,135 | 8,108 | 66.00 | 6,193 |
| 99431 | Initial care, normal newborn | 120.56 | 116.00 | 13,985 | 11,188 | 64.00 | 7,716 |
| 99433 | Normal newborn care, hospital | 57.80 | 57.00 | 3,295 | 2,636 | 30.00 | 1,734 |
| Total | All Procedures | 10,000.00 | | $35,125 | $28,100 | | $22,831 |

Discounted FFS[3]

| | |
|---|---|
| Estimated Variable Expenses | $22,831 |
| Estimated Fixed Expenses[4] | $ 3,500 |
| Estimated Total Expenses | $26,331 |
| Estimated /Revenue | $28,100 |
| Estimated Profit/(Loss) | $ 1,769 |

[1]Current Procedural Terminology.
[2]Assumed a 20% discount, therefore discounted revenue is 80% of FFS revenue.
[3]Fee-For-Service.
[4]Includes only those fixed expenses that are not already covered by remaining undiscounted FFS patients.

Column e represents the variable costs associated with performing each procedure. The last column, column f, calculates the estimated variable expenses by procedure by multiplying the assumed utilization by the variable cost. Finally, the estimated profit or loss is calculated by subtracting the estimated total expenses for the patients affected by the proposed agreement from the estimated revenue. The estimated total expenses equals the sum, for all procedures, of the variable expenses in column f plus the estimated fixed expenses that are not already covered by the revenue from the remaining undiscounted fee-for-service patients. This estimated profit or loss can be used to evaluate the attractiveness of the proposed discounted fee-for-service agreement.

Although the method illustrated previously might be considered an "ideal" analysis, physicians and physician groups may not have access to the required expense detail. An alternative analysis involves the assumption that the physician accepts the contract offered by the MCO and calculates the adjustment to the physician's revenue by the proposed discount and any anticipated change in work volume (Table 4–2). After subtracting expected total expenses from the revenue, a physician "salary" can be estimated. One method of estimating the expected total expenses involves multiplying the current variable expenses by the estimated change in volume and adding this to the current expenses. For example, in the first scenario, the current expenses total $90,000 ($40,000 of fixed expenses and $50,000 of variable expenses). Total anticipated expenses, assuming the proposed reimbursement agreement is accepted, can be estimated by multiplying the $50,000 of variable expenses by the 30-percent increase in volume (resulting in a $15,000 increase in variable expenses) and adding this amount to the current expenses of $90,000. This gives an estimated total expense of $105,000. The physician can then compare the level of the anticipated "salary" against the anticipated expense to determine if the discount is reasonable.

Alternatively, assume that the contract is not accepted and perform a similar analysis to estimate the physician's "salary" based on current undiscounted fees and a lower work volume (due to a lower patient base if physician may lose patients if the contract is not accepted, or a static patient base if physician assumes the contract will potentially increase volume). Compare the "salary" associated with more work to the "salary" associated with less work to evaluate the attractiveness of the contract. The second scenario presented in Table 4–2 illustrates this analysis.

**Table 4–2** Sample Discounted Fee-for-Service Evaluations

### Scenario I: Contracting to Increase Patient Base

|  | Current Situation | Accept Initial Contract | Counter-Offer |
|---|---|---|---|
| a. Current Revenue | $200,000 | $200,000 | $200,000 |
| b. Estimated Change in Volume | 0% | 30% | 30% |
| c. Proposed Discount | 0% | 25% | 15% |
| d. Estimated Change in Revenue [a × b × (1 − c)] | $0 | $45,000 | $51,000 |
| e. Estimated Future Revenue [a + d] | $200,000 | $245,000 | $251,000 |
| f. Current Fixed Expenses | $40,000 | $40,000 | $40,000 |
| g. Current Variable Expenses | $50,000 | $50,000 | $50,000 |
| h. Estimated Change in Variable Expenses [g × b] | $0 | $15,000 | $15,000 |
| i. Estimated Total Expenses [f + g + h] | $90,000 | $105,000 | $105,000 |
| j. Estimated Salary [e − i] | $110,000 | $140,000 | $146,000 |
| k. Estimated Percentage Increase in Salary | | 27% | 33% |

*Analysis:* If the initial contact is accepted, the physician is expected to increase his or her workload by 30% for a 27% increase in salary. Alternatively, a counter-offer of a 15% discount would lead to an expected increase in salary of 33% for the 30% increase in workload.

### Scenario II: Contracting to Retain Patient Base

|  | Current Situation | No Contract | Accept Initial Contract |
|---|---|---|---|
| a. Current Revenue | $200,000 | $200,000 | $200,000 |
| b. Estimated Change in Volume | 0% | −25% | 0% |
| c. Proposed Discount | 0% | 0% | 15% |
| d. Estimated Change in Revenue [a × b × (1 − c)] | $0 | −$50,000 | −$7,500[1] |
| e. Estimated Future Revenue [a + d] | $200,000 | $150,000 | $192,500 |
| f. Current Fixed Expenses | $40,000 | $40,000 | $40,000 |
| g. Current Variable Expenses | $50,000 | $50,000 | $50,000 |
| h. Estimated Change in Variable Expenses [g × b] | $0 | −$12,500 | $0 |
| i. Estimated Total Expenses [f + g + h] | $90,000 | $77,500 | $90,000 |
| j. Estimated Salary [e − i] | $110,000 | $72,500 | $102,500 |
| k. Estimated Percentage Increase in Salary | | −34% | −7% |

*Analysis:* If the current contract is rejected, the physician's patient base (and workload) will be reduced by 25% and the physician's salary will be reduced by an estimated 34%. Alternatively, if the contract is accepted, the physician's patient base (and workload) will be retained and the physician's salary will be reduced only by an estimated 7%.

[1]Estimated Change in Revenue is calculated by taking the Current Revenue from patients retained because of contracting and applying the proposed discount. In this case, revenue is reduced by $200,000 × 25% × 15%.

*Pros and Cons*

In general, there are several benefits to discounted fee-for-service reimbursement structures for physicians. First, it is most similar to their traditional method of reimbursement, so the physician's billing system and basic administrative procedures will not have to be significantly altered. Second, the insurance risk is retained by the MCO so the provider is still reimbursed for all services rendered. Finally, it can be used as a first step to "test the water" with a managed care organization. This allows the physician time to become familiar with an MCO to determine whether he or she would be willing to accept additional risks in return for potential gains.

There are also disadvantages associated with a discounted fee-for-service reimbursement structure. Current charge levels may not correspond to the costs associated with the service provided, so a flat discount may actually generate losses on certain procedures. The physician may be required to obtain approval from the MCO before implementing any changes to his or her charge base. If the MCO does not agree to the changes, the physician may have to maintain two schedules of charges. Finally, the negotiated discount may be large if the physician must contract to retain existing patients. This can be especially problematic if risk/reward terms are not included in the contract, because there is little potential for gains to make up for the big discount.

## Relative Value–Based Fee Schedules

Reimbursement arrangements that are based on fee schedules derived from relative unit values are called relative value–based fee schedules. These fee schedules are not based on a physician's schedule of charges. They are developed from a set of unit values that have been assigned to each procedure (CPT-4 code) in the schedule. These unit values attempt to establish relationships between procedures. For example, if one procedure has a unit value of 2 and another has a unit value of 4, this implies that the authors of the scale perceive the second procedure to be worth twice as much as the first procedure.

The unit values by themselves do not create a fee schedule. A dollar amount, called a conversion factor, must be multiplied by a unit value to produce a fee. Some relative value scales allow for one conversion factor to be applied to the unit values for all procedures, whereas others require separate conversion factors for different groups of procedures. If multiple conversion factors are used, it is common to group procedures into the following categories: surgery, anesthesia, medicine, radiology, and pathology. Other groupings can be used, depending on the scale and negotiations between the MCO and the physician. Multiplying each unit value by an appropriate conversion factor results in a fee schedule. Often, the MCO will reimburse a physician only the lesser of the actual billed charges or the fee calculated from the fee schedule.

There are several different published versions of unit values that can be used to create a fee schedule. The four most common scales are the McGraw-Hill Unit Value System, the RBRVS, the unit values published by the American Society of Anesthesiologists (ASA) for anesthesia procedures, and the California Relative Value Study (1974 CRVS).

### McGraw-Hill Unit Value System

One of the most recognized relative value schedules used through-out the country for commercial business is published by McGraw-Hill, Inc. It is commonly referred to as the McGraw-Hill unit value scale. This is the only widely used relative value system that has unit values for all procedures (CPT-4 codes), except anesthesia. McGraw-Hill, Inc. conducts extensive annual research to update existing unit values and assign unit values to new procedures. The relative values used in this system and the basis behind them, however, are not well defined. The procedures are commonly grouped into four of the five major categories described previously (no anesthesia) with the conversion factors varying significantly. Although the unit values within a particular grouping are based on a relative relationship, there is no like relationship between groupings. Thus, it would not be accurate to conclude that a procedure from one group (such as surgery) with a unit value of 3 is worth three times as much as a procedure from a different group (such as medicine) with a unit value of 1. For instance, the conversion factor for the surgery group could be $114 whereas the conversion factor for the medicine group might be more like $6, resulting in fees that differ by a factor of 57. Table 4–3 illustrates how fees are calculated for a few procedures.

### Resource-Based Relative Value Scale

Another widely recognized schedule of unit values is the RBRVS. This system was originally developed by HCFA for Medicare reimbursement. However, it is now being adopted by many MCOs for non-

**Table 4–3** Sample McGraw-Hill Fee Schedule

| CPT[1] | Procedure Description | McGraw-Hill Unit Value (a) | Sample Conversion Factor (b) | Fee Schedule (b) x (c) |
|---|---|---|---|---|
| 99202 | Office/outpatient visit, new | 9.50 | $5.50 | $52.25 |
| 99215 | Office/outpatient visit, est | 19.50 | 5.50 | 107.25 |
| 99233 | Subsequent hospital care | 20.00 | 5.50 | 110.00 |
| 99385 | Preventive visit, new, 18–39 | 16.00 | 5.50 | 88.00 |
| 99431 | Initial care, normal newborn | 22.00 | 5.50 | 121.00 |
| 33513 | CABG, vein, four | 51.00 | 126.00 | 6,426.00 |
| 35646 | Artery bypass graft | 32.00 | 126.00 | 4,032.00 |
| 58260 | Vaginal hysterectomy | 19.00 | 126.00 | 2,394.00 |
| 70553 | Magnetic image, brain | 64.00 | 21.00 | 1,344.00 |
| 72148 | Magnetic image, lumbar spine | 49.00 | 21.00 | 1,029.00 |
| 73721 | Magnetic image, joint of leg | 49.00 | 21.00 | 1,029.00 |

[1]Current Procedural Terminology.

Medicare reimbursement. Each unit value is based on the following three components: the physician's work expense, the physician's practice expense (overhead), and the physician's malpractice expense. These unit values are adjusted by regional factors to account for geographic differences in health care costs across the United States. A total unit value is calculated by adding the three area-adjusted unit values. This system is designed to use a single conversion factor for all procedures; however, this will tend to reduce compensation for certain types of physicians relative to other physicians. Thus, many MCOs develop multiple conversion factors to appease physicians in multispecialty physician groups. The biggest drawback to RBRVS is the absence of unit values for some procedures. Because this schedule was developed to accommodate Medicare-covered services, procedures such as immunizations and well-baby care are not valued. McGraw-Hill, Inc. has attempted to impute values for these procedures and includes them in *The McGraw-Hill Complete RBRVS*, which is updated annually. There are also no unit values for anesthesia and pathology procedures. Table 4–4 illustrates how fees are calculated using an RBRVS schedule.

## American Society of Anesthesiologists

The ASA publishes a relative value unit system for all anesthesia procedures. Each procedure has a base unit value assigned to it.

**Table 4-4** Sample RBRVS[1] Fee Schedule

Oklahoma Geographic Area Factors

| | Work | Practice | Malpractice |
|---|---|---|---|
| | 0.970 | 0.882 | 0.481 |

| CPT[3] | Procedure Description | Work RVU[2] (a) | Practice RVU[2] (b) | Malpractice RVU[2] (c) | Total RVU[2] (d)[4] | Conversion Factor (e) | Fee Schedule (d) × (e) |
|---|---|---|---|---|---|---|---|
| 99202 | Office/outpatient visit, new | 0.750 | 0.450 | 0.050 | 1.148 | $35.00 | $40.20 |
| 99215 | Office/outpatient visit, est | 1.510 | 0.760 | 0.070 | 2.169 | 35.00 | 75.90 |
| 99233 | Subsequent hospital care | 1.250 | 0.600 | 0.050 | 1.766 | 35.00 | 61.80 |
| 99385 | Preventive visit, new, 18–39 | 1.530 | 1.400 | 0.090 | 2.762 | 35.00 | 96.68 |
| 99431 | Initial care, normal newborn | 1.170 | 1.210 | 0.080 | 2.241 | 35.00 | 78.42 |
| 33513 | CABG, vein, four | 30.120 | 38.210 | 6.730 | 66.155 | 40.00 | 2,646.19 |
| 35646 | Artery bypass graft | 24.000 | 23.780 | 4.730 | 46.529 | 40.00 | 1,861.16 |
| 58260 | Vaginal hysterectomy | 11.390 | 9.390 | 2.070 | 20.326 | 40.00 | 813.04 |
| 70553 | Magnetic image, brain | 2.360 | 24.790 | 1.650 | 24.948 | 34.00 | 848.22 |
| 72148 | Magnetic image, lumbar spine | 1.480 | 12.520 | 0.840 | 12.882 | 34.00 | 438.00 |
| 73721 | Magnetic image, joint of leg | 0.950 | 11.110 | 0.730 | 11.072 | 34.00 | 376.44 |

[1] Resource-Based Relative Value System.
[2] Relative Value Unit.
[3] Current Procedural Terminology.
[4] Calculated as (a) × 0.970 + (b) × .882 + (c) × .481.

Additional time units are added to the base unit before a conversion factor is applied. These time units can be measured in twelve- or fifteen-minute intervals, depending on community norms and the MCO's goals. The base unit value is designed to cover the set-up time involved in a procedure, and the time units are intended to cover the actual time elapsed during the procedure. A negotiated conversion factor is multiplied by the total of the base units and the time units for a procedure to calculate the reimbursement. The ASA relative value system is the only generally recognized system for anesthesia procedures and is often used in combination with other relative value systems or reimbursement arrangements.

*California Relative Value System*

The 1974 California Relative Value System (CRVS) was developed by the California Medical Association (CMA). This was a widely recognized relative value system until the CMA stopped publishing it because of antitrust concerns. Although the unit values have not been updated since 1974, this system is still used in California and a few other states. It functions identically to the McGraw-Hill unit value system described previously. Its major disadvantage is that many new procedures developed during the past two decades have not been valued. In contracts that use CRVS, these procedures are usually reimbursed on the basis of a percentage discount from billed charges. (Of course, this can be a distinct advantage to physicians if the proposed conversion factors represent an even steeper discount from billed charges.)

*Evaluating Relative Value–Based Fee Schedules*

Table 4–5 illustrates how to evaluate a proposed fee schedule. The MCO will likely propose a unit value system and a single conversion factor, or multiple conversion factors. To evaluate the proposal, a physician must either convert his or her current fee levels into conversion factors or convert the proposed unit values and conversion factor(s) into a fee schedule. Either process will yield the overall discount being asked of the physician. (Both of these processes are included in Table 4–5. Note that some of the discounts are negative, meaning that the fee derived from the relative value schedule and the proposed conversion schedule yield a payment that is greater than the physician's own billed charge. MCOs will often try to prevent this occurrence by inserting contract language that specifies that actual

**Table 4–5** Sample Relative Value Unit Fee Schedule Evaluation

| | | (a) | (b) | (c) | (d) | (e) | (f) | (g) |
|---|---|---|---|---|---|---|---|---|
| CPT | Procedure Description | Assumed Utilization | Provider Fee | Unit Value | Provider Conversion Factor [(b)/(c)] | Proposed Conversion Factor | Resulting Fee Schedule [(c)×(e)] | Effective Discount [1-(f)/(b)] or [1-(e)/(d)] |
| 95819 | Electroencephalogram (EEG) | 15.64 | $196.00 | 23.00 | $8.52 | $5.50 | $126.50 | 35.5% |
| 96410 | Chemotherapy, infusion method | 27.54 | 109.00 | 17.00 | 6.41 | 5.50 | 93.50 | 14.2% |
| 99202 | Office/outpatient visit, new | 41.23 | 65.00 | 9.50 | 6.84 | 5.50 | 52.25 | 19.6% |
| 99212 | Office/outpatient visit, est | 140.58 | 40.00 | 6.00 | 6.67 | 5.50 | 33.00 | 17.5% |
| 99215 | Office/outpatient visit, est | 60.65 | 118.00 | 19.50 | 6.05 | 5.50 | 107.25 | 9.1% |
| 99222 | Initial hospital care | 125.40 | 151.00 | 22.00 | 6.86 | 5.50 | 121.00 | 19.9% |
| 99233 | Subsequent hospital care | 191.00 | 104.00 | 20.00 | 5.20 | 5.50 | 110.00 | –5.8% |
| 99385 | Preventive visit, new, 18–39 | 207.52 | 98.00 | 16.00 | 6.13 | 5.50 | 88.00 | 10.2% |
| 99386 | Preventive visit, new, 40–64 | 93.84 | 108.00 | 17.00 | 6.35 | 5.50 | 93.50 | 13.4% |
| 99431 | Initial care, normal newborn | 120.56 | 116.00 | 22.00 | 5.27 | 5.50 | 121.00 | –4.3% |
| 99433 | Normal newborn care, hospital | 57.80 | 57.00 | 10.00 | 5.70 | 5.50 | 55.00 | 3.5% |
| Total | All Procedures | 1,081.76 | $99.91 | 16.61 | $6.08 | $5.50 | $ 91.37 | 8.5% |

'Current Procedural Terminology.

payment is the lesser of the physician's billed charge or the fee schedule.) Once again, an assumed distribution of procedures is needed to complete this analysis. An actuary can provide assistance in this area, if utilization assumptions are needed. With this information, the methodologies outlined previously for evaluating a discounted fee-for-service arrangement (Tables 4–1 and 4–2) can be used to evaluate the attractiveness of the relative unit value fee schedule.

*Pros and Cons*

There are advantages to a relative value–based system of reimbursement. The basis of development of some unit value schedules may produce unit values that exhibit a closer relationship to the physician's variable costs per procedure than does the physician's current schedule of charges. Another advantage, as compared with some of the reimbursement methods described in the following sections is that the insurance risk is still held by the MCO.

One drawback to this type of arrangement is that the relative value unit schedule usually does not correlate well with a physician's current schedule of charges. For this reason, the physician's revenue could change drastically upon conversion to a fee schedule based on a relative value system, even if the composite effective discount is zero. Another downside to relative value–based fee schedules is the fact that unless multiple conversion factors are used, certain types of physicians may be taking bigger discounts than others. The only definite disadvantage to this system is the need to change the method of billing. A separate fee schedule needs to be maintained by the physician to reconcile payments from the MCO.

## Case Rates

Case rates are most commonly found in managed care contracts involving facilities, such as hospitals. However, they are increasingly being negotiated with physicians. A case rate is an agreed-upon dollar amount of reimbursement for a particular case. This amount is accepted as full reimbursement, regardless of the actual expenses or billed charges. A case could be defined as an inpatient stay, a surgery or transplant, a maternity delivery, an episode of disease, and so forth. The terms of the case should be specifically defined in the contract.

Payment is made to the physician for each incidence of the defined case. For example, an obstetrics case rate includes all prenatal, delivery, and postnatal care rendered or to be rendered, and is usually only differentiated by whether the delivery was a vaginal or cesarean delivery. Case rates for cardiovascular procedures are usually paid just after the procedure is performed. Other case-rate programs may not be as straightforward. A disease-specific case rate, such as for acquired immunodeficiency syndrome (AIDS), may not necessarily have a logical time for payment. The MCO and physician should agree, and the contract should state specifically what, how, and when physicians will be reimbursed.

The actual payment for a case may be adjusted for a variety of reasons. For example, the payment to a physician may also be adjusted by the actual severity of the case, defined as the ratio of actual billed charges to the case rate, the actual length of the hospital stay compared to that assumed in the case rate, or the specifics of the clinical condition of the patient. Any potential adjustments should be specifically stated and thoroughly explained in the contract.

*Evaluating Case Rates*

The evaluation of a case rate focuses on calculating the effective discount from billed charges. Most of the data necessary for an adequate evaluation should be found in the physician's patient files. If the billed charges and other pertinent information for a sufficient number of current and past patients satisfying the definition for a case can be gathered, then the analysis illustrated in Table 4–6 can be performed. The top section of Table 4–6 represents typical adjustments to case rate programs. For the example presented in Table 4–6, the age and billed charges (column a) for each qualifying patient are listed. The appropriate age factor (column b) is determined from the age-adjustment table. An age-adjusted case rate is calculated by multiplying the proposed case rate ($15,000) by the age factor (column b) for each patient. Column d represents the ratio of billed charges to the age-adjusted case rate, which is used to determine the severity factor (column e) from the severity-adjustment table. Finally, the age-adjusted case rate is multiplied by the severity factor to give the age- and severity-adjusted case rate (column f). The estimated change in revenue is calculated by subtracting the total billed charges from the total adjusted charges, and the effective discount is simply the change in revenue divided by the total billed charges.

The physician must then determine whether the effective discount is reasonable. The methodology in Table 4–2 could be used to help with this determination. The estimated change in volume would be

**Table 4-6** Sample Case Rate Evaluation

*Age Adjustment Table*

| Age Band | Factor |
|----------|--------|
| Under 16 | 0.80 |
| 16–50 | 1.00 |
| Over 50 | 1.20 |

*Severity Adjustment Table*

| Ratio of Billed Charges to Age-Adjusted Case Rate | Factor |
|---------------------------------------------------|--------|
| Less than 0.50 | 0.85 |
| 0.50–2.00 | 1.00 |
| Greater than 2.00 | 1.15 |

Case Rate   $15,000

| Patient | Age | (a) Billed Charges | (b) Age Factor | (c) Age-Adjusted Case Rate [$15,000 × (b)] | (d) Ratio [(a)/(c)] | (e) Severity Factor | (f) Age- and Severity-Adjusted Case Rate [(c) × (e)] |
|---------|-----|--------------------|----------------|--------------------------------------------|---------------------|---------------------|------------------------------------------------------|
| #1 | 13 | $24,248 | 0.80 | $12,000 | 2.02 | 1.15 | $13,800 |
| #2 | 5 | $ 5,348 | 0.80 | $12,000 | 0.45 | 0.85 | $10,200 |
| #3 | 18 | $14,521 | 1.00 | $15,000 | 0.97 | 1.00 | $15,000 |
| #4 | 34 | $26,874 | 1.00 | $15,000 | 1.79 | 1.00 | $15,000 |
| #5 | 42 | $32,857 | 1.00 | $15,000 | 2.19 | 1.15 | $17,250 |
| #6 | 53 | $24,024 | 1.20 | $18,000 | 1.33 | 1.00 | $18,000 |
| #7 | 0 | $17,425 | 0.80 | $12,000 | 1.45 | 1.00 | $12,000 |
| #8 | 25 | $14,276 | 1.00 | $15,000 | 0.95 | 1.00 | $15,000 |
| #9 | 61 | $ 8,172 | 1.20 | $18,000 | 0.45 | 0.85 | $15,300 |
| #10 | 49 | $18,422 | 1.00 | $15,000 | 1.23 | 1.00 | $15,000 |
| Total | | $186,167 | | | | | $146,550 |

Estimated Change in Revenue   ($39,617)
Effective Discount   21%

calculated by taking the estimated change in revenue from Table 4–6 and dividing it by the total current revenue. The proposed discount would be the effective discount calculated in Table 4–6.

*Pros and Cons*

The main advantage of a case rate for the physician is the potential for gains when the physician is able to manage the care of a patient less expensively than assumed in the case rate. However, the opposite is also true, leading to the potential for losses. Another risk that the physician assumes under case rate reimbursement is the risk of adverse selection. This occurs when a physician ends up with cases that have a higher severity than the severity assumed in the case rate. But, with the risk of adverse selection comes the potential for positive selection. These issues do not exist under fee-for-service, discounted fee-for-service, or fee schedule reimbursement structures.

## Capitation

The reimbursement arrangements discussed previously in this chapter pay physicians retrospectively for services rendered. Under capitation, however, physicians are paid, in advance, a fixed amount for each enrolled member to provide any of the services listed in the contract for a given period. This prepaid amount covers all of the listed services, regardless of the actual value of the services provided. Under capitation, physicians receive monthly payments for a member, even if that member does not use any physician services. This requires physicians to shift their perspective from patients (users) to members (potential users). Physicians must be able to translate their familiar patient-based data into comparable member-based data.

Capitation rates can be a fixed dollar amount or they can be based on a percentage of the premium that the MCO receives from an individual, group, or government agency. If the capitation is based on a percent of premium, then the physician should understand the rating and under-writing practices of the MCO. If the MCO is aggressively attempting to increase its membership base, the compensation to the physician may be less than anticipated because the premiums may be reduced to attract purchasers. It is sometimes possible to negotiate a flat dollar "floor" to percent of premium capitation contracts. In this situation, the MCO must pay capitation that is, at a minimum, equal to the negotiated floor. The underwriting practices of an MCO are also impor-tant in that they may indicate whether the MCO is likely to attract substandard risks by selling policies to companies or individuals who are disproportionately likely to become ill or injured.

Capitation rates are frequently adjusted for the age and sex of the member. This allows the capitation rate to reflect the real differences in per member per month (PMPM) costs by age and sex. The use of age and sex factors helps to protect the physician from MCO miscalculations about the covered population by linking the capitation rate to the characteristics of each member instead of assuming a particular distribution of age and sex of the covered population. In this way, some of the insurance risk is returned to the MCO. Age and sex factors can vary by type of capitation, such as primary care, specialty care, or a global rate. Table 4–7 illustrates a sample set of age and sex factors for

**Table 4–7** Sample Primary Care Capitation Age/Sex Factors

| Age/Sex Band | Age/Sex Factors |
|---|---|
| *Male* | |
| 0–1 | 2.775 |
| 2–6 | 0.992 |
| 7–18 | 0.623 |
| 19–24 | 0.502 |
| 25–29 | 0.644 |
| 30–34 | 0.651 |
| 35–39 | 0.714 |
| 40–44 | 0.822 |
| 45–49 | 0.932 |
| 50–54 | 1.094 |
| 55–59 | 1.368 |
| 60–64 | 1.565 |
| 65+ | 1.585 |
| *Female* | |
| 0–1 | 2.660 |
| 2–6 | 0.936 |
| 7–18 | 0.548 |
| 19–24 | 0.771 |
| 25–29 | 1.101 |
| 30–34 | 1.151 |
| 35–39 | 1.243 |
| 40–44 | 1.317 |
| 45–49 | 1.334 |
| 50–54 | 1.441 |
| 55–59 | 1.585 |
| 60–64 | 1.668 |
| 65+ | 1.812 |

primary care capitation. Physicians should carefully analyze the age and sex factors to ensure that the resulting composite rate is acceptable. Some HMOs will offer the factors within age ranges of various sizes. For example, the age ranges may run from 0 to 1,1 to 2, 2 to 18, 18 to 44, and then begin to narrow again from, 44 to 50, 50 to 55, 55 to 60, and so on. The associated factors will usually look attractively high for the age ranges that are narrow, and lower for the age ranges that are wide. This is intuitively reasonable because we all know that health care services are used by the very young and the older population at higher rates. However, the composite capitation rate may tell a somewhat different story, because it is based on the actual number of members within the age category. The wide age ranges, with the correspondingly low adjustment factors, apply to a large number of members, whereas the narrow age ranges apply to a proportionately smaller number of members. Consequently, the actual composite capitation rate may be much less than the provider assumes it to be. If the physician cannot convince the HMO to share the age distribution of the population under the proposed contract, the physician can use an actuary to calculate an approximate composite rate using population distributions that are common to the type of business under consideration.

Certain types of physicians need to be aware of a potential for adverse selection under a capitation contract. Pediatricians, for example, are especially at risk. Families with children with medical problems may be more likely to choose pediatricians as primary care physicians (PCPs), and families with children without any special problems may be more likely to choose a family practitioner who will serve as the entire family's PCP. Unless the capitation rates are adjusted to compensate for this potential adverse selection, pediatricians might fare poorly compared to other types of PCPs. PCPs with a particular specialty may also be subject to adverse selection. For example, a general practitioner who specializes in diabetes may be more likely to be chosen by patients who have diabetes as a PCP. Interestingly, an emerging pricing approach proposes attaching a risk adjustment factor to every member covered under a capitation agreement, ranging from an adjustment of "0" for those members with no history of illness to a much higher factor for those with serious illnesses.

*Primary Care*

Primary care capitation is the most common type of capitation, though specialists are increasingly accepting capitation. Typically, members are assigned to (or choose) PCPs who are responsible for managing all of a member's health care. (They are often referred to as gatekeepers.) Most of the time, specialty care physicians do not have members assigned to them. PCPs refer patients to the specialist as needed and the specialist is reimbursed for services rendered.

When evaluating a capitation proposal, physicians should consider the scope of services included in the proposed contract. This list of services may or may not be negotiable, but the physician should evaluate his or her ability to deliver all the required services. For example, if the physician does not have the capability of performing some of the listed lab procedures in his or her office, then the physician will be required to pay a lab to perform such tasks. These payments will reduce the physician's revenue from capitation. Furthermore, physicians must determine the extent to which they have control over services they do not directly provide. For example, emergency room utilization is highly dependent on the covered population and the physician's office hours. If the physician does not have the ability or desire to extend office hours, then emergency room visits may not be managed as well as the capitation rate might assume.

Physicians should also account for the cost of certain items required to perform capitated procedures. For example, under a primary care contract, are the serums included in the capitation rate when immunizations and allergy immunotherapy are covered? Some of the serums can be expensive and this should be factored into any evaluation.

Finally, in a primary care contract, the physician should ascertain whether a patient management allowance is included in the capitation rate. Because the PCP (gatekeeper) must manage all of a patient's health care, even services performed by a referral physician, he or she should be compensated for the additional time required to accomplish this task. As reasonable as this additional compensation may appear, it is clearly easier to obtain it in a marketplace where primary care physicians are in short supply and negotiating leverage is significant.

## Specialty Care

One reason that some specialists do not accept capitation is that a certain number of members are needed for the "risk of random fluctuation" to be spread sufficiently. This number is high for specialists with a low frequency of services per referral and a high average cost per service, and low for specialists with a high frequency of services per referral and a low average cost per service. Low frequency and high cost specialties include such fields as neurosurgery and transplant surgery. Examples of high frequency and low cost specialties are radiology and pathology. The number of members needed also depends on the risk tolerance of the physician.

Specialists who accept capitation must consider whether other physicians function as "gatekeepers" to the specialists' services, and whether the gatekeepers are receiving capitation reimbursement as well. If so, then care must be taken to ensure that PCPs do not unnecessarily shift care to the specialist. If PCPs routinely refer patients to specialists for ailments that PCPs should be able to treat (sometimes referred to as "dumping"), the specialist will likely begin to lose money under the capitation. For this reason, it is important that specialists understand what services are included in PCP contracts and the circumstances under which referrals should be made.

The success of specialty-based capitation is often a function of which type of physicians have control over service delivery. For example, specialty capitation in radiology is vulnerable to the actions of physicians who are not radiologists. Because a radiologist typically does not order diagnostic testing, other types of physicians control the utilization of radiologic services, potentially causing losses for radiologists accepting capitation. Anesthesiologists encounter similar issues. The physician accepting capitation reimbursement needs to have some measure of control over the utilization of his or her services to facilitate changes that might be necessary to ensure the success of the program. The physician also needs to be aware of who is responsible for out-of-area care.

### Multispecialty

Multispecialty groups frequently accept capitation reimbursement. For example, a large medical group may accept capitation for providing all physician services (including primary care). In this case, a member is assigned to (or chooses) the group and receives all physician services from this group, unless the group cannot provide a needed service, in which case the group purchases that service elsewhere for the member. Or, a group of cardiologists might accept a capitation agreement to provide all cardiovascular care to members.

### Evaluating Capitation Proposals

One method for evaluating a capitation proposal is demonstrated in Table 4–8. By applying an estimate of the number of services delivered

**Table 4–8** Sample Capitation Evaluation I

| CPT[2] | Procedure Description | Provider Fee (a) | Unmanaged | | Moderately Managed | | Aggressively Managed | |
|---|---|---|---|---|---|---|---|---|
| | | | Assumed Annual Utilization[1] (b) | Revenue[1] (a) × (b) | Assumed Annual Utilization[1] (c) | Revenue[1] (a) × (c) | Assumed Annual Utilization[1] (d) | Revenue[1] (a) × (d) |
| 95819 | Electroencephalogram (EEG) | $196.00 | 0.492 | $96 | 0.492 | $96 | 0.492 | $96 |
| 96410 | Chemotherapy, infusion method | $109.00 | 0.000 | $0 | 0.000 | $0 | 0.000 | $0 |
| 99202 | Office/outpatient visit, new | $65.00 | 122.620 | $7,970 | 122.620 | $7,970 | 122.620 | $7,970 |
| 99212 | Office/outpatient visit, est | $40.00 | 661.468 | $26,459 | 661.468 | $26,459 | 661.468 | $26,459 |
| 99215 | Office/outpatient visit, est | $118.00 | 87.873 | $10,369 | 79.000 | $9,322 | 59.000 | $6,962 |
| 99222 | Initial hospital care | $151.00 | 16.333 | $2,466 | 15.000 | $2,265 | 11.000 | $1,661 |
| 99233 | Subsequent hospital care | $104.00 | 27.465 | $2,856 | 25.000 | $2,600 | 19.000 | $1,976 |
| 99385 | Preventive visit, new, 18–39 | $98.00 | 18.218 | $1,785 | 16.000 | $1,568 | 12.000 | $1,176 |
| 99386 | Preventive visit, new, 40–64 | $108.00 | 7.761 | $838 | 7.000 | $756 | 5.000 | $540 |
| 99431 | Initial care, normal newborn | $116.00 | 15.560 | $1,805 | 14.000 | $1,624 | 11.000 | $1,276 |
| 99433 | Normal newborn care, hospital | $57.00 | 16.562 | $944 | 15.000 | $855 | 11.000 | $627 |
| | All other | $99.27 | 8,650.357 | $858,758 | 7,785.000 | $772,850 | 5,839.000 | $579,662 |
| Total | All Procedures | $95.00 | 9,624.709 | $914,347 | 8,740.580 | $826,365 | 6,751.580 | $628,406 |
| | Monthly FFSE[3] | | | $76.20 | | $68.86 | | $52.37 |
| | Proposed Monthly Capitation Rate | | | $40.00 | | $40.00 | | $40.00 |
| | Required Discount | | | 47.5% | | 41.9% | | 23.6% |

[1]Per 1,000 Members.
[2]Current Procedural Terminology.
[3]Fee-For-Service Equivalent.

per year for a covered population to the physician's regular fees, by procedure, a monthly fee-for-service-equivalent (FFSE) rate can be calculated. This is achieved by dividing the estimated total revenue by the assumed covered population. Different sets of assumed annual utilization that vary by the degree of health care management can be used to derive separate FFSEs. The FFSEs can then be compared to the proposed capitation rate. The FFSE that is closest to the capitation rate indicates the level of management that is necessary to achieve the same revenue under fee-for-service as would be achieved under capitation (assuming the physician does not wish to discount his or her fee schedule). If physicians are not comfortable with the aggressiveness of the resulting level of utilization control, they could discount their fee schedule and apply that to the level of management they desire. The discount is determined by dividing the capitation rate by the FFSE for the desired degree of health care management.

An alternative method of evaluation focuses on the effect the acceptance of the capitation agreement might have on revenue and workload. Table 4–9 illustrates this type of analysis for a primary care physician. The goal of this analysis is to estimate the increased revenue and effective discount that might result from accepting the contract. Once again, the increased revenue should be balanced against the increased workload. The physician will be required to obtain or estimate items a through g to use this method of evaluation. Physician capacity (item h) represents the maximum number of visits per year that the physician can currently handle. Excess capacity (item k) is the difference between this physician capacity and the current number of visits per year (item d). The expected number of visits under capitation (item i) is derived by multiplying the new members under capitation by the average number of visits per member per year (item e). The new members from capitation that will absorb excess capacity (item l) is obtained by dividing the excess capacity (item k) by the average number of visits per member per year (item e). The remaining members are assumed to have shifted from the current patient base (item m). Estimated revenue consists of the following three components: revenue from current patients moving to capitation (item n), revenue from new capitated members that are not currently patients (item o), and revenue from non-capitated patients (item q). The calculation of items n and o are fairly straightforward. Item q, estimated revenue from non-capitated patients, is estimated by multiplying the expected number of visits per year for these patients by the average revenue per visit (item j). The expected number of visits is estimated by subtracting the product of the

**Table 4–9** Sample Capitation Evaluation 2

| | | | |
|---|---|---|---|
| a. | Proposed Capitation Rate (per member, per month) | input | $12.00 |
| b. | Estimated Number of Members Expected Under Capitation Agreement | input | 250 |
| c. | Current Annual Revenue | input | $125,000 |
| d. | Current Number of Visits Handled Per Year | input | 2,400 |
| e. | Average Number of Visits per Member per Year | input | 3.5 |
| f. | Maximum Number of Visits per Week | input | 60 |
| g. | Weeks Worked per Year | input | 48 |
| h. | Physician Capacity (Visits per Year) | $f \times g$ | 2,880 |
| i. | Expected Number of Visits Under Capitation | $b \times e$ | 875 |
| j. | Current Average Revenue per Visit | $c / d$ | $52.08 |
| k. | Excess Capacity (Visits per Year) | $h - d$ | 480 |
| l. | New Members Absorbing Excess Capacity | $k / e$ | 137 |
| m. | Members From Current Patient Base Moving to Capitation | $b - l$ | 113 |
| n. | Estimated Revenue for Patients Moving to Capitation | $a \times m \times 12$ | $16,272 |
| o. | Estimated Revenue for New Capitated Members Absorbing Capacity | $a \times l \times 12$ | $19,728 |
| p. | Estimated Revenue from Capitation | $a \times b \times 12$ or $n + o$ | $36,000 |
| q. | Estimated Revenue for Non-capitated Patients | $(d - m \times e) \times j$ | $104,401 |
| r. | Estimated Total Revenue | $p + q$ | $140,401 |
| s. | Estimated Revenue as a Percent of Current Revenue | $r / c$ | 112.3% |
| t. | Current Revenue From Patients Moving to Capitation | $e \times j \times m$ | $20,599 |
| u. | Average Discount Assumed in Capitation | $1 - n / t$ | 21.0% |

number of current patients moving to capitation (item m) and the average number of visits per member per year (item e) from the physicians' current workload (item d). The estimated change in revenue resulting from the capitation agreement is calculated in item s. Finally, the average discount assumed in the capitation rate is calculated in item u by looking at the ratio of the estimated revenue for patients moving to capitation (item n) to the current revenue from these patients (item t).

*Pros and Cons*

Capitation shifts the insurance risk from the MCO to the physician with mixed consequences. It offers the potential for financial gains if the physician is able to deliver quality care to members more efficiently than that assumed in the capitation rate. On the other hand, it also leaves the physician at risk for potential losses due to such factors as adverse selection or the inability to manage care sufficiently. Despite the disadvantages, a properly designed capitation contract does provide incentives to physicians to manage health care services appropriately. This is an admirable goal. However, the incentives in the contract should not promote the rationing of care. This is crucial if the physician is to profit from the contract while still providing quality health care.

A few other advantages to capitation deal with the prospective nature of this type of reimbursement. The physician under capitation will experience a more regular cash flow than with his or her traditional business. In addition, bad debt risk will be reduced because there is no collection process—the physician is paid before services are rendered. Finally, there is a potential for reduced office expenses associated with billing because the physician will no longer have to bill the MCO and patient for providing services. These savings must be evaluated against the costs associated with additional office procedures necessary to operate capitation contracts and with any additional reports physicians must produce to monitor the success of capitation agreements.

## Risk-Sharing Arrangements

Risk pools are designed to share risk and reward with providers. In its simplest form, a risk pool is funded at the beginning of a contract period and claims are charged against the pool during that period. At the end of the period, any surplus in the pool is distributed to the participating providers and the MCO, and any deficits are funded by the providers and the MCO according to agreed upon schedules. Who participates in the pool, how the pool is funded, what services are included in the pool, how the surplus and deficits are distributed, and other specifics will vary for different risk-sharing arrangements.

The primary reason MCOs offer risk-sharing arrangements to providers is to provide incentives to physicians to provide only those services that are medically necessary. The goal is to make physicians more financially accountable for the services they deliver and prescribe.

Physicians enter into risk-sharing arrangements to gain the potential to share in the fruits of their labor. If they are able to provide efficient, quality health care to the MCO's members at a cost that is less than the budgeted expense, they are able to share in the savings.

Depending on the degree of health care management in a community, a physician has the potential to share in some significant financial gains. On the other hand, risk-sharing arrangements usually include the potential to experience financial losses as well. Agreements structured to safeguard physicians against losses due to uncontrollable events are the most attractive arrangements, although such safeguards are generally not free.

As with capitation, precautions must be taken to limit or eliminate the physician's financial incentive to ration care or otherwise compromise the quality of health care. MCOs sometimes include quality assurance measures in the risk-sharing agreement to provide additional incentives to maintain high quality services. The amount of any surplus paid to a physician or physician group may be affected by the level of quality attained by the physicians. The selection of the types of quality measurement should be jointly agreed to by the physicians and the MCO.

*Common Incentive Structures*

There are two major classifications of physician incentives: negative and positive. Negative incentives are based on penalties and positive incentives are based on rewards. The most common type of negative incentive is the provider withhold. Although the terms of withhold programs can vary widely among MCOs, a common version withholds a small portion of the physician's negotiated reimbursement to fund a risk pool that is tied to a specified set of health care services. Withhold percentages usually range from 10 to 20 percent of the negotiated reimbursement.

Actual claims that exceed the budget for services are charged against this pool and any amounts remaining in the pool at the end of the agreed upon period (usually a year) are refunded to the physicians. If the pool is completely depleted, the MCO is usually at risk for covering any deficit. Under this type of risk-sharing arrangement, physicians who manage the delivery of health care services within the budget established by the MCO have the potential to have their entire withhold refunded. If physicians are not able to deliver care within the established budget, because of poor management, catastrophic claims, or adverse selection (or insufficient budget), they are penalized by losing a portion or all of their withhold. This results in reduced overall reimbursement to the physicians. Put simply, under a best case scenario, physicians can expect to receive only their agreed upon

**Table 4–10** Withhold (Negative Incentive)

| Withhold % | Unused Withhold Split | | Negotiated Discount |
| | Plan | Providers | |
| 15% | 0% | 100% | 5% |

| | Case 1 | Case 2 | Case 3 |
|---|---|---|---|
| a. Target Budget (Expected Claims) | 500,000 | 500,000 | 500,000 |
| b. Actual Claims | 500,000 | 600,000 | 400,000 |
| c. Paid Claims [b × 85%] | 425,000 | 510,000 | 340,000 |
| d. Withhold [b × 15%] | 75,000 | 90,000 | 60,000 |
| e. Unused Withhold [d – (b – a), minimum = 0 and maximum = d] | 75,000 | — | 60,000 |
| f. Total Provider Reimbursement [c + e] | 500,000 | 510,000 | 400,000 |
| g. Estimated Billed Charges [b / 95%] | 526,316 | 631,579 | 421,053 |
| h. Effective Provider Discount [1 – f / g] | 5.0% | 19.30% | 5.0% |

reimbursement for services rendered, and under the worst case scenario, physicians are expected to give up their withhold. This type of incentive system is illustrated in Table 4–10.

Withholds are advantageous to MCOs in that they provide some protection against adverse experience and less-than-optimal medical management, and yet they allow the MCOs to retain any savings due to favorable experience. Most physicians, however, view withholds as discounts rather than incentives. They assume that they will never receive their withhold and tend to practice accordingly. Consequently, withholds are rarely used as a stand-alone incentive system.

Positive incentives, on the other hand, provide the physician with the potential to gain financially from the efficient delivery of health care services. A bonus pool is the most common form of a positive incentive arrangement and is illustrated in Table 4–11. The pool is funded by any savings generated from actual claims compared to the target budget (based on expected claims) for a specified set of services. At the end of the agreed upon period, any amounts in the bonus pool are distributed to the physicians. (If the bonus pool includes hospital services, often referred to as a Hospital Incentive Fund, the surplus funds are usually shared between the physicians and the MCO. The MCO receives a share of the pool because it is at risk for any claims that are in excess of the target budget. The physician's share is intended to reward him or her for managing hospital costs well.) Under this positive incentive system, physicians stand to profit from any plan savings but are not at risk for any plan losses. For this reason, bonus

**Table 4–11** Bonus Pool (Positive Incentive)

| | Bonus Pool Split | | | | |
|---|---|---|---|---|---|
| | *Plan* | *Providers* | *Negotiated Discount* | | |
| | 50% | 50% | 5% | | |

| | | *Case 1* | *Case 2* | *Case 3* |
|---|---|---|---|---|
| a. | Target Budget (Expected Claims) | 500,000 | 500,000 | 500,000 |
| b. | Actual Claims Paid | 500,000 | 600,000 | 400,000 |
| c. | Bonus Pool [(a − b), minimum = 0] | — | — | 100,000 |
| d. | Provider's Share of Bonus Pool [c × 50%] | — | — | 50,000 |
| e. | Total Provider Reimbursement [b + d] | 500,000 | 600,000 | 450,000 |
| f. | Estimated Billed Charges [b / 95%] | 526,316 | 631,579 | 421,053 |
| g. | Effective Provider Discount [1 − e/f] | 5.0% | 5.0% | (6.9%) |

pools are generally popular with physicians. Conversely, under the negative incentive system described previously, physicians are at risk for plan losses, up to the withhold, but are not able to share in any plan savings.

A hybrid incentive arrangement that capitalizes on the strengths of both the negative and positive incentive systems while minimizing the weaknesses is illustrated in Table 4–12. This alternative methodology uses both the withhold concept and the risk-pool concept. The physicians are at risk for adverse experience, up to the withhold amount, yet they are allowed to share in any surpluses from favorable experience. Because physicians are able to share in both the utilization risk and reward, this incentive system is more equitable than the negative incentive system for physicians and it is more equitable than the positive incentive system for health plans. This compromise provides the incentive for the physicians and MCO to work together toward the common goal of providing quality health care efficiently.

Some MCOs have developed complex systems of risk pools with varying programs of positive and negative incentives. These systems may have (1) a withhold arrangement for a primary care risk pool, (2) a separate withhold arrangement for specialist physicians in combination with a bonus arrangement for primary care physicians for cost savings obtained in the specialty services fund, and (3) a bonus arrangement tied to a hospital services pool. Still other MCOs have implemented deficit funding terms that require physicians to recompense MCOs for plan deficits. Physicians are advised to carefully

**Table 4–12** Withhold and Risk-Sharing Pool (Combination)

| | Unused Withhold Split | | | | Risk Pool Split | |
|---|---|---|---|---|---|---|
| Withhold % | Plan | Providers | Negotiated Discount | | Plan | Providers |
| 15% | 0% | 100% | 5% | Gains | 50% | 50% |
| | | | | Losses | 0% | 100% |

| | Case 1 | Case 2 | Case 3 |
|---|---|---|---|
| a. Target Budget (Expected Claims) | 500,000 | 500,000 | 500,000 |
| b. Actual Claims | 500,000 | 600,000 | 400,000 |
| c. Paid Claims [b × 85%] | 425,000 | 510,000 | 340,000 |
| d. Withhold [b × 15%] | 75,000 | 90,000 | 60,000 |
| e. Unused Withhold [d − (b − a), minimum = 0 and maximum = d] | 75,000 | — | 60,000 |
| f. Risk Pool [a − b] | — | (100,000) | 100,000 |
| g. Provider's Share of Pool [f × 50%][1] | — | — | 50,000 |
| h. Total Provider Reimbursement [c + e + g] | 500,000 | 510,000 | 450,000 |
| i. Estimated Billed Charges [b / 95%] | 526,316 | 631,579 | 421,053 |
| j. Effective Provider Discount [1 − h / i] | 5.0% | 19.3% | (6.9%) |

[1]The provider's share of a deficit is limited to the Unused Withhold.

---

review risk pool terms in provider contracts to ensure a thorough understanding of the risk terms and the potential impact on physician practices.

*General Concerns and Features*

The size and composition of the physician risk pool should be considered when evaluating proposed risk-sharing arrangements. The pool of physicians (often referred to as "PODs" for pool of doctors) needs to be large enough to limit random fluctuation and yet small enough for physicians to feel that they have some control over the pool's performance. Ten to twenty physicians create a POD that is conducive to effective peer review and peer pressure. Because the group's compensation is based on performance, the inefficient providers will be encouraged by the others to modify their behaviors. In addition, the POD, to the extent possible, should be based on a "natural" group because effective peer review is based on sound working relationships.

The health plan executives will often want to include the out-of-network claims in the risk-sharing pool. They think that this will eliminate any tendencies for participating physicians to refer members to nonparticipating providers in an effort to keep the pool "healthy." However, physicians may not want to agree to this because they exercise little control over the services performed by out-of-network providers and/or the prices charged by out-of-network providers.

Physicians should also pay close attention to the negotiated value of services that are charged against risk pools. This is particularly true for risk pools covering services that physicians do not directly provide, but for which they carry some financial risk. The most straightforward example of this situation is embodied by the Hospital Incentive Fund. Many MCOs will distribute savings (or require some deficit funding) from this fund to contracted physician groups. However, the physicians may have no direct control over how hospitals bill for services. At a minimum, physicians should insist on information regarding the negotiated reimbursement between affected hospitals and the MCO before agreeing to participate in these incentive arrangements.

## STOP LOSS AND REINSURANCE

As risk transfer reimbursement methodologies grow in popularity, it is essential that physicians understand how to protect themselves financially. Risk-protection strategies include the following elements: (1) accurate prediction of the extent of risk (which is fundamental to the evaluation of reimbursement proposals), (2) adequate risk-management strategies (which include programs of medical management, utilization management, demand management, and utilization trend review), and (3) actual risk reduction (through the implementation of a stop loss, reinsurance, or other risk-reduction program). The remaining sections of this chapter will focus on a variety of risk-reduction strategies.

The terms *stop loss* and *reinsurance* are often used interchangeably in managed care contracts, which is usually due to variable state regulatory requirements governing the sale of insurance. Insurance companies and HMOs (as primary insurers) usually do not assume the full risk of a member's medical losses. Typically, a portion of the primary insurer's risk of loss is insured with other insurance companies under a policy of reinsurance. Reinsurance is simply an insurance policy for insurers designed to cover catastrophic and overall (aggregate) losses. It is usually offered on an excess-loss basis, whereby the reinsurance coverage begins once a certain loss threshold has been breached.

Most of the risk-protection programs available to physicians are modeled closely on the products purchased by insurance companies and HMOs. Indeed, under a full-capitation program, the physician or physician group becomes, in effect, the primary insurer, whereas the HMO or insurance carrier often assumes the role of reinsurer through its offers of programs of stop loss, reinsurance, and/or other risk-reduction programs. Medical provider reinsurance offers provider groups protection from catastrophic losses associated with an individual member over the course of a year or episode of disease (specific reinsurance), as well as protection from overall program losses, usually by protecting the physician risk pools (aggregate reinsurance). These programs include deductible requirements and coinsurance, but generally at much lower levels than the HMOs themselves might purchase.

## Specific Reinsurance

Specific reinsurance applies to a specific case or individual. (This form of coverage is often referred to merely as "stop loss.") The primary insurer is responsible for all medical claims up to a specified deductible. Medical claims in excess of the deductible amount are reimbursed by the reinsurer, up to the base policy maximums. Under specific reinsurance, the primary insurer (physician group) shares risk with the reinsurer (often, an MCO) by absorbing the cost of the deductible and by sharing the costs of the claims once the deductible and/or loss threshold have been breached. For example, the physician group may continue to be responsible for 10 to 20 percent of the costs above the deductible or threshold. The reinsurer may insist on this form of cost-sharing to ensure that the physician group continues to take an interest in the case after the submission of claims to the reinsurance carrier. Coinsurance features will also modify the price of the reinsurance coverage.

A typical specific reinsurance policy for a physician group or individual physician might include a $5,000 to $7,500 deductible for primary care and specialty care combined, and a $50,000 deductible for the hospital risk pool (covering hospital care and ancillary services). The value of capitated services is converted into a fee-based equivalent based upon a fee schedule (usually an RVU schedule), which is agreed to and made part of the physician's contract with the HMO. The basis upon which hospital services are calculated should also be defined as part of the reinsurance contract.

Physicians pay for specific reinsurance either through direct premium payments, or through deductions from their capitation payments or the risk pool. For example, if the medical group receives monthly capitation payments of $40 per member, the HMO might deduct $2 per member per month to cover the costs of the reinsurance program. Thus, the medical group's effective capitation rate is $38. Physicians should compare this charge with the market premiums charged by commercial reinsurance carriers to identify whether the HMO is offering a competitive rate for comparable protection.

## Aggregate Reinsurance

Reinsurance coverage on an aggregate basis covers the provider group's cumulative medical claims risk. The reinsurance carrier is responsible for all of the provider group's claims that are greater than a threshold amount. In this arrangement, the threshold amount is a percentage amount tied to the total expected claims for a specified period, usually a year.

Aggregate reinsurance for physicians is usually offered to protect the various professional services risk pools and the Hospital Incentive Fund. The reinsurer specifies a threshold amount, usually ranging from 110 to 125 percent of the anticipated pool amount for a given period. For example, if the Hospital Incentive Fund is funded at $45 PMPM and the physician group enrollment averaged 5,000 members during the year, the approximate anticipated pool would equal $2.7 million ($45 x 5,000 members x 12 months). At a threshold of 120 percent, the threshold amount would be $3,240,000. That is, paid claims amounts that exceeded $3,240,000 would be subject to reimbursement under the reinsurance policy.

Under HMO-sponsored plans, aggregate reinsurance is often paid for through a funding deduction. For example, the HMO specifies by contract that it is funding the Hospital Incentive Fund at $45 PMPM, and that it will pay hospital and related charges from this fund. The HMO charges $2 PMPM for the aggregate reinsurance, so the effective net funding payment is actually $43 PMPM. Commercial reinsurance carriers typically charge a premium, payable on a monthly or quarterly basis.

## Sources of Stop Loss and Reinsurance

Several types of companies sell commercial reinsurance policies: professional reinsurance companies, reinsurance departments of primary insurance carriers, underwriting organizations and other risk-pooling associations, and the London-based reinsurance consortium, Lloyds of London. Although specific and aggregate reinsurance policies are available to medical providers from these sources, by far the most common source is HMO- or primary insurer-sponsored reinsurance. (Many of these programs are not specifically labeled reinsurance, or even stop loss. This is due to the variable and sometime onerous state regulations governing the sale of reinsurance products. In an effort to avoid the regulatory requirements, some primary insurers [whether HMOs or insurance companies] refer to these programs as "capitation protection," and others refer to these programs as "income guarantee" programs.)

Physicians should be aware, however, that HMO-sponsored programs are not always competitively priced. The common capitation-deduction form of payment is, in fact, a premium charged by the HMO for access to this form of risk protection. In particular, physicians should pay close attention to reinsurance programs that are offered by the HMO seemingly at no charge. If the HMO is not charging for the program, either through a specified capitation payment deduction or some other form of separate charge, then the capitation rate itself has been adjusted to cover the costs of this program. This makes it particularly difficult for the physician group to evaluate the actual charge for the program. Physician groups should be prepared to probe the HMO to uncover the real charge for the protection.

Increasingly, licensed reinsurance carriers are fashioning programs for larger physician groups and sometimes offer a better deal than the HMO. HMO-sponsored policies are off-the-shelf arrangements with little advantage to the physician group with superior claims experience. One advantage to direct purchase of reinsurance is the ability to "experience rate" the reinsurance policy. That is, most direct reinsurance arrangements require detailed historical utilization and claims information, and are based on these data. Physician groups with superior risk-management histories and programs will benefit from lower premiums and possibly dividend roll-backs. Conversely, groups with little experience with risk-sharing programs or with checkered histories may do better with HMO-sponsored programs.

## CONSIDERATIONS IN REINSURANCE

When evaluating a reinsurance program, physicians need to consider several aspects of the program.

### The Deductible

Although the typical deductible for specific reinsurance programs ranges from $5,000 to $7,500 for professional charges and anywhere from $30,000 to $75,000 for Hospital Incentive Fund protection, it is sometimes possible to negotiate for higher or lower limits. The same is true for the threshold levels set in the aggregate policy. Higher limits should reduce the "premium" charges, but will increase the risk for the physician group. Lower deductibles and thresholds will increase the premium but will lower the overall risk for the group. Typically, physicians and physician groups new to managed care contracting will opt for lower deductibles and thresholds for the first couple of years until they have had enough experience with the contract to adequately evaluate its terms and feel more comfortable accepting greater risks.

### The Coinsurance

Nearly all stop loss and/or reinsurance programs contain some provisions for coinsurance or cost-sharing once the deductible or threshold has been met. Typically, the coinsurance will require 10 to 20 percent sharing of the reinsured liability. This is to ensure that the physician group remains interested in effective risk management even after the deductible or threshold has been met and the reinsurance coverage is activated. It is clearly in the physician group's interests to minimize this cost sharing, especially if this can be achieved without increasing the premium charge for the coverage. It is sometimes possible to negotiate for a reduction in coinsurance without affecting any other provisions of the reinsurance program. Exhibit 4–1 shows an example of coinsurance.

### Service Valuation

The decision regarding how services are charged against reinsurance deductibles is a common topic of negotiation between the health plan

**Exhibit 4-1** Calculating Coinsurance

Assume aggregate reinsurance threshold level of 125 percent of anticipated claims and 10 percent coinsurance after threshold has been breached.

Total Anticipated Claims = $1 million

Total Actual Claims = $2 million

Claims in Excess of Threshold = Actual Claims less 125 percent of Anticipated Claims ($1 million × 125%)

$$= \$2,000,000 - \$1,250,000 = \$750,000$$

Coinsurance Amount = 10 percent of Claims in Excess of Threshold

$$= \$750,000 \times 10 \text{ percent} = \$75,000$$

and the physician or physician group. Under a capitation contract, for example, the parties must agree on how capitated services are converted into fee-based equivalents for service valuation. This conversion calculation is necessary for reinsurance deductibles to be calculated, cost sharing to occur, and reinsurance claims to be paid. It is clearly in the reinsurer's interest to minimize the service valuation as much as possible. If the charges toward the deductible are based on a low fee schedule, it will take much longer for the deductible to be met, and the per unit reinsurance liability will be minimized. Conversely, physicians want to maximize the fee schedule used for service valuation to have the opposite effect.

The terms specifying how hospital services are charged against Hospital Incentive Funds are equally important, but can have unintended effects if not handled thoughtfully. Although the physician group may not be directly involved in hospital-rate negotiations, the reimbursement to hospitals can have a profound effect on physician bonuses and reinsurance reimbursement. For example, if hospital claims are reimbursed generously, reinsurance deductibles are met more quickly for the purposes of specific reinsurance coverages (this is good news). However, a high reimbursement to hospitals will tend to deplete the overall fund quickly, leaving little or nothing for physician bonuses (bad news). In this case, it may be advantageous for physicians to support moderate reimbursement to hospitals and take a bit more risk regarding the specific coverage.

In addition, some reinsurance contracts include maximum ceilings of reimbursement for certain conditions. For example, a reinsurance contract might stipulate a per diem maximum on the reimbursement for an inpatient day for selected conditions. To the extent that the hospital charges for the "day" exceed the reinsurance-stipulated per diem, the Hospital Incentive Fund would be responsible for the excess.

## Timing and Submission of Claims

Most reinsurance policies are actually reimbursement policies. The reinsurer requires the primary insurer to pay for all services and to submit a reinsurance claim to begin the reimbursement process. The reinsurance contract should specify the precise manner and requirements for claims submission as well as precise details concerning the coverages.

The terms of reinsurance and/or stop loss coverage are variable and should be carefully reviewed. In addition to the terms mentioned previously, some reinsurance policies require the insured's medical claims to be closed and completely paid before reimbursement can commence. Others will begin payment on claims as soon as the deductible or threshold has been met. The latter form of coverage is clearly preferable because reinsurance claims may be submitted and paid during the course of a long illness, protecting the cash flow of the physician group.

Some reinsurance policies have strict time guidelines for claims submission, for example, within 60 to 90 days of the close of the reinsurance contract year. Unless physician groups are certain that they can accurately track all claims associated with an individual insured, attach appropriate documentation, value the claim, and send it off within the allotted time frame, they should negotiate for a longer time frame.

## Coverage Guidelines

Another common variation concerns the nature of the coverage. Some reinsurance contracts specify that the insurance applies only to a single continuous episode of care or disease process, whereas others cover cumulative medical claims expense during the contract year regardless of the nature of the claims. The latter type of coverage is clearly the preferable one, unless the physician group is experienced and is willing to "self-insure" for all but the most catastrophic expenditures.

Another common variation excludes primary care services from the reinsurance claim calculation, covering only specialty professional services. For physician groups that use specialty physicians for tertiary level diagnoses and treatment plan development, and rely on primary care physicians for most medical treatment implementation and chronic care management, this approach can be disastrous. It penalizes, in effect, those physician groups that have made the greatest use of their primary care specialties.

## Evaluating Stop Loss and Reinsurance Proposals

How can physicians adequately evaluate stop loss and reinsurance proposals? Evaluation is somewhat easier currently because of the recent development of a more competitive marketplace for reinsurance products for physicians. A few years ago, practically the only entity offering reinsurance to physicians was the HMO itself. Currently, a number of commercial reinsurance carriers have developed products specifically for physicians and physician groups. And a number of large physician groups and hospitals have developed captive reinsurance companies located in a variety of offshore locations.

First and foremost, physicians should compare quotes from a number of reputable reinsurance carriers, as well as the MCO. Physicians should take care that quotes are made on identical reinsurance terms (an obvious point but frequently overlooked). Current customers of the carriers should be contacted to investigate the timeliness of payment and the degree to which the carrier complies with its own procedures and contract terms. Physicians should also investigate any risk-management programs the carrier has developed—first, because these programs are often well-structured and useful, and secondly, because some reinsurance contracts stipulate that participation in company-sponsored, risk-management programs is a mandatory prerequisite for reimbursement under the reinsurance contract.

Finally, an actuary can be useful in evaluating the structure of deductibles and thresholds and the "reasonableness" of the reinsurance premium. Although the physician or physician group should examine historical claims data from its closed-panel insurance programs (like HMOs), in an effort to anticipate future experience, the actuary can also provide population-based disease incidence, as well as predictions regarding future health services resource use and corresponding pricing, to anticipate future costs. The actuary is also a credible ally when negotiating stop loss terms with an MCO.

## OTHER FORMS OF RISK REDUCTION

Reinsurance or stop loss are not the only forms of risk reduction available to physicians. HMO contracts frequently reduce capitation risk by providing certain business guarantees to the physicians and/or physician groups they seek contracts with. The most common of these guarantees fall into the following two broad categories: low-enrollment guarantees and fee-for-service guarantees.

## Low-Enrollment Guarantees

As noted previously, under capitation contracts, physicians assume the role of insurer by becoming financially responsible for the provision of health care services to populations of insureds, regardless of the actual cost of such services. Fundamental to the practice of insurance, however, is the requirement to "pool" large numbers of people together. By combining groups of insureds into a large pool, insurers can make the insurance risk an acceptably predictable business risk. State regulatory agencies require especially large reserves for start-up insurance companies, precisely because the insurance risk is so volatile and unpredictable until the populations of insureds are appropriately large. But what about the individual physician and/or group that is acting like an insurer? It may take months, or even years, until the populations of patients covered under capitation contracts are large enough to effectively "spread the risk." Until that time, these individuals and groups are managing significant amounts of insurance risk, often without sufficient reserves or even an in-depth understanding of their risk positions.

Some HMOs will attempt to minimize the start-up risk of physician practices under capitation through programs known as "low-enrollment guarantees" or "capitation guarantees." In their simplest form, these programs postpone the implementation of the capitation reimbursement until the number of enrollees or insureds is large enough to form an adequate "pool" for the purposes of risk prediction and management. Convention suggests that 200 enrollees are sufficient for individual primary care physician risk and approximately 2,000 enrollees are sufficient for a moderately sized physician group. Until these numbers are reached, the physicians are reimbursed according to a negotiated fee schedule stipulated in the provider contract. When the member threshold is reached, the payment converts to a capitation methodology. (Physicians should attempt to negotiate a caveat to this protection that stipulates that the capitation payment is maintained until the enrollment falls below the required level. This provision will come into play only if the HMO is losing enrollment, at which time the sickest of the members are likely to stay while the healthier members have left for other insurance programs.)

It is important that the physicians review in detail the contract language describing these types of programs. Some HMOs will guarantee fee-for-service payments until their enrollment in a particular geographic area reaches the specified minimum, but this is of little use unless the particular physician group is the sole provider in the area and is receiving all the enrollees. Other HMOs will link the low-enrollment guarantee to a time frame, for example, six months, but not to the actual number of insureds. Still others will attempt to link the low-enrollment guarantee to a fee schedule that is uncompetitively low. Physicians should be prepared to negotiate the terms of these guarantees like any other terms of the provider contract.

### Fee-for-Service Guarantees

Some HMOs offer bottom-line, fee-for-service guarantees to their capitation contracts. This represents a form of aggregate reinsurance in that it assures the physician that his or her income has some overall protection. It operates much differently than traditional forms of aggregate reinsurance, however. In its most straightforward form, the physician is required to submit mock claim forms called "encounter forms" specifying all services performed for patients from an enrolled population. These services are then valued through a fee-for-service equivalency calculation based upon a pre-negotiated relative value schedule, like RBRVS. The total calculated value of the services are then compared to the total of capitation payments paid to the physician for the same period and for the same population. Should the capitation payments represent less than some percentage (typically 60 to 80 percent) of the fee-for-service equivalency, the HMO pays the physician additional reimbursement to meet the guarantee. Conversely, some contracts stipulate maximums on the capitation revenue, as a percentage of billed charges. For example, a contract might require physicians to return capitation revenue that was in excess of some pre-set percentage of billed charges, for example, 125 percent.

Although this form of guarantee is useful, it should not lead physicians to underestimate the level of financial risk they are assuming under capitation contracts. First, the fee schedule used to evaluate the fee-for-service equivalency usually produces reimbursement that is substantially less than billed charges. Furthermore, the typical guarantee usually pegs a percentage of the fee schedule as the threshold of the guarantee. It is not uncommon, for example, for the guarantee to represent a 40-percent discount from an already heavily discounted fee schedule. Ultimately, this may represent a huge discount from a physician's usual and customary fees. This form of fee-for-service guarantee functions more like a financial safety net than an income guarantee.

## Disease-Specific Protection

Some HMOs offer to protect a physician's reimbursement from catastrophic expenditures associated with a specific disease. Diseases like AIDS or conditions that require organ transplants can deplete physician funds quickly, particularly if the physician is responsible for specialist and consult expenditures associated with enrollees. As an alternative to specific reinsurance, which covers any expensive disease or condition, some HMOs will "carve-out" the financial risk associated with specified diseases and pay for these expenditures out of a special fund. One California HMO, for example, deducts a small amount from physician capitation payments to cover patients with HIV. Any enrollee with a positive HIV test result is referred to the carve-out program, which is staffed with specialized providers, and any expenses associated with treatment are paid for out of the special fund. Similar funds are available from some HMOs for organ transplants and other selected conditions.

Specialized reinsurance or risk-protection programs can be extremely helpful, particularly to individually contracting physicians. However, it is important to evaluate whether the "premium" paid for the program is competitive within the industry, and whether the coverages are redundant. It may not be worthwhile to participate in these disease-specific arrangements if a good policy of specific reinsurance can be obtained at a reasonable premium.

## CONCLUSION

Physician reimbursement systems are undergoing constant modification as the health care industry continues its rapid evolution. Although it is nearly impossible to keep abreast of each new change, physicians who thoroughly understand the financial incentives and mechanisms underlying these reimbursement methods will be better able to comprehend and evaluate the possible impact on practice revenues and resulting physician income.

**NOTES**

1.  Starr, P. 1982. *The social transformation of American medicine*. New York, NY: Basic Books, 383–388.
2.  1995 AAHP HMO & PPO Trends Report. 1996. *Medical Benefits*. Vol. 13. Gaithersburg, MD: Aspen Publishers, Inc.
3.  HCFA Release. Office of Managed Care. September, 1996.
4.  Dorary, P., et al. 1995. *Understanding Medicaid. Research Report*. Seattle, WA: Milliman & Robertson, Inc.

# Analyzing Financial Arrangements— Comments from the Field

*Richard M. Weinberg*

The previous chapter offers a clear summary of the major type of arrangements under which physicians are compensated in managed care contracts and provides good examples of reasonably accessible methods physicians can use to determine the financial value of these contracts. Physicians and physician groups who have matured through the process of managed care contracting often identify other factors that may facilitate or hamper the process, depending on how well the physicians or their contracting representatives understand these factors. Although these criteria may not withstand strict financial scrutiny, they are important in evaluating financial proposals from managed care organizations (MCOs).

## UNDERSTANDING AND COMPARING FEE STRUCTURES

It is important to have an understanding of the relationship among the fees offered (or fee equivalents in capitation or case rate contracts), the premium structure of the product being analyzed, and the baseline to which the physician compares the offer. Physicians often choose a baseline of their traditional indemnity fees or a usual, customary, and reasonable (UCR) fee schedule; this generally raises expectations to unrealistic levels. Managed care premiums are typically lower than those of the indemnity products they are replacing. In the absence of effective utilization management by providers, these lower premiums cannot support fees equivalent to those paid under indemnity coverage. Physicians resist this principle, citing stability in their income levels as proof such changes in fees need not occur. Most do not follow the unit revenue of all services over long periods, however. Careful analysis inevitably reveals that physician income is sustained by increased volume of work or by the addition of new services (the fees for which are also decreasing, but for which the physicians do not even have a basis for comparison).

The traditional fee comparison has another shortcoming—it does not address the disparity in fees between primary care physicians (PCPs) and specialty care physicians (SCPs). Despite increased productivity and new services, the total revenue of a group practice declines to the point where PCPs begin to demand a redistribution of the available dollars. At this point, provider organizations must reexamine their initial internal fee schedule (which is usually based on historic fees or a SCP-friendly relative value scale) and replace it with a resource-based relative value scale (RBRVS) schedule. This type of fee schedule will increase payments for PCPs relative to SCPs. Doing this exercise early may reduce some of the inevitable conflict between PCPs and SCPs, and give provider organizations a more realistic baseline against which to compare new contracts.

Even nonorganized physicians must reconcile their fees against those of physicians in other specialties. Because regulatory limitations have prevented nonorganized physicians from sharing and negotiating these fees, the early adoption of an acceptable fee schedule may offer some reassurance to these physicians. Eventually, both organized and nonorganized physicians must recognize that a fee schedule based on an average monthly managed care premium of $130 (per enrollee compared to $230 monthly premium for an indemnity enrollee) will result in lower physician fees unless utilization is dramatically reduced. This reflects the market value of the physician services in a market with an oversupply of physicians. Physicians in a marketplace with substantially reduced average premiums who continue comparing managed care fees to their UCR are likely to reject contracts they should be accepting.

## RISK CONTRACTING

Physicians, or their representatives, should also be aware of regional managed care economic factors as they make contract decisions. Large MCOs are often reluctant to move toward full capitation in a market where there is still substantial over-utilization in the system. By refusing to capitate physicians early, the MCO does not have to share the savings of efficient patient management with providers. For example, those physicians and hospitals that are on the periphery of a relatively high-cost metropolitan area may not be offered capitation because the MCO is experiencing the savings from reductions in utilization. This delay means a longer period in the "death spiral" of reduced fee-for-service for those physicians who already have reduced their utilization and patient length of stay. Armed with this understanding, the physician or contracting representative might be wise to accept a lower initial fee structure in return for a quick (and contractually guaranteed) conversion to capitation, particularly if the hospital fund is included in the risk pool calculations.

In addition to effective utilization management, the success of a risk contract depends on the physician's understanding of the structure and funding of risk pools, risk-sharing mechanisms with the payer, controls over out-of-network utilization, and the method and timing of financial reconciliation. Nonrisk contracts also require close examination. The inclusion of financial penalties for late claim payment may reduce work for the physician's office staff, as will attention to the number of different agencies the staff may have to contact for eligibility, benefits, and authorization issues. This is particularly true with preferred provider organizations (PPOs), which are brokers for many insurers.

## NEGOTIATING EXPERTISE

Rarely does the individual physician or small group have the time or expertise to negotiate favorable contract terms or perform the strict financial due diligence that may increase physician revenue. For these reasons, it is imperative for physicians to organize and provide professional representation for themselves in the negotiating process.

Physicians are loathe to delegate the power to contract on their behalf to anyone, even another physician. This is due, in part, to the understandable fear that even another physician may not appreciate all the nuances applicable to the represented physician's interests. More poignantly, this reluctance to delegate contracting authority may be due to the fiercely independent nature of some physicians who, historically, have not placed much value on collaboration. Because payers are often represented at the negotiating table by a team of seasoned negotiators, physicians cannot expect to negotiate favorable terms until they delegate contract negotiation duties to trusted and experienced administrative representatives.

Physicians may need to give up some business autonomy in return for more successful contract outcomes, such as an earlier implementation of global capitation. Only under these arrangements do physicians have a reasonable prospect of regaining their professional autonomy.

## THE VALUE OF DATA

Finally, physicians are beginning to experience the added value of the data derived from the care of a population of patients. Initial fears about data sharing are fading with the recognition that data are a valuable competitive tool. Data are essential to improve the value of care rendered, to secure new contracts, and to ensure financial success in risk contracts already acquired. Other types of arrangements, such as single-specialty care networks and episode-of-care compensation, further increase the value of data. Physicians and other health care providers must understand their costs and utilization patterns to bid successfully for inclusion in these types of programs, and to manage their existing contracts profitably. As premiums equilibrate, the "ownership" of these data may be the most important competitive advantage for MCOs or provider organizations.

Data sharing has been a particularly effective tool when used in the small "virtual" group setting, or pool of doctors (POD). Under a risk contract, groups of ten to fifteen physicians will meet regularly to review utilization and outcome data with their "podners." This process is dependent on the integrity, timeliness, and format of the data. Physicians must consider the availability and usefulness of data in their analysis of the contract, particularly if they are at risk. A capitated contract that looks good before the first patient arrives may not seem so terrific after the PCPs discover they cannot obtain the data necessary to determine which of their SCPs practice cost-effectively. Timely and reliable data may prove to be the secret to great success in a risk contract, even if the capitation rates or their equivalent are not extraordinary.

# 5

# Exploring Issues for Group Contracting

*Dolores M. Blanco*
*Michael J. Alper*
*Richard A. Gold*

The ongoing evolution of managed care throughout the country has resulted in a continued trend toward physician group organization. Physicians continue to join or form independent practice associations (IPAs) to become part of integrated single- or multispecialty groups, to join management companies or for-profit physician practice management organizations, and to become part of integrated health systems. The continued growth in health maintenance organization (HMO) enrollment compels physicians to examine their practice options to ensure retention of existing patients or access to new patients. In 1995, enrollment in pure HMOs increased 13.6 percent (to more than 52 million lives) and open-ended HMO enrollment increased 48 percent representing more than 6 million lives.[1] In addition, government programs continue to encourage the movement of Medicare and Medicaid beneficiaries toward managed care programs. Taken together, this movement toward managed care and the increasing pressure on physicians to manage care clinically and fiscally, improve the quality of care delivered, and consolidate administrative services contribute to the formation of organized physician entities. This chapter discusses the various corporate structures, internal provider reimbursement mechanisms, managed care contracts, and reimbursement strategies that pertain to provider groups.

## PROVIDER ORGANIZATIONAL STRUCTURES

Physicians in today's health care environment have never been faced with so many practice options. This section describes the various group provider organizational structures and summarizes each structure's strengths and weaknesses.

## Independent Practice Associations

An IPA is a legal entity that is comprised of independent physicians for the purpose of negotiating managed care contracts with managed care organizations (MCOs) and sharing risk under such contracts to provide or arrange for the provision of professional services to assigned members. Except for business generated through the IPA contracts, the physician remains an independent and autonomous entity from the other IPA physicians regarding practice management activities. IPAs are typically organized as professional corporations, medical partnerships, or limited liability companies in compliance with state laws and corporate practice of medicine concerns. IPAs can be either single- or multispecialty. Many markets across the country have recently seen a burst of single-specialty IPAs such as cardiology, orthopedics, and ophthalmology. These IPAs typically service a large geographic area under a risk-sharing arrangement with the MCOs. Exhibit 5–1 lists the strengths and weaknesses of IPAs.

## Integrated Medical Groups

The integrated medical group operates as a single legal entity for both managed care and non-managed care sources of business under a single tax number and provider structure. All sources of revenue (managed care and non-managed care) flow through the group practice. Integrated group practices are typically organized as professional corporations, general partnerships, limited liability companies, or limited liability partnerships. As with an IPA, group practices can be either single- or multispecialty. Exhibit 5–2 lists the strengths and weaknesses of integrated medical groups.

## Physician-Hospital Organizations

The physician-hospital organization (PHO) operates as a centralized contracting organization on behalf of its member hospital and physicians. The PHO can negotiate with MCOs on a risk basis for the

**Exhibit 5–1** Strengths and Weaknesses of IPAs

| |
|---|
| **Strengths** |
| • Physician practice remains independent and autonomous concurrent with participating in managed care risk contracts. |
| • IPAs are easy to organize; relatively low capital is required to develop an IPA. |
| • Wide geographic presence of PCPs is attractive to MCOs. |
| • Physicians can negotiate capitation contracts collectively with MCOs. |
| **Weaknesses** |
| • IPAs are not as operationally efficient as integrated medical group practices. |
| • IPAs need continuous commitment from physicians to ensure appropriate utilization of medical resources. |
| • IPAs need capital support during start-up and enrollment growth phases. |

provision of both professional and institutional (that is, hospital) services. Depending on the regulatory climate of the state, the PHO may be limited to negotiating the contract and restricted from being a party to the contract. The PHO may be organized on an independent contract basis with individual physicians or with a distinct physician entity. The independent-contract PHO enters into professional service agreements directly with interested solo or small-group practices. Other PHOs may enter into professional service agreements with an IPA or integrated group practice. Exhibit 5–3 lists the strengths and weaknesses of PHOs.

**Exhibit 5–2** Strengths and Weaknesses of Integrated Medical Groups

| |
|---|
| **Strengths** |
| • Integrated medical groups can produce more operational efficiencies than IPAs. |
| • Integrated medical groups have a centralized management and business office. |
| • There is a single administrative and clinical system among physicians. |
| • There is a cooperative environment for on-call coverage, scheduling, and other administrative issues. |
| • Greater leverage exists to negotiate managed care contracts. |
| **Weaknesses** |
| • Physicians lose some autonomy as they are subject to group governance. |
| • Single-site location may not be attractive to MCOs. |
| • Physicians need to distinguish managed care activities from practice management activities. |

**Exhibit 5–3** Strengths and Weaknesses of PHOs

---

**Strengths**

- PHOs facilitate joint physician and hospital managed care contracting.
- PHOs encourage joint managed care strategic planning between the physicians and hospital.
- PHOs align economic incentives of physicians and hospitals under risk contracts with MCOs.
- Physicians can negotiate capitation contracts collectively with MCOs.
- PHOs offer MCOs a single contracting entity.
- There is a centralized administration of managed care contracts.

**Weaknesses**

- Physicians lose autonomy as part of a large organization.
- Hospitals often insist on "controlling" the organization.
- Hospital-dominated PHOs may lack experience in administration of risk-based capitation contracts.
- It is difficult to achieve cost-efficiencies.
- Large physician panel size may hinder decision-making process.

---

## Management Services Organizations

The management services organization (MSO) model is a relatively new entity that offers management services to physicians, IPAs, integrated medical groups, and other health care providers. Services can range from the administration of capitation and other managed care arrangements to complete physician practice management. MSOs are not providers of health care services, but are vehicles to consolidate administrative functions.

MSOs can be structured in a number of ways with a combination of nonphysician (referred to as "lay") or physician ownership. These structures include a physician equity model; a wholly owned hospital subsidiary; and a joint venture among physicians, hospital, and other organizations. With an MSO model, the physician organization maintains the provider contracts with the MCO and signs a management services agreement with the MSO to provide administrative support. Exhibit 5–4 lists the strengths and weaknesses of MSOs.

### Foundation Models

A medical foundation is a legal entity organized under various structures depending on state jurisdiction. It is the most highly integrated model of physician and hospital organizations. A typical medical foundation is a not-for-profit, tax-exempt entity that con-

**Exhibit 5–4** Strengths and Weaknesses of MSOs

| |
|---|
| **Strengths** |
| • MSOs may provide joint physician and hospital managed care contracting. |
| • MSOs may encourage joint managed care strategic planning between the physicians and hospital. |
| • MSOs may align economic incentives between physicians and hospitals under risk contracts with MCOs. |
| • Integration allows physicians to participate in managed care activities with the hospital. |
| • Physician remains independent and retains ownership of his or her practice. |
| • Physicians may have equity in the entity. |
| • MSOs may access capital through the public sector via initial public offerings (IPOs). |
| • MSOs may offer management services to other third parties. |
| **Weaknesses** |
| • MSOs may require large capital investment to develop. |
| • MSOs are limited to providing management support; the physician organization remains the provider of care. |
| • Physicians need to differentiate the goals of the physician organization from the MSO. |

tracts to provide professional services. Participating physicians usually operate under an employment relationship with the foundation. Exhibit 5–5 lists the strengths and weaknesses of foundation models.

**Exhibit 5–5** Strengths and Weaknesses of Foundation Models

| |
|---|
| **Strengths** |
| • A foundation model is a fully integrated physician-hospital entity. |
| • A foundation model usually operates under a tax-exempt status. |
| • A foundation model may operate in states that prohibit corporate practice of medicine. |
| • A foundation model encourages joint managed care strategic planning between the physicians and hospital. |
| • A foundation model aligns economic incentives under risk contracts with MCOs. |
| • A foundation model offers MCOs a single contracting entity and centralized administration of managed care contracts. |
| **Weaknesses** |
| • Physicians lose autonomy as part of a large organization. |
| • Hospitals often insist on "controlling" the organization. |
| • A foundation model requires significant capital investment to purchase physician practices. |
| • Strict Internal Revenue Service (IRS) requirements due to tax-exempt status exist. |

## THE RELATIONSHIP BETWEEN PROVIDERS AND MANAGED CARE ORGANIZATIONS

The typical provider organization is developed as a mechanism to contract with MCOs on behalf of the providers. The success of these organizations is based, in part, on their ability to assemble and manage an integrated network of providers. Each MCO may have specific methods for contracting with provider organizations that may dictate different approaches in developing relationships. However, maintaining the integrity of the physician panel should be paramount to the provider organization.

In many areas of the country, the MCO will set the premium charge to the purchaser and develop a contracted provider fee schedule. The provider will be paid directly by the MCO for all approved and covered services, bypassing the provider organization. The role of the organization in this case is merely the assemblage of providers. If the MCO chooses to modify its fees or policies, it has the contractual right to do so. Any surplus funds derived from the effective management of services and costs are retained by the MCO.

### Preferred Provider Organizations

Preferred provider organizations (PPOs) constitute one of the most basic forms of managed care. The typical PPO is a wide-ranging network of physicians and hospitals that agree to accept a discounted fee schedule in return for being a "preferred" provider. Many PPOs develop a proprietary fee schedule and network of physicians that they market (usually as a leasing arrangement) to other MCOs, health insurance companies, or purchasers. From a provider's perspective, if the fee schedule is reasonable and the timing of payments is acceptable, entering into a PPO agreement is not detrimental or risky.

In many markets, PPOs have dominated the market share until the recent surge in HMO and POS enrollment. Because PPOs lack opportunities for providers to share in savings from risk contracts and do not have incentive programs to reward providers for appropriate utilization and costs, PPOs have not been able to offer the competitive premiums of HMOs.

Most PPOs contract with individual providers directly; therefore, the provider organization's contracting relationship to the MCO is limited. Often, PPOs represent purchasers of health benefits that self-insure or self-fund the cost of these benefits. In this scenario, the purchaser pays the PPO a network access fee. Although the PPO may act as a third-party administrator (TPA), it most often contracts with a TPA or other party to perform administrative functions. Finally, antitrust regulations (although becoming less stringent) often preclude independent providers from banding together to set fees in non–risk-based contracts. (See Chapter 11 for a detailed discussion of antitrust issues.)

A typical contracting relationship between a provider network and a PPO includes the following elements:

- A PPO or independent party develops a minimum fee schedule for the provider organization to review.
- Individual providers within the group can opt out of each PPO contract negotiated by the group.
- The medical management functions are performed by the PPO or its contracted TPA. Notification of referrals, prior authorization for hospitalizations, and second surgical opinions are often required.
- Each provider bills and collects payments from the PPO (or its TPA) directly.

Giving each provider the option to opt in or out of the MCO contract is best accomplished through a "negative acceptance" approach; the individual provider is given notice of the negotiated contract and ten to fifteen days to opt out of the contract. If the provider organization does not receive a notice from the provider, the provider is assumed to be in agreement with the contract, and thus participating providers. Conversely, the provider organization can use the negative acceptance approach to contract with the PPO on behalf of all providers. Having the physicians bill the PPO directly precludes the provider organization from collecting and aggregating claims data (or at least, makes this task difficult). However, direct physician billing prevents the provider organization from duplicating the billing and accounts receivable activities in existence at each provider's office.

## Point-of-Service Plans

Point-of-service (POS) plans have become popular in the last few years. These plans combine the elements of HMOs, PPOs, and in some cases, indemnity insurance plans. The benefit packages can vary tremendously. For example, one POS benefit design might require members to see their primary care physician for all routine services, and before accessing hospital or specialty care. It might cover preventive care services and require a $10 co-payment for all services, but not include coinsurance or a deductible.

A second POS benefit design might allow patients to access contracted specialty care providers directly. Instead of a flat co-payment, the plan might require coinsurance and deductibles for services, for example, 20 percent of the fee schedule. The negotiated fee schedule might be a "preferred" rate.

The benefit designs will impact the contracting relationship between the provider organization and the MCO offering the POS plan. Important factors to consider when negotiating contracts to provide services under POS benefit designs include the following:

- Will there be varying fee schedules or reimbursement arrangements for the different POS products?
- Will the provider group assume financial risk when members receive care outside the group or outside the network? If so, what is the expected out-of-network usage?
- Will the benefit design be clear on the member's identification card?
- Will the utilization management and referral authorization requirements for the different product lines be easy to differentiate and follow?

Their tremendous flexibility makes these plans popular; however, administration of POS products can be complicated for employers, MCOs, and providers alike. Often, the patient is unclear regarding the coverage and requirements of the POS plan because of its complexity.

In an attempt to make POS plans less complicated and affordable, several HMOs are beginning to offer "scaled down" versions of POS plans. These open-access plans afford patients HMO-like coverage combined with the opportunity to access network specialists directly. In exchange for the enhanced access to specialty care, members will often pay a higher co-payment for specialty services.

## Health Maintenance Organizations

HMO products are available for commercial enrollees, individuals, Medicare beneficiaries, and Medicaid beneficiaries. An organized provider network offers the HMO an effective way to arrange for services to beneficiaries. Furthermore, the provider organization offers individual providers the opportunity to manage risk-based contracts while sharing that risk with their colleagues. The effective management of risk-based contracts affords the provider network the arbitrage opportunity previously gained by insurers exclusively. A group of providers working together can also facilitate a more organized approach to the delivery of patient care. This can help to reduce costs and improve quality through limiting unnecessary or duplicative diagnostic services, improving communication between providers and improving access to services.

In many markets, the relationship between a provider organization and an HMO involves a risk-based contract. The HMO will sell a benefit package(s) to an employer (or, increasingly, to an individual subscriber) for a determined premium amount. The HMO usually allocates a certain percentage of that premium dollar for its administration and other overhead expenses, such as taxes, broker commissions, licensing fees, marketing, enrollment costs, salaries, and office space. A portion of the premium is also allocated for medical services for which the HMO is directly responsible or for which the HMO capitates provider organizations to manage. The percentage of premium allocated for medical services is typically known as the "medical loss ratio." Most HMOs experience direct medical costs of between 60 and 90 percent of the premium dollar.

## Noncommercial Products

There is relatively little distinction in the relationship between a provider organization and an HMO offering commercial, Medicare risk, or Medicaid products; however, the types of health care services or providers the provider organization must offer in a risk-based contract for these different populations may vary. For example, a provider group accepting full capitation under a Medicare-risk contract with an MCO will want to establish contractual relationships with skilled nursing facilities (SNFs), hospice programs, and a physician therapist, because elderly members often need these services.

## Administrative Services-Only Products

Several HMOs also offer administrative services-only (ASO) products to their commercial purchasers. Usually, these programs afford the member HMO-style benefits and access to the HMO's provider network, but the purchaser reimburses the HMO on a claims-made basis plus an administrative fee. In this manner, the employer has the benefits of self-insuring (for example, improved cash flow, retention in the savings of premium versus actual expenses, tax benefits) while accessing a traditional HMO network. From a provider organization's perspective, its relationship with the HMO is usually the same for ASO and fully insured plans, with one significant distinction—those provider organizations receiving full capitation for insured business will likely be paid on a fee-for-service basis for ASO business. Because the HMO is not collecting premium dollars (an advance payment for estimated services), it is usually unwilling to make that same advance payment to the provider organization.

## RISK-BASED ARRANGEMENTS

Under a risk arrangement, an MCO will contract with a provider organization to provide a defined set of medical services at a negotiated capitation rate and other arrangements that will obligate the provider organization for the care of enrolled members. Capitation rates can be negotiated as a flat amount per member per month (PMPM); a table of PMPM rates based on age, sex, and benefit option adjustments to the flat PMPM; and a percentage of the employer premium to the MCO. This capitation rate is offered to the provider organization as a direct capitation payment or budget, depending on the arrangement negotiated. When the funds are held by the MCO, the capitation rate serves as a budget rather than a direct capitation payment. Different portions of the medical services can be allocated as capitation rates, budgets, or risk pools.

### Risk-Sharing Models

In risk-based relationships with provider networks, several financial and organizational models exist for managing and distributing funds.

*Primary Care Physician Capitation and Shared-Risk Pool*

Under this arrangement, only the primary care physicians (PCPs) are paid a capitation rate, whereas the other providers are paid at a discounted fee-for-service rate determined by the MCO. Figure 5–1 shows the distribution of funds under a PCP capitation and shared-risk pool model. Often, the MCO will retain a percentage of the allowed payment as a "withhold" to be used in case the network costs exceed the budget. When the costs are less than the budget, the

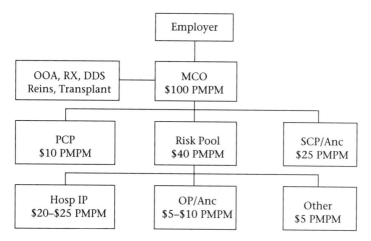

**Figure 5–1** PCP Capitation. *Source:* Courtesy of Meridian Health Care Management, LF, Thousand Oaks, California.

---

withhold, and perhaps additional amounts up to the total budget, are returned to providers.

*Provider Organization Capitation and Shared-Risk Pool*

A common type of risk-based arrangement between MCOs and provider organizations is a provider group capitation for professional services and a risk pool for hospital and other services. The provider organization capitation and shared-risk pool arrangement is illustrated in Figure 5–2. Hospitals are typically paid on a fee-for-service basis. Under a fee-for-service–based hospital contract, the hospital is paid per diems or case rates or some combination of the two. In this type of contract, the MCO has a hospital budget pool and deducts payments to the hospital from that pool. If there is a surplus (savings) in the pool, the savings are shared between the health plan and the physicians. Fee-for-service contracts, therefore, can have the effect of limiting the hospital's incentive to work toward creating savings in the pool by controlling utilization and costs. This is at cross purposes to the medical group, which is capitated for the membership in question and which is seeking to benefit from surpluses in the hospital shared-risk pool. As a result, many providers are seeking global capitation contracts to align the incentives of the parties to the contract.

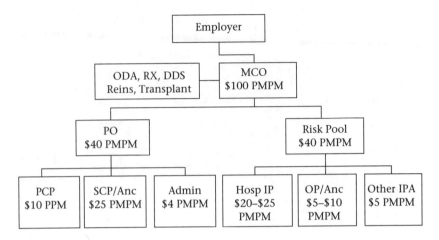

**Figure 5–2** Provider Organization Capitation. *Source:* Courtesy of Meridian Health Care Management, Thousand Oaks, California.

---

*Full-Risk Capitation*

In a full-risk (or global) model, the provider organizations are given the negotiated capitation rate to manage directly. The capitation fee paid by the MCO includes professional and institutional services. Figure 5–3 illustrates the full-risk capitation model.

With full-risk arrangements, the provider organization is also responsible for administering the capitation payment. This will include tracking and monitoring member eligibility and benefits information, authorizing and tracking referrals to specialists, paying and processing claims, and preparing financial and utilization reports. As such, the provider organization will need to establish appropriate information and financial management systems to administer these functions.

As physician and hospital providers continue to integrate through the formation of joint ventured medical groups, MSOs, and PHOs, there is significant movement to develop joint contracting strategies aimed at aligning the interests of all parties. Increasingly, provider organizations are seeking to obtain global capitation (physician and hospital services). In many states, an insurance or HMO license is required for a provider organization to receive a capitation payment for all services. For some large, well capitalized physician groups, this is a viable strategy. However, for most providers, the first step toward global capitation involves capitating the hospital and the physicians

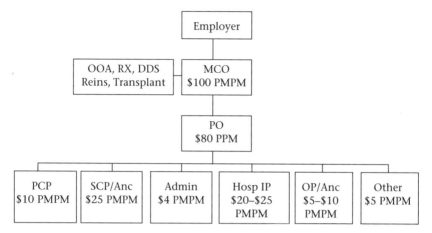

**Figure 5-3** Provider Organization Full-Risk Capitation. *Source:* Courtesy of Meridian Health Care Management, Thousand Oaks, California.

for their respective portions of the services under the MCO contract. This provides the hospital with access to shared-risk savings and allows the physicians and the hospital to arrive at the optimum division of financial responsibility for the capitated medical services.

## Division of Responsibilities

When entering into a capitated contract of any kind, and particularly when entering into a full-risk (or global) capitation contract, the hospital, physicians, and MCO should agree on a division of responsibilities for each service.

The distribution of health care services outlined in the contract will enable the parties to develop a matrix of financial responsibilities. This matrix should be incorporated into the agreement between the MCO and the provider organization, as well as the shared-risk agreements between the provider organization and the hospital, and the provider organization and its member physicians.

A matrix of service and financial responsibility should be developed for all products that fall under the contract (that is, commercial, Medicare risk, Medicaid). It should reflect the benefits available to the member and should be as specific as possible. The matrix will help the parties identify any service gaps so that the necessary contracting can occur before members receive care. This may result in fewer retrospective payment disputes between the MCO and provider organization.

## Distribution of Shared-Risk Funds

In global capitation contracts, a contract must be established between the physician group and the hospital defining the rates to be charged against the hospital capitation, and the distribution of shared-risk surpluses and deficits. The distribution will define how the surplus/deficit will be split between the two parties and the timing for performing the calculation and making the payments.

There are two levels of surplus and deficit distribution to be considered. The first level involves the distribution between the MCO and the provider group, or, if the hospital is capitated, between the hospital and the group. The second level involves the distribution among the providers at the group level.

Once a shared-risk surplus or deficit occurs, there must be a mechanism for allocating or collecting the funds. Many organizations are not prepared to deal with this issue when it arises, often at great political cost to the organization. If possible, providers should be informed in advance of the risk-sharing methodology. This sets forth the understanding (in advance) of the group's policy and procedure regarding surplus and deficit distributions.

*Provider Organization Distributions*

Depending on the risk-sharing arrangement negotiated, a provider organization will share risk with the MCO (if there is a hospital risk pool) or the hospital (if it is capitated by the MCO). When a hospital risk pool budget is established with a provider organization, all inpatient and outpatient facility expenses are allocated to the hospital pool. From this pool, a budget for inpatient hospital expenses is determined with target utilization and average per diem rates. Based on comparisons of actual versus budgeted utilization and costs, a surplus or deficit occurs in which the MCO or hospital and physicians share according to a pre-negotiated contractual split.

A typical distribution involves a fifty-fifty split between the MCO or hospital and the physicians, that is, each receives or pays half. As stronger integration occurs between physicians and hospitals, physicians are receiving a higher percentage of the surplus. In a deficit situation, the MCO or hospital generally bears the full risk, even though the physicians may be liable for a percentage of the deficit. In successive years, physicians would make retrospective settlement payments to the MCO or hospital to cover prior deficits. However, this traditional methodology is based on volume of business rather than on individual cost-effectiveness. The overall size of the pool is based on the performance of the entire group; therefore, individual physicians who are particularly cost-effective may not experience any return of funds. This model is a strong disincentive for physicians that could result in a loss of the risk-pool dollars ultimately, with no change in costs and utilization patterns.

An alternative distribution model involves distributing funds based on product lines, in addition to total costs. For example, the group may decide to split surplus funds for commercial members 60 percent to PCPs and 40 percent to specialists because the PCP is doing the bulk of the work for these members. For Medicare members, the group may divide the pool 40 percent to PCPs and 60 percent to specialists under the assumption that the senior population requires more specialty care than the commercial population.

### Internal Provider Distributions

After the initial allocation of funds is determined between primary and specialty care, a number of factors can be used when distributing the pool funds to individual physicians. One model establishes performance for PCPs in the areas of PMPM costs, patient satisfaction survey results, availability of the practice to new enrollment, and completion of a specialist survey. Providers are scored and a distribution formula is established and applied against the total dollars available in this portion of the pool. The performance targets established for specialists may include a satisfaction rating by referring physicians, a patient satisfaction rating, and participation in the development of clinical guidelines.

Other methods for risk-pool distribution include the following:

- If the PCP receives a full professional capitation rate (professional primary and specialty care services), he or she will receive all available surplus dollars. Strong medical management is required for this arrangement to succeed.
- Grouping physicians for collective risk-pool distributions. It is recommended that five to fifteen physicians be grouped into a POD (pool of physicians). Risk-pool funds are set aside based on

utilization of hospital, specialty, ancillary, pharmacy, and emergency services of the entire group and dispersed evenly among the physicians.

Legal counsel should be consulted on the specific laws and regulations surrounding physician and hospital risk-pool distributions.

## INTERNAL PROVIDER CONTRACTS

Internal provider contracts are those agreements between the provider organization that holds the risk contract with the MCO and the physicians who are members of that provider organization. Typically, the internal provider contracts mirror those between the MCO and provider organization, carrying forward applicable state, federal, and MCO requirements. The agreements between the provider organization and its member physicians should distinguish the responsibilities of each party clearly regarding the provision of services and the financial and administrative obligations of each.

### Key Contract Terms

The contract provisions in the agreement between the provider organization and its member physicians should be as comprehensive as necessary to ensure that the provider organization is in compliance with its responsibilities under its contracts with MCOs. Appendix 5–A is an example of a primary care contract. Key contracting issues in professional service agreements include the following:

- *Utilization management.* Member physicians agree to comply with the provider organization's (or MCO's) utilization management (UM) policies and procedures.
- *Termination.* This sets forth the termination provisions between the provider organization and the member physician, including when and how each may terminate a relationship and what, if any, obligations continue after the termination.
- *Contracting authority.* This provision specifies the member physician's decision to grant the provider organization the authority to enter into managed care contracts on behalf of the physician.
- *Covered services.* Physicians that are capitated for certain services must have a thorough understanding of the definition of those services.

## Reimbursement

The reimbursement section(s) of the agreement should state the type of reimbursement, the amount of reimbursement, the services included under reimbursement, and the payment time frame. Other important considerations affecting reimbursement include the physician's responsibility to collect co-payments and deductibles (reimbursement from the MCO may not include an adjustment for co-payments), balance billing of members, claims submission guidelines, and utilization or authorization requirements affecting reimbursement. Agreements where providers are compensated under a capitation arrangement should also include which services are being capitated, when the capitation payment will be made, what adjustments may be made to capitation payments, and how noncapitated services will be reimbursed.

Primary care physicians who are capitated to provide primary care services must have a thorough understanding of the definition of primary care services. Services typically covered under a primary care contract include the following:

- routine office visits, including well-baby care (family practice and pediatrics), complete physicals, preventive medical care, and routine chest radiographs;
- physician office visits for treatment of acute and chronic illness;
- care for minor injuries, including minor burns, simple lacerations, suture removal, and treatment of epistaxis;
- surgical procedures, including biopsy or removal of cysts, moles, and growths (except facial), electrosurgical/cryosurgical destruction of lesions (except facial), and simple incision and drainage procedures;
- miscellaneous medical supplies related to treatment in the physician's office;
- professional services for inpatient and outpatient hospital care;
- telephone consultations as necessary with members;
- office visits for urgent medical problems outside normal office hours;
- home visits when necessary;
- routine outpatient lab tests (unless capitated);
- twenty-four–hour on-call coverage; and
- preventive medical care and health education.

Many provider organizations will capitate high-cost, high-frequency specialties in an effort to fix expenses and control utilization. Such specialties frequently include cardiology, orthopedics, physical therapy, general surgery, urology, ophthalmology (if there is a significant Medicare-risk population), and hematology/oncology. The services to be provided under specialty capitation should be as broad as possible. The contract should also list those services that are excluded from the capitation payment.

Critical sections of the internal provider contracts involve how the provider organization will be reimbursed by the MCO and how the provider organization will compensate its member physicians. Arriving at an acceptable reimbursement methodology will be critical to the success of the contract. The reimbursement methodology must balance diverse market factors such as current provider fee schedules, competitor capitation rates, ease of administration, providers' familiarity with selected methodology, volume of business anticipated from the MCO, and projected utilization.

A wide array of payment methodologies exist. The most common methods are fee-for-service and capitation.

*Fee-For-Service*

A fee-for-service reimbursement arrangement typically involves a discount from the physician's current fees. Sometimes fee-for-service payments include a withhold that generally ranges from 10 to 25 percent of the fees. They are used to fund withhold pools to cover any expenses over the budget ("overages") that may occur. Withhold pools can be used to cover overages for the entire group, or can be apportioned along specialties, that is, primary care, specialty care, subspecialty care. (See Chapter 4 for a detailed discussion of withhold arrangements.)

To build a fee-for-service fee schedule, it is important to understand the relative level of discounts assumed in the fee schedule and how the fee schedule compares to those of other MCOs and to "reasonable and customary" reimbursement levels in the community. Steps involved in developing a fee schedule include the following:

- establishing a benchmark fee schedule for participating physicians based on prevailing charges in the area;
- obtaining an understanding of how the fee schedule might be adjusted so the group can compete successfully in the managed care market; and
- using the information to adopt a fee schedule as a basis for negotiating actual fee proposals from MCOs. Negotiated fees

should strike the best possible balance between competitive pricing and reasonable reimbursement to the member physicians.

The Health Insurance Association of America (HIAA) or other charge profiles can be used to develop the benchmark fee schedule. HIAA data are specific to geographic areas and are defined and gathered uniformly across the country. They consist of fees that are submitted by physicians to commercial health insurance companies. Because these data are geographic-specific, the HIAA fee profile is more suitable and uniform for use as a standard in developing a fee schedule and usually produces higher fee values than those of other charge profiles.

Once the benchmark fee schedule has been established, it is advisable to use the McGraw-Hill Relative Value Unit (RVU) Scale or Medicare's Resource-Based Relative Value Scale (RBRVS) to convert the benchmark levels to a basis that can be modified easily. (See Chapter 4 for a detailed discussion of RVU and RBRVS fee schedules.)

An RBRVS fee schedule relies, for the most part, on a single conversion factor. A single conversion factor has the following several advantages:

- It is usually credible because it is based upon all services.
- It is easy to administer and coincides with Medicare's reimbursement system.
- It is flexible and easy to adjust, especially when testing multiple prospective fee schedules.

When evaluating the appropriateness of the McGraw-Hill basis, there are also the following several issues to consider:

- The underlying basis of the McGraw-Hill RVUs is purely historical costs. Contrary to the development of the RBRVS, there were no charge-related objectives intended when the McGraw-Hill RVUs were developed.
- McGraw-Hill relies on several different conversion factors for various service categories (that is, medical, surgical, radiology, pathology). As a result, more traditional physician fees, that is, for surgical procedures, are reimbursed more than those for medical procedures.
- McGraw-Hill conversion factors are based on less volume when divided into the various service categories.

- The multiple conversion factor system is more burdensome when creating multiple fee schedules, and is more complex to administer.

It is crucial for the long-term success of the group that the member physicians understand and accept the fee schedule. Soliciting input from physicians at the start of the fee development process enhances the efficiency of obtaining their acceptance "buy-in."

*Capitation*

Under capitation, the MCO or provider organization pays the provider a fixed amount PMPM for managing the health of enrolled members and providing all defined services required for those members. The capitation payment does not fluctuate with the utilization of services or cost structure. (See Chapter 4 for a detailed discussion of capitation.)

When determining the acceptability of capitation rates, it is important to build a cost and utilization model. The model includes a breakdown of services by specialty by Current Procedural Terminology (CPT) code; utilization rates for each service category; provider reimbursement; and co-payment, deductible, and coinsurance levels. This information then can be calculated as a PMPM expense for each service category.

A number of factors must be considered when developing a capitation model, including the following:

- understanding the strategic objectives of capitation both from the provider group's and MCO's perspective;
- defining the covered population, that is, commercial, Medicare, Medicaid, workers' compensation. (Because the covered services, utilization rates, and reimbursement will vary according to the population covered, each requires a separate analysis.);
- defining the capitated services as specifically as possible, that is, CPT and ICD9 codes;
- defining the products, that is, HMO, POS;
- collecting and projecting utilization data adjusted for incurred-but-not-reported (IBNR) claims, benefit design, population, and utilization management;
- defining the risk-sharing arrangement among primary care physicians, specialists, hospital, and MCO;
- applying the targeted provider reimbursement;

- applying product design adjustment such as co-payments, coinsurance, deductibles, and coordination of benefits (COB) payments;
- adjusting for stop loss costs and recoveries;
- valuing administrative capabilities and costs of performing these services. (This may include additional staffing requirements, utilization management costs, reporting [internal and external] costs, eligibility tracking costs, and audit fees.); and
- applying health-risk adjusters (if applicable) such as age and sex factors and industry factors.

All of these factors taken together will form the basis for the group's evaluation of the capitated rate as well as for establishing individual capitation rates for the providers. Capitation of specialists within a provider group is growing. The most frequently capitated specialties are psychiatry, ophthalmology, radiology, cardiology, urology, allergy, orthopedics, general surgery, otolaryngology, and dermatology.

Any combination of reimbursement methodologies can be used within a provider group. Many groups capitate PCPs and reimburse specialists on a fee-for-service or modified fee-for-service methodology. Some groups receiving global capitation payments from MCOs do not capitate their providers at all, whereas others capitate all the providers in the group, including specialists. Finally, to curtail growing specialty costs, some groups are beginning to capitate PCPs for all professional services including specialty services or to pay PCPs on a fee-for-service basis and capitate key specialists.

In summary, the capitation rates developed should be fair and equitable, consistent with provider and MCO objectives, based on valid assumptions and methods, and monitored and updated on a regular basis.

## CONCLUSION

The managed care marketplace and the contracting process for provider groups are complex. Many issues must be taken into account when forming an appropriate physician entity and securing managed care contracts. Success in securing viable managed care contracts requires careful consideration of governance and corporate structure;

market demographics; competition; experience in managed care; internal provider reimbursement and incentive programs; and contractual, reimbursement, and legal issues.

---

**NOTE**

1. *The InterStudy Competitive Edge. Part II: HMO Industry Report 6.2.* 1996. St. Paul, MN: InterStudy Publications, 5.

# Appendix 5-A _____

## Sample Primary Professional Services Agreement

This Professional Services Agreement ("Agreement") is made and entered into this _____ day of _____ , 19 _____

by and between _____ ("IPA")

located at _____ and

_____ ("Professional"), whose

speciality is in the field of _____

and having his/her principal place of business at _____

_____ .

### Recitals

WHEREAS, IPA intends to enter into agreements with Health Care Service Plans, Hospital Service Plans, and Federally Qualified Health Maintenance Organizations ("Plan[s]") which are licensed under the laws of the State of California, for the provision of medical services to persons enrolled as Members ("Members") of Plans; and

WHEREAS, IPA and Professional desire to enter into a contract whereby Professional agrees to provide Covered Services on behalf of IPA to Members of the Plans which contract with IPA;

NOW, THEREFORE, in consideration of the mutual convenants and promises contained herein, the parties agree as follows:

### ARTICLE I—DEFINITIONS

1.1 "ASA Guide" means a Relative Value Guide, published by the American Society of Anesthesiologists, which is a payment mechanism for assigning unit values to anesthesia services.

1.2 "BR" is an abbreviation for "by report," used in the 1974 CRVS for procedures not accompanied by unit values that are too variable in the nature of their performance, to permit the assignment of unit values because the fees for such procedures need to be justified by report.

1.3 "Capitation Fee" means a predetermined monthly fee, to be multiplied by the number of Members assigned to Professional for Covered Services.

1.4 "Conversion Factor" means a set rate, to be multiplied by a unit value, to equal a reimbursement amount.

1.5 "Co-payment" means those charges for professional services that shall be collected directly by Professional from Member, as payment in addition to the fee paid to Professional by IPA, in accordance with the Member's Evidence of Coverage.

1.6 "Covered Services" means those health care services and supplies that a Member is entitled to receive under a Plan's benefit program and that are described and defined in the Plan's Evidence of Coverage and disclosure forms, subscriber and group contracts, and in a Plan's Provider Manual.

1.7 "CRVS" is an abbreviation for "1974 California Relative Value Studies" published by the California Medical Association, and is a payment mechanism for assigning unit values to medical procedures in categeories of medicine, surgery, radiology, pathology, anesthesiology, and radiology/nuclear medicine.

1.8 "Emergency" means the sudden onset of a symptom, illness, or injury requiring immediate diagnosis and/or treatment.

1.9 "Evidence of Coverage" means the document issued by a Plan to a Member that describes the Member's Covered Services in the Plan.

1.10 "Fee-For-Service" means Professional will be paid according to a determined payment schedule for all authorized services rendered.

1.11 "Flat Rate" means a set fee paid to Professional for a specific procedure.

1.12 "Global Rate" means a set fee paid to Professional for multiple procedures.

1.13 "Medical Director" means a Participating Physician who is authorized by IPA to be responsible for administering IPA medical affairs and for serving as IPA's medical liaison to contracting Plans.

1.14 "Medically Necessary" means medical or surgical treatment that a Member requires as determined by a Participating Provider, in accordance with accepted medical and surgical practices and standards prevailing at the time of treatment and in conformity with the professional and technical standards adopted by the Utilization Management Committee of IPA.

1.15 "Medicare Fee Schedule" means a payment mechanism, listing by procedure number, the flat rate payable by geographic area, and ZIP code of the Professional, that is administered by the Health Care Finance Administration.

1.16 "Member" means a person who is enrolled in a Plan, also referred to as an Enrollee, including enrolled dependents, and is entitled to receive Covered Services.

1.17 "Non-Covered Services" means those health care services that are not benefits under the Evidence of Coverage.

1.18 "Participating Hospital" means a duly licensed hospital that has entered into an agreement with a Plan and/or IPA to provide Covered Services to Members.

1.19 "Participating Physician" means a physician (duly licensed to practice medicine or osteopathy in accordance with applicable California law) who has entered into an agreement with IPA to provide Covered Services to Members.

1.20 "Participating Provider" means a Participating Physician, Participating Hospital, or other licensed health facility or licensed health professional, that has entered into an agreement to provide Covered Services to Members.

1.21 "Primary Physician" or "Primary Care Physician" means a Participating Physician selected by a Member to render first contact medical care and to provide "primary care" as that term is defined by IPA in Exhibit "C". "Primary Physician" or "Primary Care Physician" may include, as determined by IPA, internists, pediatricians, family practitioners, and general practitioners.

1.22 "Referral/Authorization" means the process by which the Participating Physician directs a Member to seek and/or obtain Covered Services from a health professional, a hospital, or any other provider of Covered Services.

1.23 "RNE" is an abbreviation for "relativity not established" used in the 1974 CRVS codes for procedures that are well-defined services, but either are too recently developed or are performed with insufficient frequency for a determination to be made about the relationship between charges for them and for other services listed in the CRVS. Also, fees for procedures listed on an RNE basis may need to be justified "by report."

1.24 "Specialist Physician" means a Participating Physician who is professionally qualified to practice his/her designated specialty and whose agreement with IPA includes responsibility for providing Covered Services in his/her designated specialty.

1.25 "Subscriber" means a person or entity that is responsible for payment to a Plan or person whose employment or other status, except for family dependency, is the basis for eligibility for enrollment in a Plan.

## ARTICLE II—SERVICES TO BE PERFORMED BY PROFESSIONAL

2.1 *Professional Responsibilities.* Professional shall provide Primary Care Physician Covered Services and related administrative services to Plan Members in accordance with applicable legal and professional standards and in compliance with IPA's professional and administrative rules, regulations, requirements, policies, and procedure manuals. Failure by Professional to comply with IPA's professional or administrative requirements after reasonable notice and opportunity to comply, shall constitute grounds for termination of this Agreement by IPA upon ninety (90) day written notice to providers. Professional agrees to be bound by the Primary Care Physician responsibilities set forth in Exhibit "C". These procedures may be amended from time to time by administrative notice from IPA.

2.2 *Covering Physician*. If Professional is, for any reason, from time to time, unable to provide Covered Services when and as needed, Professional may secure the services of a qualified covering physician, who shall render such Covered Services otherwise required of Professional; provided, however, that the covering physician so furnished, must be a licensed physician capable to provide Covered Services to Members. Professional shall be solely responsible for securing the services of such covering physician and paying said covering physician for those Covered Services provided to Members. Professional shall ensure that the covering physician: (1) looks solely to Professional for compensation; (2) will accept IPA's peer review procedures; (3) will not bill Members for Covered Services under any circumstances; (4) will obtain authorizations as required for Covered Services and hospitalizations, in accordance with the IPA's utilization management program; and (5) will comply with the terms hereof.

2.3 *Referral/Authorization*. Professional agrees to be bound by the Referral/Authorization procedures as set forth in Exhibits "D" and "E", hereof, and any other procedures adopted by IPA to comply with its Plan contracts. These procedures may be amended, from time to time, by administrative notice from IPA.

## ARTICLE III—REPRESENTATIONS

3.1 *Representations by IPA*. IPA hereby warrants and represents that it is a California Corporation, in good standing with the California Secretary of State.

3.2 *Representations by Professional*. Professional hereby warrants and represents that Professional is a physician, or California professional corporation, duly licensed to practice medicine in the State of California, and is in good standing with the Medical Board of California. Professional warrants and represents that Professional is currently and for the duration of this Agreement, shall remain a member in good standing of the medical staff of the Participating Hospital, with appropriate privileges.

## ARTICLE IV—IPA'S ROLE AND RESPONSIBILITY

4.1 *Prompt Payment.* IPA will be responsible for prompt payment of all authorized billed services from Professional.

4.2 *Administration and Management.* IPA will organize, operate, and market a commercially competitive product, consisting of physician and related health care services to various Plans. IPA will be responsible to provide or arrange all program marketing, administration, financial management and control, claims processing, billing and collections, and the operation of comprehensive quality assurance and utilization management programs consistent with IPA's institutional objectives and with the requirements of Plans. IPA will develop and maintain written policies and procedures relating to such activities and relating to Participating Provider compensation, and will make such written policies and procedures available to Professional and other participating physicians and providers.

## ARTICLE V—CONTRACTING AUTHORITY

5.1 *Contracting Authority.* Subject to the other terms of this Agreement, and to IPA's general policies regarding third-party contracting payers, Professional hereby delegates to the IPA the authority to bind Professional to contracts with third-party payers, including, but not limited to, Preferred Provider Organizations and Competitive Medical Plans, and to negotiate on Professional's behalf, regarding such contracts; provided, however, that the Professional compensation terms of such agreements must be more favorable to Professional than the Professional compensation terms set forth in IPA's contracts with Plans.

## ARTICLE VI—COORDINATION OF BENEFITS

6.1 *Definition.* Coordination of Benefits ("COB") refers to the determination of which of two or more health benefit plans will apply, either as primary or secondary coverage, for the rendition of hospital, surgical, or medical services to a Member. Such coordination is intended to preclude the Professional from receiving an aggregate of more than one hundred percent (100%) of covered charges from all coverage when the primary and secondary benefits are coordinated.

Determination of liability will be in accordance with the usual proce-dures employed by the California Department of Insurance and applicable state regulations.

6.2 *COB Obligations of Professional.* Professional agrees to coordinate with IPA for proper determination of COB, and to bill and collect from other payers such charges for which the other payer is responsible. Professional shall report all collections received to IPA in accordance with this Paragraph 6.2.

## ARTICLE VII—COMPENSATION

7.1 *Compensation.* Professional agrees to look solely to IPA for any and all remuneration, subject to the division of financial responsibility between IPA and Plan, and agrees not to bill Plan Members for covered services, except where co-payments are required. Payment shall be made in accordance with Exhibit "A" (and/or Exhibit "A/1" when applicable).

7.2 *Patient Billing.* Professional agrees to accept payment from IPA as payment in full, for all Professional Covered Services rendered to Plan Members and agrees not to bill such Plan Members for Covered Services, except to the extent that co-payments, deductibles, coordi-nation of benefit charges, or other payments are expressly permitted to be billed by Professional, separately pursuant to written rules and procedures adopted by IPA. Professional specifically agrees not to institute any legal collection proceedings against Plan Members in violation of this provision. Professional agrees that it will not main-tain any action at law against Plan Members to collect sums that are owed by IPA to Professional.

7.3 *Billing.* Professional agrees to comply with the billing procedures set forth in Exhibits "A" and "D". These billing procedures may be amended, from time to time, by administrative notice from IPA.

## ARTICLE VIII—OBLIGATIONS OF PROFESSIONAL

8.1 *Hours.* Professional shall make available Professional services to Plan Members during office hours, and shall provide on-call coverage to Members on a twenty-four (24) hour, seven (7) day a week basis.

8.2 *Malpractice Insurance.* Professional shall provide, unless otherwise agreed to by Professional and IPA, at Professional's sole cost and expense, throughout the entire term of this Agreement, a policy of professional malpractice liability insurance with a licensed insurance company, admitted to do business in the State of California, in an amount of not less than one million dollars ($1,000,000) per claim and three million dollars ($3,000,000) aggregate to cover any loss, liability, or damage alleged to have been committed by Professional, or Professional's agent, servant, or employees.

8.3 *Comprehensive Insurance.* Professional shall provide, unless otherwise agreed to between Professional and IPA, at Professional's sole cost and expense, throughout the entire term of this Agreement, a policy or policies of insurance, in an amount acceptable to IPA, covering Professional's principal place of business, insuring Professional against any claim of loss, liability, or damage committed or arising out of the alleged condition of said premises, or the furniture, fixtures, appliances, or equipment located therein, together with standard liability protection against any loss, liability, or damage as a result of Professional's, Professional's agent's, servant's, or employee's operation of a motor vehicle for business purposes.

8.4 *License to Practice/Hospital Privileges.* If at any time, during the entire term of this Agreement, Professional shall have Professional's license to practice medicine in the State of California, suspended or Hospital Privileges revoked, impaired, reduced, or suspended, this Agreement, at the sole option of IPA, shall terminate immediately and become null and void, and of no further force or effect, except as otherwise provided herein.

8.5 *Professional Roster.* Professional agrees that IPA and Plans may use Professional's name, address, phone number, type of practice, willingness to accept new patients, and other marketing information, in the IPA and/or Plan roster of Professional participants. The roster may be inspected by, and is intended to be used by, prospective patients, prospective IPA physicians, and others.

8.6 *Compliance with California and Federal Statutes.* Professional agrees to cooperate with IPA, so that IPA may meet any requirements imposed on IPA by state and federal law, as amended. Such obligations shall not be terminated upon termination of this Agreement.

8.7 *Non-Discrimination.* Professional shall not discriminate against any Plan Member, any contract party, prospective contracting party, or person reasonably expected to benefit from any such contract, because of race, color, national origin, ancestry, religion, sex, marital status, or age; and Professional agrees to cooperate with IPA and Plans in programs designed to monitor access and quality of care for Plan Members.

8.8 *Notice of Changed Circumstances.* Professional agrees to notify IPA, in writing, within thirty (30) days of any changes in Professional's medical staff privileges, professional licensure status, including, but not limited to, controlled substances registration certificate and state license, office address, availability of office facilities and services, mental and physical health status, teaching appointments, clinical privileges, or board certification status.

## ARTICLE IX—MEDICAL RECORDS

9.1 *Record Retention.* Professional agrees to maintain such records, books, and papers and provide such information to IPA, Plans, or to the California Commissioner of Corporations as may be necessary for compliance by Plans with the provisions of the Knox-Keene Health Care Services Plan Act of 1975, as amended, and the regulations, promulgated thereunder. The Professional further agrees that such obligation is not terminated upon termination of this Agreement, whether by rescission or otherwise, and that such records will be kept for a minimum of seven (7) years.

9.2 *Access to Records.* Professional agrees to provide access to an inspection by IPA, Plans, the California Department of Corporations, the California Department of Health, the United States Department of Health and Human Services, and the Controller General of the United States, at all reasonable times and upon demand, to the books, records, and documents of the Professional, relating to the Covered Services provided to Plan Members, and access to the cost thereof, and to the amounts of any payments received from Members or from others, on such Member's behalf. Such records and information shall be open to inspection during normal business hours, and, to the extent feasible, all such records shall be located in the State of California.

9.3 *Standards for Medical Records.* Professional shall maintain, with respect to each Plan Member receiving Covered Services hereunder, a single standard medical record. Professional agrees to comply with the standards for medical records referenced in Exhibit "D". These procedures may be amended, from time to time, by administrative notice from IPA.

## ARTICLE X—TERM AND TERMINATION

10.1 *Term and Termination.* The effective date of this Agreement shall be the FIRST day of 19__. The initial term of this Agreement shall extend for twelve (12) months following the effective date. This Agreement will automatically be renewed for successive periods of twelve (12) months each, on the same terms and conditions contained herein, unless sooner terminated, pursuant to the terms of this Agreement.

10.2 *Termination with Notice.* This Agreement may be terminated by Professional by the giving of ninety (90) days prior written notice, served to IPA by registered or certified mail; provided, however, IPA may, at its sole and absolute discretion, shorten this notice period, upon receipt of written request by Professional, to shorten said notice period. This Agreement may be terminated by IPA by the giving of ninety (90) days prior written notice served to Professional by registered or certified mail.

10.3 *Continuity of Care.* Professional agrees that upon termination of this Agreement, Professional will continue to provide Covered Services to Plan Members who retain eligibility under their Subscriber's Contract, or by operation of law, and who are receiving Covered Services from the Professional at the time of termination, until such Covered Services are completed.

10.4 *Plan Contract Termination.* IPA agrees to notify Plan in the event that its contract with the Professional is amended or terminated. Notice to Plan is considered given when electronically submitted, faxed, or when deposited in the United States mail, by IPA.

## ARTICLE XI—UTILIZATION MANAGEMENT AND GRIEVANCE PROTOCOL

11.1 *Participation in Quality Assurance and Utilization Management.* Professional agrees to participate fully in formal quality assurance, utilization management, and disciplinary peer review activities, relating to the program conducted by or on behalf of IPA. Such participation includes preparation of reports and documentation, attendance at meetings, conduct of investigations, assessments, and such other activities as IPA may prescribe, from time to time, through written rules and procedures. Professional agrees to keep all IPA documents and information (including documents and information related to quality assurance, utilization management, and peer review) strictly confidential, and not to disclose such documents or information without IPA's written consent.

11.2 *Grievance Resolution.* Professional agrees that all disputes or disagreements between Professional and any Plan or Member, shall be resolved in accordance with such grievance resolution process as an applicable Plan may establish, from time to time. Likewise, Professional agrees that all disputes or disagreements between Professional and IPA, relating to this Agreement or to the Plan, shall be resolved according to the grievance process established, in writing, by IPA, from time to time.

## ARTICLE XII—GENERAL PROVISIONS

12.1 *Arbitration.* Professional agrees to accept and be bound by the Member's Arbitration Agreement, referenced in Exhibit "B."

12.2 *Dispute Resolution/Legal Fees.* Any dispute between the parties relating to or arising out of this Agreement or the parties' actions under this Agreement shall be resolved exclusively in accordance with the terms of this Paragraph 12.2.

12.2 (a) If either party (Complaining Party) to this Agreement considers the other party to be in breach of any provision of this Agreement or if a Complaining Party asserts any claim or demand against the other party relating to this Agreement, the Complaining Party shall transmit written notice to the other party (Responding Party) setting forth in detail the basis of the Complaining Party position.

12.2 (b) Within ten (10) business days following receipt of such written claim the Responding Party shall either comply or agree to comply with the claim or shall give the Complaining Party written notice of the Responding Party position.

12.2 (c) If the Complaining Party claim remains unresolved for fifteen (15) business days following receipt of the claim by the Responding Party, each party shall promptly appoint a representative. The two representatives shall then promptly consult with each other and shall designate an arbitrator. The arbitrator shall then promptly resolve the claim in accordance with such procedures and conditions as the arbitrator shall adopt.

12.2 (d) Neither party shall initiate legal proceedings against the other party until the dispute resolution provisions of this Paragraph 12.2 have been completed.

12.2 (e) If any legal action or any arbitration or other proceeding is brought for the enforcement of this Agreement, or because of an alleged dispute, breach, default, or misrepresentation in connection with any of the provisions of this Agreement, the successful or prevailing party or parties shall be entitled to recover reasonable attorneys' fees and other costs incurred in that action or proceeding, in addition to any other relief to which it or they may be entitled.

## ARTICLE XIII—ENTIRE AGREEMENT

13.1 *Entire Agreement.* This Agreement supersedes any and all agreements, either written or oral, between the parties hereto, with respect to the subject matter contained herein, and contains all of the covenants and agreements between the parties. With the sole exception of IPA's rules, regulations, requirements, policies, and procedure manuals relating to Provider Medical and administrative services (as described in Exhibits "A", "A/1", "B", "D", and "E" ), this agreement may not be modified, without a written statement, executed by both parties.

Executed this _____ day of _____ , 19__ , at _____

_____ , California.

APPROVED:

NAME OF IPA PROFESSIONAL

_____

                                                  PROFESSIONAL SIGNATURE

_____

DATE                                      PRINT NAME

                                         _____

                                         DATE

**ADDENDUM #1**

This addendum shall become a part of the Professional Services Agreement between NAME OF IPA ("IPA") and

_____

("Professional") entered into on _____ .

*Nondiscrimination Requirement.* Professional shall not discriminate against Medi-Cal members because of race, color, creed, religion, ancestry, marital status, sexual orientation, national origin, age, sex, or physical or mental handicap, in accordance with Title VI of the Civil Rights Act of 1964, 42 USC Section 2000d rules and regulations, promulgated pursuant thereto, or as otherwise provided by law or regulation. For the purpose of this contract, discrimination on the grounds of race, color, creed, religion, ancestry, marital status, sexual orientation, national origin, age, sex, or physical or mental handicap, include but are not limited to, the following: denying any member any covered services, or availability of a facility; providing to a member any covered services which are different, or are provided in a different manner or at a different time, from that provided to other members under this contract, except where medically indicated; subjecting a member to segregation or separate treatment, in any manner related to the receipt of any covered service; restricting a member in any way, in the enjoyment of any advantage or privilege enjoyed by others receiving any covered services; treating a member or eligible beneficiary differently from others in determining whether he or she satisfies any admission, enrollment, quota, eligibility, membership, or other requirement or condition, which individuals must meet in order to be provided any covered service; the assignment of times or places for the provision of services on the basis of race, color, creed, religion, ancestry, marital status, sexual orientation, national origin, age, sex, or physical or mental handicap of the participant to be served. Professional will take affirmative action to ensure that members are provided covered services, without regard to race, color, creed, religion, ancestry, marital status, sexual orientation, national origin, age, sex, or physical or mental handicap, except where medically indicated. For the purposes of this section, physical handicap includes the carrying of a gene which may, under some circumstances, be associated with disability in that person's offspring, but which causes no adverse effects on the carrier. Such genes will include, but not be limited to, Tay-Sachs trait, sickle cell trait, thalassemia trait, and X-linked hemophilia.

*Notification to IPA of Tort and Workers' Compensation Cases.* Professional agrees to notify IPA regarding any Members for whom the Plan will be able to recover monies from tort or workers' compensation liabilities, and that IPA shall be notified promptly after case identification.

APPROVED:

NAME OF IPA                          PROFESSIONAL

_____            _____

_____            _____

DATE                                 PRINT NAME

                                     _____

                                     DATE

# Exploring Issues for Group Contracting— Comments from the Field

*Donald H. Hutton*

The Morgan Health Group (MHG), a 350-member primary care physician (PCP) group, selected the independent practice association (IPA) model to position themselves to respond to the managed care marketplace. In large part, this was because the most desirable physicians did not want to sell their practices to hospitals, publicly traded companies, or managed care organizations (MCOs). While these physicians valued their independence and had many options available to them, they acknowledged the need to be a part of a group to retain their patients in the dynamic managed care marketplace. The IPA model allows the physicians to remain independent, managing their own practices on a day-to-day basis, while being part of a larger group that marketed the physicians to MCOs. As a group, the physicians are better organized to manage risk contracts and deliver cost-effective care to patients than are single physician practices. Therefore, they are more valuable to MCOs.

## ORGANIZATIONAL STRUCTURE

Rather than contract with an outside company to provide the medical and practice management services for the individual practices, MHG built these capabilities internally through creation of a management services organization (MSO). The MSO has the capabilities to assist the individual physicians in managing their practices, and better caring for their patients, and is dedicated to assisting the individual physicians in gaining efficiency and increasing their practice revenue. Combining the medical group and the MSO increased the physicians' control over their own organization and enhanced their opportunity to gain financially from risk contracts.

Through nonexclusive direct contracts with other providers, the group built an integrated delivery system (IDS). The IDS comprises primary care physicians, specialists, hospitals, nursing homes, outpatient surgery centers, home health care companies, durable medical equipment suppliers, and other ancillary care providers. The providers are reimbursed in the following ways:

- The primary care physicians are paid a capitation rate that approximates their current charges.
- The specialists and ancillary care providers are reimbursed on a discounted fee-for-service (FFS) basis equal to 115 percent of Medicare's Resource-Based Relative Value Scale (RBRVS) reimbursement levels for medicine.
- The facilities, hospitals, nursing homes, and outpatient centers were paid according to a Diagnostic Related Groupings (DRG) schedule, a case rate, or a per diem rate.

Because the MSO is owned and controlled by the PCPs, the financial arrangement allows the PCPs to increase their revenue through the appropriate reduction of specialty care services and hospitalizations. After approximately two years of operation, when the appropriate utilization rate for specialists could be ascertained, MHG contracted with groups of single-specialty physicians on a capitated basis. This reduced the exposure of the MSO and give the specialists an opportunity to further improve their utilization and gain financially from these efforts.

A successful MSO will reduce specialty and hospital costs by 30 percent. As incentive for reducing the unnecessary use of specialty care services and hospitalizations, profits earned were distributed to the PCPs based on a formula that recognized each physician's contribution. Most MSOs take approximately three years to achieve profitability, as it takes that long to affect the practice patterns of physicians.

## CONTRACTING STRATEGY

The first step in contracting with MCOs is to determine if the plan values contracting directly with large, well-organized provider groups. Many MCOs do not contract with large organized provider groups; therefore, it is necessary to determine if there is a good business fit with a targeted MCO. When contracting with MCOs, MHG embraced two key principles: (1) negotiate an agreement that aligns the goals of the MCO and MSO, and (2) do not accept risk that the group cannot totally control.

More MCOs are seeking contracts with provider organizations that can effectively control medical costs. MHG contracts with MCOs solely on a capitated basis. The organization realized that contracting on an individual FFS basis and on a group capitated basis requires two different mind sets. In the former, physicians see patients as revenue opportunities, that is, one receives more money when more services are provided. Group contracting on a capitated basis forced the provider organization to see patients as an expense that needs to be managed appropriately. To avoid this conflict, the organization accepted only capitated agreements with MCOs.

MHG entertained two kinds of capitated agreements: a full professional contract and a global risk contract. The professional capitation contracts reimburse the group for all physician services. Frequently, risk pools for inpatient hospital or specialty services are included as an incentive to control these costs. These risk pools can be good tools to align the incentives of the MSO and the MCO. It is not uncommon for a PCP group to earn a bonus of up to 25 percent of their professional capitation rate by aggressively managing these other costs. Although this kind of arrangement requires minimal risk and resources, the reward (i.e., profit potential) is limited. Under a global capitation agreement, MHG assumes the responsibility for providing all professional and technical services to enrolled patients, including both inpatient and outpatient hospital services. These arrangements are much more complex and require more management expertise to be successful.

MHG's experience yielded them the following contracting lessons:

- actuarial expertise is important for the group to understand its business exposure;
- all parties should understand the contract terms fully; and
- no contract should place physicians at a financial or operational disadvantage.

The actuarial review is the key to understanding the associated risks of managed care contracts. Additionally, hiring individuals with health maintenance organization (HMO) experience gives the MSO an excellent knowledge base with which to negotiate managed care contracts. Finally, MHG found that the actual time between identifying an MCO and seeing its patients was approximately twelve months, sometimes longer. Because the MCOs were not willing to reimburse the MSO administrative expenses associated with managing the capitation contract, the group needed to reduce the existing medical costs of the MCO by at least 15 percent to cover the administrative costs and make a profit.

## CONCLUSION

It is worthwhile for physicians to organize themselves in such a way that they can contract with MCOs on a group basis rather than as solo practitioners. This can bring about a positive situation for all parties. Group contracting on a risk basis puts the physicians back in control of managing the care of their patients. Well-managed physician groups can often deliver care more effectively than single practitioners. As a result, MCOs benefit from the lower medical costs and associated employer premiums. Lastly, the patients win as the physicians can control the patients' care without interference from an MCO.

# 6

# Specialty Care Contracting

*Michael J. Benenson*
*Steve Gutman*

Although much specialty care contracting involves contracts directly between managed care organizations (MCOs) and individual specialty care providers, the focus of this chapter is on arrangements between MCOs and organized groups of specialty care providers rather than on individual provider arrangements. Because of current MCO interest in the restructuring of specialty care using single-specialty networks with disease-management and medical-management capabilities, we have included as a secondary focus information pertaining to the formation of such networks.

In emerging and relatively mature managed care markets not dominated by multispecialty independent practice associations (IPAs) and large medical group practices, single-specialty contracting organizations in cardiology, orthopedics, oncology, mental health, ophthalmology, and radiology are being established to address continued ineffectiveness and inefficiencies in these specialties. Because they are characterized by broad professional latitude (with the exception of radiology) and have historically consumed relatively large shares of the health care dollar, these specialties are considered fertile areas for specialty contracting. In addition, the large surpluses of specialty physicians in most areas create buyers' markets for MCOs seeking to transfer risk to specialists, reduce oversight of specialty care, and gain greater predictability of specialty costs.

MCOs typically contract with specialty provider organizations to build provider networks quickly, and later may negotiate individual contracts when they have significant market share or time to engage in individual contracting. Conversely, tightly managed MCOs that have built specialty networks of individually contracted providers may be persuaded to contract on a capitated basis with specialty networks once they have brought utilization and costs under control and enjoyed (without sharing with providers) the savings that were once available by significantly reducing hospital inpatient admissions and lengths of stay. MCOs that are unable to bring their specialty care utilization and costs under control are even more likely to consider contracting with specialty provider organizations if such organizations have true medical- and disease-management capabilities, superior providers, and a willingness to accept capitated reimbursement. Consequently, specialists should pursue every contracting option that is reasonable in the context of the moment, because contracting modalities can change rapidly.

## DEFINITIONS

Because of the confusion that exists concerning different interpretations of managed care terminology and acronyms in managed care markets across the country, the following definitions pertain to our exploration of specialty care contracting in this chapter:

- *Specialty care contracting* refers to managed care contractual arrangements between MCOs and specialty care providers.
- *MCO* refers to an entity such as an insurance company, health maintenance organization (HMO), or other health-benefit plan sponsor, as well as an "intermediary" organization such as the provider network management company that arranges for the "managed" delivery and reimbursement of contracted health care services on behalf of health-benefit plan sponsors.
- *Specialty care providers* will be understood to include the full spectrum of physician specialists and specialty-related ancillary care providers either individually contracted or affiliated with single-specialty or multispecialty contracting organizations established to arrange and manage contracts on behalf of participating physicians and other providers.
- *Specialty provider organizations and single-specialty networks* refer to contracting organizations used by groups of providers to market, contract, and manage the delivery of contracted specialty care.

## THE PARTICIPANTS

The primary participants in specialty care contracting are specialty care providers and MCOs (supported by their respective consultants and lawyers). In addition, a number of entities have emerged as intermediaries in the contracting process. These entities represent both MCOs and providers.

## Managed Care Organizations and Intermediaries

Traditionally, entities arranging managed care contracts with specialty care providers were limited to MCOs that directly fund or reimburse health care services, such as health insurance companies, HMOs, and sponsors of self-insured health benefit plans.

In the late 1980s, MCO intermediaries emerged to arrange contracts with providers and re-market such arrangements to health insurance companies and self-insured benefit plan sponsors. By contracting with MCO intermediaries, such health plan sponsors and administrators are able to delegate the burden of provider recruitment, contract negotiation, and network maintenance to third parties. These arrangements enable health plans to develop provider panels expeditiously and to enter new markets without the need to develop and maintain significant local network operations in every market.

## Management Services Organizations

The management services organization (MSO) is a relatively new participant that emerged to fill the unmet need of provider organizations for utilization management, contract negotiation, and administrative infrastructure necessary to operate  successfully in a risk contracting environment. Many have evolved from physician practice management companies and, consequently, have a solid foundation of claims adjudication experience and management information systems operations.

In numerous managed care markets, especially in the emerging mid-Atlantic markets, MCOs hire MSOs to provide specialty care restructuring and ongoing management. Such MSOs operate as "hired guns" for MCOs. Typically under contract with the MCO, these MSOs maintain existing contracts between MCOs and providers but implement capitated reimbursement arrangements in targeted specialties. The MSO is generally responsible for medical and disease management, utilization review, claims pre-adjudication, and payments to providers, provider network maintenance, and specified reporting. The following are typical objectives:

- to arrange for and administer provider services agreements that transfer financial risk to providers (and sometimes to the MSO) through capitated reimbursement arrangements;
- to reduce (or "de-select") certain numbers of specialists from their existing multispecialty panels; and
- to create and provide specialized medical and disease management and administrative support for providers in targeted specialties.

A number of MSOs represent physician interests primarily. In this capacity, they facilitate the development and operation of managed care functions for the full spectrum of physician organizations. This may include establishing information and utilization management systems, managing capitation payments, and educating member physicians.

In the increasingly crowded and competitive MSO marketplace, many MSOs are exploring strategies to service both MCO and provider clients. MSOs with "physician-friendly" reputations are likely to be successful in serving both sectors, whereas MSOs with reputations as "hired guns" for MCOs encounter resistance from individual and organized physicians in certain markets.

## Specialty Provider Contracting Organizations

A growing number of specialty providers are forming contracting organizations to facilitate marketing, contracting, and the managed delivery of specialty care services. The most common organizational forms that engage in specialty care contracting include the following:

- provider-owned professional associations that are permitted by law to participate in the practice of medicine, including the professional association (PA), professional corporation (PC), and professional limited liability corporation (PLLC or LLC);
- single-specialty networks (or provider organizations);
- broad-based provider organizations, such as the multispecialty medical group practice and independent practice association (IPA);
- hospital-centered groups, such as the physician organization (PO) and physician-hospital organization (PHO); and
- the integrated delivery system (IDS), typically sponsored by a hospital system to encompass a broad spectrum of professional capabilities and health care facilities.

Although a number of broad-based provider organizations in mature managed care markets have developed significant management capabilities to become successful in managing the delivery of specialty care, many MCOs consider use of IPAs, POs, and PHOs a short-term strategy because of their historic inability to control growing specialty costs.

Often, the motivations of hospital-based contracting organizations are at odds with those of MCOs, which have come to perceive physicians, who control upwards of 85 percent of health care spending, as their logical partners in managed care, not hospitals. Moreover, hospital-based organizations are often fragile because of fluctuating hospital and physician commitments, unstable funding, lack of effective marketing, inadequate medical and data-management capabilities, and limited administrative support.

Despite the shortcomings described previously, broad-based provider organizations such as IDSs and multi-county hospital/physician "alliances" may become viable entities for specialty care contracting over the long term because of their structural ability to assume global risk for physician services and facilities-related expenses, and their potential to significantly streamline contract administration for MCOs.

In recent years, single-specialty provider organizations and networks, especially those in high-cost specialties, have emerged in response to growing MCO interest in controlling specialty costs and improving clinical effectiveness and outcomes through disease-management approaches. The coordination and delivery of specialty care based on clinical pathways and protocols require a highly trained and disciplined specialty physician panel and a well-organized infrastructure. These capabilities are presently the exception rather than the rule in broad-based organizations, especially those centered on the hospital. The increasing availability of single-specialty networks facilitates the ability of MCOs to coordinate and deliver specialty care for its members. Single-specialty networks that develop superior disease-management capabilities and are responsive to the other needs of MCOs are likely to enjoy long-term success in competition with broad-based multispecialty provider organizations.

Providers in effect become MCOs in markets such as California where health benefit plan sponsors contract with broad-based provider organizations to provide (or arrange for) the majority of health care services for their health benefit plan members under risk contracts. In these markets, single-specialty networks must market to entities who typically receive such contracts from MCOs. These include (a) large primary care physician groups, (b) broad-based provider organizations, and (c) IDSs interested in purchasing managed specialty care services to better control costs in risk contracts, some of which encompass all professional and technical components, including facility and ancillary expenses.


## UNDERSTANDING THE MARKETPLACE

### Market Research

A thorough understanding of the marketplace is critical to the successful design, marketing, and maintenance of specialty contracting organizations. Effective market research can generate information essential to developing specialty networks, and can be an opportunity to establish long-term marketing relationships with prospective clients. Involving prospective MCO clients in the development of the specialty contracting organization can be helpful in securing contracts with the MCOs once the specialty contracting organization is established.

The most productive market research is conducted by individuals who have a sustainable role in marketing the provider organization. These individuals are likely to have a vested interest in obtaining accurate information and integrating design specifications revealed by MCOs into the organizational development. They will also be best able to capitalize on the relationships established during the research stage, provided that they maintain frequent contact with the MCOs. Including MCO representatives on the provider organization's committees charged with developing crucial functional capabilities, such as utilization management and management information systems, is one way to invest prospective MCO clients in an emerging specialty contracting organization.

Recent market research, test marketing, and marketing for a broad range of managed care provider organizations in various emerging markets by Benenson & Associates, a health care consulting firm specializing in developing provider organizations, have revealed circumstances that reflect a growing interest in specialty contracting. These considerations should be investigated and thoroughly understood before committing to the specific design of a specialty contracting organization in a given area.

Our market research focuses on the following several key areas.

*Continuum of Managed Care Products*

MCOs are interested in specialty care arrangements that can facilitate the movement of members along the continuum of managed care products—preferred provider organization (PPO) products, point-of-service (POS) programs, and HMOs. For example, a specialty provider organization can offer an MCO a select panel of physicians for HMO "lock-in" products, which can be augmented by a second tier of providers to service products requiring larger panels, such as POS plans and PPOs. For these products the small panel may be packaged as a "providers of excellence" panel if its standards are sufficiently high. This enables health plan members to maintain continuity with their specialists as employers move toward increasingly restrictive plan designs.

*Broad-Based Provider Organizations*

Although contracting with PHOs and large nonselective IPAs (such as those sponsored by county or statewide medical societies) is a desirable initial strategy to build large provider networks rapidly, this is not necessarily perceived by most MCOs to be a viable long-term strategy in ensuring the highest quality of specialty care and controlling specialty costs. In addition, it is questionable whether hospital and physician partners are committed to funding such cost centers indefinitely (some are already declaring bankruptcy), or are capable of operating them effectively.

*Physicians as the Legitimate Partners of MCOs*

In many respects, MCOs engaged in outcomes-oriented care are recognizing that physicians are more appropriate partners than hospitals. "Heads on beds" rates are viewed by many MCO managers as commodities to be purchased at market or below market rates. It is cheaper for MCOs to "rent" beds at per diem rates than to build or buy and operate their own hospitals. There is also increasing sensitivity to the growing public perception that the financial incentives of primary care physicians (PCPs) and the monitoring of specialty referrals by MCOs can create inappropriate barriers between patients and specialists.

*Seamless Geographic Coverage*

Physicians in many markets have a strong interest in arranging specialty care coverage in wide geographic areas to attract MCOs and other clients with multistate or regional service areas. There is growing awareness that organizing provider networks along state or county borders does not always satisfy the needs of employers whose employees live in one state or city and work in another.

*Select Groups of Physicians*

There is emerging interest in contracting with select groups of physicians who have the highest qualifications and best clinical outcomes, as well as positive attitudes toward managed care participation. There is also growing recognition that at-risk patients need to be intensively managed by highly qualified referral specialists in collaboration with PCPs.

*Broadly Defined Specialties*

Some MCOs are allowing specialty groups to define their specialties as broadly as possible for risk contracting and enable them to include the full spectrum of subspecialties and ancillaries under a single capitated contract. This facilitates the coordination of specialty treatment involving multiple therapeutic modalities and eliminates the need for MCOs to contract directly with ancillary providers.

*Delegation of Administrative Functions*

Some MCOs are interested in delegating administrative and medical management functions to MSOs and other network management vendors. Often such delegation includes the management of financial risk associated with the delivery of specialty care in capitated arrangements.

## Forces Promoting Change in Specialty Care Contracting

In the past, most MCOs have endeavored to control as many managed care contracting and administration functions as possible. This has required MCOs to make significant investments in provider network development and maintenance and utilization management. Traditionally, PCPs have been recruited to serve as gatekeepers to prevent unnecessary use of specialty care.

Despite some initial successes and significant capital investments, specialty care costs continue to climb for many MCOs. Moreover, the PCP gatekeeper approach has erected real and perceived barriers between patients and specialists, and has created momentous unfavorable publicity for the managed care industry. With renewed attention to improving clinical outcomes and minimizing disruptions to specialty care treatment, MCOs are considering specialty management changes that involve restructuring of specialty panels, introduction of third-party medical and disease management, and contracting with single-specialty networks and MSOs as options to directly arranging and managing the delivery of specialty care. These changes in the marketplace are prompting MCO executives to replace the PCP gatekeeper strategy with alternative mechanisms for controlling specialty costs. Their motivations include the following.

*Organizational Redirection*

Changing business objectives are causing many MCOs to redesign their businesses to focus on their original mission of generating and managing cash flow resulting from the development and marketing of health benefit plans. The desire to deliver cost-effective, quality care is prompting many MCOs to develop "carve-out" or "carve-in" specialty care services arrangements. This often involves arranging for care management and related administrative functions through contracts with outside vendors such as provider organizations, and MSOs acting on behalf of MCOs or provider organizations.

*Surplus of Physicians and Hospitals*

Because there is a significant oversupply of specialists and hospitals in most heavily populated areas, it is truly a buyer's market for specialty care in most urban and suburban markets.

*Variety of Managed Care Contracting Vehicles*

Hospitals and their medical staffs have made competing PHOs readily available to MCOs interested in assembling large provider panels. Single-specialty networks have emerged in primary care and high-cost specialties like cardiology and orthopedics. Physicians, specialty care organizations, and MSOs are replacing hospitals as the preferred principal partners of MCOs. In risky and expensive attempts to retain control in a changing environment, some hospital systems have established IDSs. The result is that MCOs can now choose from a variety of competitive contracting vehicles to implement their specialty care initiatives.

### Entrance of the Management Services Organization

The needs of the burgeoning number of PHOs and specialty provider organizations, plus the needs of MCOs interested in shifting management and financial risk to qualified third parties, have created a new managed care contracting participant—the MSO. The success of MSOs is promoting the formation of specialty contracting organizations and causing MCOs to contract with them to manage the restructuring of specialty care in certain markets. Emerging managed care markets typically prefer broader access.

### Need to Manage Costs in Large Provider Panels

In most managed care markets, MCOs with the greatest choice of providers are the most popular. However, it has proven to be difficult, if not impossible, to control quality and costs of care when panels are large and nonselective. Although many MCOs would like to improve their performance by downsizing their provider networks, they must maintain reasonable access to physicians to remain competitive. Therefore, MCOs are challenged with servicing their various managed care products with appropriately sized provider panels and setting their premiums accordingly, so that members who desire the broadest choice of providers pay more for that privilege.

## Objectives of Specialty Care Initiatives

MCOs have several objectives in implementing specialty care initiatives. They include the following:

- reducing costs associated with the medical and surgical specialties that consume the greatest part of the health care dollar;
- maintaining competitive premium rates, market share, and profitability;
- developing new products for price-sensitive populations, such as Medicare, Medicaid, workers' compensation, and small businesses;

- motivating specialty providers to cooperate with MCO-driven cost management initiatives;
- improving clinical outcomes of care delivered by contracted physicians;
- maximizing patient satisfaction and maintaining high retention of members in an increasingly competitive marketplace; and
- streamlining provider contract administration while maintaining adequate control over costs, quality of care, customer service, and patient satisfaction.

An overriding concern of most MCOs contemplating specialty care initiatives is to avoid disrupting existing relationships with contracted PCP groups and key individual practitioners or with selected PHOs and other provider groups critical to their networks.

## STRATEGIES FOR SPECIALTY CARE CONTRACTING

MCO strategies exist on a continuum ranging from tight management of existing panel specialists ("maximum control strategy") to delegation of care management and financial risk ("transfer of control strategy"). Certain strategies can co-exist.

### Individual Contracts With Specialists

The MCO continues to contract with individual specialists separately and manage utilization by applying increasingly rigorous prior authorization and retrospective review procedures. Although the MCO may not generally partner with large physician organizations or MSOs, the MCO may contract with a single-specialty organization on a limited basis after tight utilization management has removed most of the excess utilization. These MCOs are no longer concerned about sharing a substantial surplus with contracted physicians or their MSOs because the potential for savings has been minimized.

### Specialty Network "Carve-In" Contracts

In a "carve-in" approach, the MCO capitates an existing panel of physicians for a particular specialty, such as physical therapy or radiology. To minimize provider unrest, the capitated networks are generally not downsized to a significant degree. These capitated networks are managed by the MCO or a designated MSO or specialty management vendor.

## Specialty Network "Carve-Out"

In this arrangement, the MCO replaces its individual specialist contracts with single-specialty networks operated by separate entities. The MCO will often use the specialty network on an exclusive basis, requiring the organization to provide the full spectrum of services within a particular specialty. Small physician panels can function as "physicians of excellence" programs that can be overlaid on larger specialty panels for PPO and POS products. They can also be exclusive panels for lock-in capitated programs that require members to trade latitude of choice of specialists for reduced premium.

## Multispecialty Medical Group

MCOs will often contract with a variety of multispecialty organizations to obtain combined primary and specialty care coverage in a given service area with relatively few contracts. Although these contracting arrangements pose relative ease in contract administration, they offer limited opportunity to implement consistent disease-management protocols for high-cost specialties because they are relatively closed referral systems. However, specialty care management can be achieved by overlaying "providers of excellence" care programs in targeted specialties.

## Integrated Delivery System

In some markets, MCOs have the option of contracting with IDSs for managed care. IDSs offer MCOs one-stop shopping for all required care. Because the arrangement involves one contract, it can be the most expedient and accessible way for MCOs to enter a market or cover a service area. However, IDSs often maintain a powerful negotiating position and may force the MCO to compromise on key contract terms to obtain essential concessions. In addition, there is a danger in contracting with a potential competitor, as the IDS can in the future obtain an HMO license and market directly to the employer groups directed to the IDS by the MCO.

## ORGANIZATIONAL DEVELOPMENT CONSIDERATIONS

It is critical for a provider group considering the establishment of a specialty provider organization to perform a feasibility study before committing resources to complete the development of an organization. Usually, a core group is clear about the essential nature of the organization it desires to create, but thorough consideration of market conditions relevant to the underlying design and necessary capabilities of the specialty organization is necessary to maximize marketability.

### Local Environment

Because market needs and opportunities vary widely, an analysis of each market should be performed before establishing a single-specialty network. When assessing the potential for developing a specialty organization in a given market, the group should seek answers to the following questions:

- What is the managed care penetration? How much has managed care enrollment increased over the past two years?
- How sophisticated are the MCOs and providers? How many years have they engaged in capitated contracting?
- How many MCOs are there? Are more seeking licensure?
- Are MCOs interested in seamless geographic coverage across state or county lines? Regional coverage? Statewide? Multistate?
- Are MCOs interested in integrated disease-management services?
- What is the availability of practicing specialists in the proposed service areas? Is this sufficient to provide reasonable accessibility for members in mature markets? Are there significant surpluses of specialists?

### Access to Specialty Providers

Because the assessment of provider accessibility is a popular means by which employers and members measure the quality of managed care plans, MCOs are concerned with meeting standards for member access to providers. Industry standards for access are developed by the National Committee for Quality Assurance (NCQA) and other groups as a way for employers and others to judge the performance of health plans. Large provider panels do not guarantee access to specialty care; however, because of market pressure to meet employer demands and satisfy accreditation requirements, MCOs are reluctant to deviate from access standards established or endorsed by these organizations.

Appropriate access to care can be ensured in other ways including the following: (a) acceptable matching of specialty provider organization practice sites with member residences; (b) acceptable waiting times for appointments; and (c) a disease-management model of specialty care delivery that removes barriers between members and specialists.

## Optimum Panel Size and Composition

From the perspective of employers (and, therefore, many MCOs), the most desirable specialty panel is the largest. However, smaller and more selective specialty panels are often better able to manage and deliver quality care than are larger panels. Balancing marketplace demands for large panels and the efficient manageability of smaller networks is challenging.

Frequently, the marketplace wants more physicians and other providers than are necessary to provide appropriate access. Under risk contracts, an excessively large panel (compared with plan membership) dilutes the patient volume available to all providers and increases financial risk to individual providers as well as their provider contracting organization.

To best control utilization and costs in markets where lean networks have limited market appeal, selective specialty organizations may consider forming expanded panels customized for specific MCOs that add to the organization's "core panel" of participating providers. The additional providers, selected by mutual agreement of the MCOs and the specialty provider organization, increase the density of provider coverage for benefit plans requiring larger specialty panels. Some of the additional providers may be invited to participate as equity members of the provider organization when the organization requires better core coverage, whereas others may be invited to participate as contract affiliates only. Contracting arrangements may be implemented by having the MCO assign the contracts of its desired additional physicians to the specialty provider organization, and then contract with the specialty organization to provide medical management and reimbursement administration for those physicians as well as equity and contract participants in the specialty organization.

The specialty provider organization's original "select" panel can be packaged as a physicians of excellence program to service PPO and POS benefit plans. However, to justify such designation, the specialty provider organization must establish participation criteria (especially for interventionists and other subspecialists) that exceed payer/MCO standards. In addition, the organization should provide sophisticated medical and disease-management capabilities and attractive reimbursement packages such as case rates and global package prices.

One way to determine the appropriate size of specialty panels and generate recruitment targets for populated markets is to apply provider-to-population ratios in each county. Observed ratios in cardiology and orthopedics are 1:25,000 in mature markets, that is, one orthopedist can serve 25,000 people. For example, if there are 100,000 people in the community, four orthopedists are needed in the network. In general, it is advisable to limit the number of specialists selected to 20 percent of the active providers in each county to leave room to add providers recommended or required by prospective clients. Obviously, in areas where there is a shortage of specialists, the MCO will not have the luxury of selecting from among several physicians and may be fortunate to find one or two physicians in key specialties.

A geo-access analysis of member concentrations and provider practice sites measures coverage adequacy and deficiencies. The provider organization can target additional specialty physicians and other providers as necessary if deficiencies exist. It is wise to ascertain whether participating providers in adjacent (noncompeting) areas may be interested in obtaining privileges at one of the contracted hospitals in the service area before offering participation in the network to additional competing practices.

In addition, an effort should be made to include practices that collectively can manage admissions at (a) 100 percent of the tertiary care programs in the specialty; (b) 100 percent of "preferred" hospitals designated by MCOs; and (c) 75 to 90 percent of remaining hospitals participating in managed care contracts. Some participating physicians will have limited opportunity to participate if their admitting hospitals do not contract with an MCO or specialty provider organization.

However, their participation will enable the provider organization to assume take over cases when patients are inappropriately admitted to a nonparticipating hospital ("leakage") and move such patients to participating hospitals. These physicians can add significant value to the specialty provider organization by addressing the leakage, which is a major concern of MCOs.

## Structure

Specialty providers may choose from a broad array of templates when organizing for specialty contracting participation. They include professional corporations, professional associations, regular corporations, and professional limited liability corporations. Depending on state regulations (which vary widely), provider organizations may have to reorganize for each risk contract.

## Ownership and Control

In general, specialty provider organizations are owned and controlled exclusively by participating physicians. Sometimes ancillary providers have ownership stakes in such organizations. In specialties where nonsurgical specialists perform the majority of the diagnosis and treatment, surgeons are often excluded from equity participation and management opportunities. Cardiology is an example of this arrangement. This approach has the potential to create an adversarial relationship instead of a treatment partnership among allied subspecialists. It also encourages surgical specialists to create their own networks and attempt to negotiate separately. When nonsurgical and surgical specialists are represented by competing MSOs, contract negotiations are complicated and may motivate MCOs to form their own integrated specialty networks. Nonprovider joint venture partners and outside investors can be offered equity opportunities in the form of shares in a nonphysician MSO that supports the physician-owned provider organization.

## Governance

Many physician organizations adopt a one-person–one-vote management structure, requiring a separate class of stock for each practice. Each stock class (that is, practice) designates a representative to serve on the board of directors, and the board elects an executive or management committee. Executive committees should be limited to a workable number to manage the day-to-day operations of the organization.

## Exclusivity

Exclusivity can be a divisive and volatile issue. In general, individual specialists and specialty provider organizations should seek diversity of managed care contracts and not be exclusive to any MCO. This means that individual specialists should pursue managed care contracting opportunities through physician-hospital organizations, medical society IPAs, multispecialty practice groups, and any other available contracting vehicles.

This notwithstanding, emerging specialty provider organizations should not allow member physicians to participate in other single-specialty networks that cover similar service areas. If leading specialty practices belong to multiple (and competing) single-specialty organizations, then the principal differentiation between competing organizations shifts from the excellence of their respective provider panels to price. This forces participating physicians to compete among themselves regarding price alone, to the detriment of both the local specialty reimbursement structure and the personal incomes of specialists.

## Standards for Participation of Specialty Practices

Recruitment of member physicians is the responsibility of the committee charged with forming the organization. The most important factor in identifying desirable specialists and ancillary providers is the reputation of the practice or facility. A specialty provider organization's chances for success are heavily influenced by its ability to recruit the most highly regarded physicians and ancillary providers.

Another important consideration is the size of the prospective participating practice, relative to its local competitors, and the breadth of subspecialty care provided within the practice and its affiliates. In general, the larger and broader the practice, the better. It is much easier for a specialty organization to manage a network of relatively few large practices with broad subspecialty participation than a network of one- or two-physician practices. Typically, larger practices have better managed care capabilities, especially regarding the experience of administrative staff and the quality of information systems.

Formation group members should seek practices whose physicians and business managers have developed an understanding of managed care and a willingness to participate in managed care contracts without compromising their clinical and service values. Practices that have "reengineered" to improve their clinical outcomes and cost-effectiveness are models for other participating practices to emulate.

## FORMATION OF A PROVIDER NETWORK

Confidentiality is critical during the formative stages of a specialty provider organization. Premature disclosure of organizational development plans and names of candidate participants can promote an immediate competitive response from other physician entrepreneurs concerned that they may be excluded. Nondisclosure agreements with strong liquidated damage provisions should be signed by all individuals who attend meetings or receive written information on the emerging organization. In general, oral presentations at meetings and personal telephone calls should be used to share information about the emerging organization to candidates, rather than written correspondence.

### Formation Group Meeting

After identifying target numbers of specialists to be recruited, members of the formation group should individually prepare lists of practices they believe meet the organization's criteria for participation. When the formation group meets, names of specialists identified before the meeting as potential invitees are reviewed and consensus is reached on practices to be invited.

### Initial Information Meetings

Physicians identified as candidate members should be invited to attend an "information meeting." It is critical for legal counsel to prepare guidelines for the information committee members for contacting prospective physicians to ensure that violations of U.S. Securities and Exchange Commission regulations pertaining to the sale of securities are not inadvertently committed.

The initial meeting (or round of meetings if travel distances within a service area are considered excessive) usually involves a formal presentation to prospective physicians. Before beginning the presentation, legal counsel should require all attendees to sign the nondisclosure agreements. Those unwilling to sign should be asked to leave the meeting. The presentation should include the following: (a) demographic characteristics of the marketplace, including commercial and Medicare/Medicaid populations; (b) comparison of the number of available specialty practices and the number of physicians needed for participation in managed care contracts highlighting the surplus of specialists in the area; (c) findings of the feasibility study assessing MCO interest in specialty contracting initiatives and the nature of the organization required to be able to respond to the market opportunity; (d) organizational concept and other legal issues; and (e) anticipated organizational development costs and available funding mechanisms. After the formal presentation, and before concluding the initial information meeting, the formation group should seek to ascertain the level of physician interest in developing the specialty contracting organization.

In addition, draft legal documents are distributed to those who pay a processing fee to indicate their interest in participating (and keep their competitors off the panel). These are to be reviewed by business advisors and legal counsel for the practices before the preorganizational meeting.

## Organizational Meeting

At the last meeting (or series of meetings), executed shareholder and physician services agreements are submitted, payments for stock are received, and the board of directors is elected. Obtaining complete applications from candidate providers is time consuming and labor intensive. Completion of initial credentialing and preparation of an accurate provider database and directory are perhaps the most challenging start-up tasks facing new provider organizations. The return of completed detailed applications should be a condition of attendance at organizational meetings. Failure to implement this requirement will delay credentialing and add significantly to network development costs. If appropriate, the board elects an executive committee and other committees are formed. A work plan for the critical initial activities is reviewed and meetings are scheduled for the initial months of operation.

## Leadership

The quality of the initial leadership is the major determinant of the long-term success of an emerging specialty care organization. Premier physicians attract peers of similar quality. Start-up organizations lacking such leaders may not be able to attract a superior panel readily and the recruitment process may take much longer than expected.

Physicians considering leadership roles in establishing specialty care organizations should understand the demands that will be placed on them. In addition to requiring significant amounts of time for meetings, phone calls, and written communications, leaders of new specialty networks become "lightning rods" who attract the wrath of peers not invited to participate and hospital executives threatened by the formation of the organization. They must also deal with reluctant physicians who are vital to the organization's ability to secure critical geographic coverage. Perhaps most importantly, leaders in subspecialties who are dependent on referrals from other specialists in their discipline may risk alienating their referring physicians who are not invited to participate.

Forceful and impassioned leaders are essential in establishing strong and effective specialty contracting organizations. However, such leaders often have difficulty involving others in their vision and in restraining their personal agendas. Specialty care organizations must find ways to harness the brilliance and charisma of such leaders and channel their efforts for the common good of the group.

## CRITICAL EARLY OBJECTIVES

### Development of a Care Delivery Model

Development or adoption of a care delivery model to define a specialty contracting organization's disease-management approach is the principal characteristic that differentiates a managed care delivery system from an association of doctors willing to contract. The care delivery model is the structural framework that gives shape to the organization and its operating functions. Development of the model should address the following issues:

- MCO care management requirements;
- disease-management objectives appropriate for the specialty;
- methods of early identification of patients at risk who require specialty management;
- clinical pathways for diagnoses that consume significant specialty care dollars; and
- appropriate role of PCPs.

## Specialty Gatekeepers

Committees of the most respected practitioners should develop clinical pathways for the most common procedures and highest-cost diagnoses. Many specialty societies have promulgated such standards, as have major health care consulting and actuarial firms such as Milliman & Robertson. These can be used as starting points for peer discussions leading to the adoption of treatment guidelines for the specialty provider organization. Treatment guidelines must then be communicated to participating providers with procedures for seeking exceptions.

## Capitated Reimbursement Allocation Model

From a provider perspective, the most important change in contemporary health care is the shift from fee-for-service to capitated and other at-risk reimbursement. Capitation is possible in markets characterized by surplus providers where plan sponsors shift some of their financial risk to providers in exchange for exclusive contracts. From the outset, existing and emerging specialty provider organizations must prepare to secure capitated managed care contracts aggressively and service them successfully.

It is undeniably in the best interests of quality, efficient providers in immature managed care marketplaces to participate as early as possible in capitated contracts (that are properly evaluated) because of the potential profit opportunity if they are successful in managing inappropriate utilization and costs. Capitation may in fact be the last dying gasp of truly profitable (to providers) health care delivery.

Once committed to capitated reimbursement, the specialty provider organization is challenged to develop and formally adopt a methodology for distributing service pools and risk pools to participating physicians and other providers. Development of reimbursement strategies that appropriately compensate specialists participating in risk contracts is among the most challenging tasks facing emerging specialty provider organizations. The many payment strategies and their implications for the delivery of specialty care are found in a separate section of this chapter.

## Committees

Committees are the heart and soul of an effective specialty care organization. Critical issues are delegated to standing and special committees for development of policy recommendations for board approval. Under a committee structure, key managers can provide organizational oversight without micromanaging every issue. It also builds a cadre of knowledgeable physician managers. In addition to the board of managers or executive committees, standing committees of a specialty care organization should include the following:

- finance committee—oversees the development of operating budgets and monitors financial performance;
- marketing committee—oversees marketing and contracting activities;
- provider relations committee—oversees communications with member physicians and other providers (This function is sometimes merged with the marketing committee because a specialty provider organization has two markets—MCOs and member physicians and their support staffs.);
- reimbursement committee—charged with developing, updating, and administering the organization's capitated reimbursement allocation model;
- clinical protocols committee—responsible for developing and implementing the clinical pathways and protocols that define the organization's medical and disease-management approach;
- utilization management committee—in conjunction with the organization's medical director is responsible for developing and overseeing implementation of the organization's utilization management plan; and
- quality assessment and quality improvement committee—charged with overseeing continuous measurement and improvement of clinical outcomes and patient service.

It is best to structure initial committee meetings as educational forums to establish a knowledge basis for committee members, most of whom may have limited understanding of managed care operations. Organizing these early committee meetings as educational seminars requires extensive support from the organization's administrative staff.

## Credentialing

As soon as completed applications are available, emerging specialty provider organizations must arrange to verify the credentials information submitted by candidate providers. Although it seems duplicative for the specialty organization to do this when many MCOs will re-credential specialty providers already participating in their provider panels, it is nonetheless an essential activity for the provider organization to obtain credibility and limit its liability.

To be valuable to prospective MCO clients, credentialing reviews must meet standards set by the NCQA in every respect. Many MSOs provide this service for their partner physician organizations, and numerous free-standing "primary source verification" contractors are available as well.

## Clinical and Administrative Support Services

The existence of an effective clinical and administrative support infrastructure differentiates a specialty care delivery system from a group of specialty physicians willing to accept a discount from billed charges. There is significant MCO interest in specialty organizations that have these capabilities. In competitive marketplaces with excessive numbers of quality specialty physicians, the long-term survival of the specialty care organization will depend on the sophistication and effectiveness of such clinical and administrative systems.

Therefore, selection of a clinical and administrative management infrastructure strategy is one of the most critical decisions made by emerging specialty care organizations. The decision to develop administrative support capabilities internally or purchase them through an MSO should be made before the formation stage of the organization. Groups that delay this decision are likely to paralyze the new board of directors and executive committee for months during the start-up phase when the assistance of an MSO can streamline and shorten the organizational development process greatly.

## Insurance

In today's litigious environment where selective managed care contracting can radically reduce the practice volumes of physicians excluded from successful specialty provider organizations, it is necessary for specialty organizations to secure appropriate insurance coverage regardless of how carefully the organization is structured. This will minimize antitrust, restraint of trade, and medical malpractice liability exposure. Insurance coverage should be secured for committee members, directors, officers, and employees from an insurance carrier experienced in such coverage. In addition, vicarious medical malpractice coverage should be purchased in the event the organization is sued for promulgating standards and guidelines for care that fall outside existing local norms.

### Communications With Participating Providers

The balance between saying too little and saying too much must be carefully weighed, but it is essential that the organization's management and staff begin to develop functional relationships with participating providers and their practice managers at an early date. Failure to do so during the often painfully long wait for the first managed care contract can jeopardize the organization's credibility with providers and prospective MCO clients.

Emerging specialty provider organizations should make concerted and early efforts to establish committees and hold educational seminars to begin building a managed specialty care delivery system out of an association of competing physicians and other providers.

## SPECIALTY PROVIDER REIMBURSEMENT

Reimbursement modalities have significant implications for the delivery of care by individual physicians in single and multiple specialty provider contracting organizations. Specifically, they present different motivations for physicians to (a) appropriately use expensive resources; (b) efficiently provide medically necessary care; (c) deliver care of highest quality; and (d) satisfy patients regarding quality of care and quality of service.

Individual physician reimbursement strategies may be placed along a continuum that runs from procedure-based reimbursement to capitation as follows:

*By Procedure—By Points—By Case—By Visits—By Referrals—Subcapitation*

These may be combined in a number of ways to maximize incentives and reward appropriately high-quality physicians who provide medically necessary services and produce high levels of satisfaction among their patients. The various strategies for distributing specialty capitation revenues to physicians have different implications for the delivery of high-quality managed specialty care.

## Procedure-Based Reimbursement

*Description*

Payments to providers are calculated using a fee schedule developed by the reimbursement committee. Such reimbursement represents discounted fee-for-service and is typically used in PPO contracts and in conjunction with risk withholds. It is usually based on a relative value schedule (RVS).

*Rationale for Use*

This is the easiest reimbursement method to use when a specialty provider organization is beginning operations and has not yet had time to develop more sophisticated reimbursement strategies. Because it is most closely related to fee-for-service reimbursement, physicians are most familiar with and like this method.

*Managed Care Implications*

This mode of reimbursement provides no incentives for providers to reduce unnecessary medical care nor does it motivate providers to become optimally efficient. Indeed, it motivates physicians to perform and bill maximum numbers of procedures, especially when they are competing for a limited pool of dollars. When used with a fixed conversion factor, this productivity-based payment modality leaves the provider organization holding most of a capitated contract's financial risk.

## Point System Reimbursement

*Description*

The reimbursement committee develops a simplified relative value schedule for the specialty, assigning points to procedures and groups of procedures reflecting the group's perception of their relative degrees of complexity, risk, and overhead intensity. Existing RVS structures are in effect "customized" to reflect the committee's views on these factors.

*Rationale for Use*

This method enables the specialty provider organization to depart from generic relative value schedules when designing its reimbursement methodology, and to gain some protection from creative billing practices used by aggressive physician offices.

*Managed Care Implications*

These are similar to those for procedure-based reimbursement; however, a properly designed point system reimbursement structure will eliminate adverse effects of many inappropriate billing practices such as "upcoding" and "testing" intended to generate higher levels of payment.

## Case Rates

*Description*

Using input from MCOs, the reimbursement committee designates a number of major case types to be paid by flat fees that cover all care immediately before and after diagnosis of a condition. This includes preoperative care, hospital visits, office aftercare visits, home care, and ancillary fees.

*Rationale for Use*

This reimbursement strategy is attractive to MCOs desiring to contain and gain better predictability of costs of expensive procedures. A limited number of leading provider groups in a specialty can constitute centers of excellence, and the plan can include strong financial incentives to channel patients to these providers. This strategy is attractive to sponsors of noncapitated plans and those pursuing "carve-out" approaches and providers of excellence contracts.

*Managed Care Implications*

This modality motivates participating physicians to reengineer the delivery of care to be optimally efficient for designated high-cost, high-volume procedures.

## Flat-Fee Reimbursement

*Description*

The reimbursement committee develops a fee schedule that pays physicians one flat fee for all office visits, regardless of the type of visit or diagnostic resources used. A flat fee can also be paid for all visits within a specified time frame such as thirty days or for all hospital visits, regardless of the length of the visit or type of patient.

*Rationale for Use*

This method removes incentives for unnecessary repeat visits and overutilization of diagnostic tests in doctors' offices.

*Managed Care Implications*

This type of case rate reimbursement motivates physicians to schedule only medically necessary office and hospital consultations, and to be optimally efficient in the use of diagnostic and treatment resources related to office visits.

## Per Referral Reimbursement

*Description*

Per referral reimbursement is a limited form of "subcapitation," often referred to as "contact capitation." The group pays the physician a flat fee, pro rated over the number of months remaining in a course of treatment, to provide all care for each patient referred for a given condition, regardless of the number of visits or resources consumed.

*Rationale for Use*

Such arrangements motivate physicians to see patients only as frequently as is medically necessary, and to be optimally efficient in delivering care.

*Managed Care Implications*

This method of payment protects a capitated provider contracting organization against physicians seeing patients more frequently than may be necessary or overutilizing in-office diagnostic testing.

## Subcapitated Reimbursement

*Description*

Under subcapitation, a specialty network subdivides its service area geographically or by PCP referral base and distributes pro rata shares of the organization's monthly capitation payments to the practice groups covering these areas. In turn, the groups agree to assume financial responsibility for delivering specified specialty care to patients in their designated service areas.

*Rationale for Use*

This method provides a way for a provider contracting organization to allow large and efficient practice groups to be financially rewarded for their performance and protects the organization against poor performance by other participating physician groups.

*Managed Care Implications*

Subcapitation motivates groups of physicians to deliver care appropriately and efficiently and shifts financial risk from the provider organization to participating physicians. However, it requires that the organization (and the MCO) maintain a particularly strong commitment to assessing and ensuring quality of care and patient satisfaction as subcapitated groups under financial pressure may be motivated to reduce access to needed medical services, resulting in reduced clinical outcomes and patient satisfaction. This modality also requires the group to develop a way to charge responsible practice groups for those services that they do not directly provide, such as out-of-area emergency care and certain ancillary services.

## DESIGNING INDIVIDUAL PHYSICIAN REIMBURSEMENT STRATEGIES

Few, if any, financial issues are more important to physicians than reimbursement. When physician organizations participate in prepaid capitated contracts, participating physicians need to feel comfortable that the reimbursement allocation methodology is as reasonable and fair as possible. Through a reimbursement committee, physicians themselves need to take full responsibility for developing the reimbursement methodology they use to distribute risk and reward. This function cannot and should not be delegated to outside parties, although consultants can provide the educational foundation and expertise required to complete the process.

### Funding a Service Pool

First, the organization should identify the specific specialty services to be provided. This should also involve developing clinical protocols to govern referrals from PCPs when there is potential for PCPs to "dump" patients on specialists, and the development of other protocols that promote shared delivery of care by PCPs and specialists to best manage disease-oriented care.

Second, the group should define the amount of monthly capitation payments received by the specialty contracting organization to be allocated for payments to participating providers for defined specialty services, and for payment of the organization's administrative costs (often a percentage withhold).

### Establishing a Risk Pool

The group should decide on the amount to be withheld from the service pool and reserved to pay costs of higher-than-expected utilization. Twenty percent of monthly capitation payment is the traditional norm.

Next, they should separate the risk pool from the service pool. It is best to establish a risk pool that can be augmented at the end of the year by a percentage of year-end and end-of-contract balances in accounts reserved by plan sponsors for hospital services. The specific formula for sharing such hospitals (and other technical components), savings among participating hospitals, the specialty provider organization, and a plan's PCP gatekeepers is negotiated with the plan before the effective date of a capitated contract. Although some recommend that hospitals not be allowed to participate in distribution of such savings, we believe that hospitals should indeed be given incentives to be part of the treatment partnership and contribute efficiencies in many ways that are not within the control of physicians.

## Paying Participating Specialists

The group should develop a monthly reimbursement strategy using any of the methods described previously. A hybrid approach can be used to compensate outpatient and inpatient services differently. For example, inpatient procedures can be reimbursed on a case-rate basis, and outpatient visits can be reimbursed based on a flat rate per referral, on a per-visit basis regardless of the resources used per visit, or on a point system.

## Distributing Risk Pool Annual Balance

A specialty provider organization should not consider distributing risk pool amounts to physicians until the end of the second contract year. At that time, the organization's board of managers and directors may decide not to distribute the total risk pool balance at the end of this initial two-year contract period and subsequent contract years, and may retain some amount to build a long-term reserve fund.

The amount of the contract risk pool to be distributed among participating physicians is calculated at the end of the contract period. Distributions may be based on any combination of the following indices:

- Pro rata shares of physicians' individual total monthly distributions—Each physician receives a share of the risk pool equivalent to the physician's share of total reimbursement distributed during the contract period;
- Pro rata shares of total numbers of patients treated during contract period—Each physician receives a share of the risk pool equivalent to the physician's percentage of all the organization's patients treated during the contract period;
- Relative performance of physicians regarding patient satisfaction—Each physician's risk pool distribution may be modified to reflect patient satisfaction. This requires implementation of a strong patient survey program to obtain statistically significant results; and
- Relative performance of physicians regarding resources consumed—The relative numbers of referrals for diagnostic services and other ancillary services are evaluated, by physician. Physicians who prescribe relatively few resources earn a larger share of the risk pool than do physicians who prescribe more services.

## SPECIALTY CONTRACTING ISSUES

Specialists and specialty contracting organizations must address a number of important issues when negotiating managed care contracts. Aside from legal issues, some of the most commonly encountered issues are as follows.

### Risk-Reward Potential

Contract opportunities must be evaluated for the risk-reward potential: Does a risk-bearing contract ensure sufficient volume, by legal exclusivity or strong financial and other patient channeling mechanisms, to make the acceptance of risk acceptable? The governing rule is "the higher the volume, the more manageable the risk."

### Services To Be Provided

Care must be taken to ensure that services to be delivered and the circumstances of referrals are clearly specified. This is necessary to avoid miscalculation of the quantities and types of services for which the provider organization is responsible, and to prevent "dumping" by other providers seeking to shift their risk. In addition, medical- and disease-management models require clear definitions of protocols for identifying and managing cases that are appropriate for shared patient management and treatment by PCP gatekeepers and specialty care providers.

### Reliability of Utilization Data From MCOs

Data available from MCOs on which to base capitation proposal calculations have historically been inadequate. In such cases, a provider organization can purchase commercially available databases that are matched with MCO membership demographics, and include actuarial projections of utilization and capitation proposals. It is critical to consider the impact of Medicare populations in such calculations because of their high rate of consumption of specialty services. Without reliable data and actuarial projections of specialty utilization and costs, the specialty provider organization may be able to negotiate a capitation agreement that includes a "corridor of risk" and periodic budget reconciliations that prevent either the MCO or the specialty provider organization from making undue profits or taking an unacceptable financial loss during the initial phase of the contract, pending acquisition of reliable utilization data.

## Patient Channeling

For nonexclusive contracts such as PPOs and POS plans, contracts must include at least a 20 percent patient-payable co-payment differential plus reduced or waived deductible to have an effective patient steering mechanism. The PPO approach is to offer a broad, not limited, choice of providers. Consequently, providers in a PPO still compete for patient volume and must continue to cultivate referral sources.

## Minimum Number of Patients

The economics of capitation are based on the law of large numbers: There have to be enough patients to ensure that cost overruns on "bad" cases will be offset by savings on "good" cases. Actuarial assistance should be sought when determining whether projected volume is adequate for capitation, and for recommendations related to establishing corridors of risk or obtaining stop-loss reinsurance.

## Minimum Contract Duration

Contract periods for capitated contracts should be a minimum of two years. An effort should be made to ascertain whether there may be a "pent-up demand" for services that are newly covered benefits. This could lead to utilization that is much higher than expected during the first contract year, followed by a fall-off during the second year allowing the provider to "play catch-up."

## CONCLUSION

Perhaps the only definite pronouncement that can be made about prospects for specialty contracting in managed care is that contracting modalities preferred by MCOs vary greatly from market to market. Because the nature of specialty contracting in virtually any market can be markedly different one year from today, it is critical that specialists and MCOs pay careful attention to their respective market-places and respond rapidly to the opportunities that are revealed.

# Specialty Care Contracting— Comments from the Field

*Vance J. Weber*

---

After the first election of President Clinton, much of the early political rhetoric emanating from the Administration centered on the topic of transforming the nation's health care system. Although I shared with most of my physician colleagues a cynicism about the new attempt by politicians, "pin-striped suits," and others with little practical knowledge of the dynamics of medical care delivery, to re-engineer our health care system, I saw a serious threat and a clarion call to the marketplace to accelerate the changes that were transpiring—that is, an increasing penetration of managed care in the erstwhile largely fee-for-service reimbursement structure.

Fortunately, my transformation from a typical, hard-working physician with little previous interest in the "business" aspects of medicine, to a self-appointed physician leader, motivator, managed care expert, and visionary had begun during the presidential campaign in the spring of 1992. As a long-term avid reader of financial journals with a frustrated and unfulfilled penchant for entrepreneurship and a pragmatic nature, certain self-preservation qualities sharpened in an effort to convert these impending threats to my financial livelihood into marvelous opportunity. The major stumbling block to success, for physician leaders such as myself, has been the oftentimes unyielding nature of physicians, who through years of training and subsequent successes are disinclined toward the rapid change necessary to compete effectively in a predominantly managed care environment.

## CHANGES IN THE CARDIOVASCULAR MARKET

The rapid market changes promoted by managed care organizations (MCOs) and their clients, and the motivations of physician leaders who are trying to forge consensus and meet the challenges for the common good, were reshaping the delivery of cardiovascular care in the greater New York and Philadelphia marketplace. Indeed, the marketplace was shifting elsewhere as well. In California, Atlanta, and Florida, cardiologists were experiencing secular practice alterations with devastating consequences on practice profitability. The oversupply of specialists for a managed care market was manifested clearly in the cardiovascular market. Given the substantial part of the premium dollar attributable to cardiovascular disease, the cardiologist was destined on a national scale to be a target—if not poised for extinction or retribution, then certainly due for unusual hardship.

To develop and guide our strategy, we sought out the best possible talent in the health care consulting business and selected Benenson & Associates, a California-based consulting firm. Our initial strategy centered around consummating the merger of several cardiology groups, including our own. A California law firm with vast health care experience was retained to complete the merger, despite the criticism of my cynical colleagues for bringing in west coast experts. In a short period, the merger began to pay dividends, if not financial, then in terms of perception of market force and leverage. We quickly developed a relationship with a coalition of employers for package pricing and soon thereafter gained entrance (along with our cardiac surgeons and hospital partners) in an entity called the National Cardiovascular Network. Although the latter relationship has been an unmitigated failure in terms of generating new business, it gave our group a certain notoriety, which was advantageous in the network formation detailed in the following.

Concurrent with this group formation, the consulting firm performed a pre-marketing analysis of the New Jersey marketplace and concluded that the cardiovascular services could be capitated successfully. A common theme voiced by area MCOs was their inability to control specialty costs. As the market transitions to pure health maintenance organization (HMO) products and direct contracting with employers, the opportunities seem plentiful for carving out high-cost specialties, such as cardiology. This background work was the foundation for the formation of a state-wide cardiology network specifically suited to deal with the opportunity (or threat) of specialty carve-out capitation.

Using our group as an example of some small success, we began to engage and solicit cardiologists from around the state. Quantitative models were developed to determine the appropriate numbers of cardiologists needed for this entity. Cardiologists-to-population ratios and county-by-county hospital coverage parameters were also used. Each group of cardiologists in the network was given a geographic domain based on which it would receive exclusive capitation. This early work required an enormous expenditure of time and effort. From these early organizational efforts came our first full meeting in October of 1994. A near unanimous vote by the solicited cardiologists propelled us to proceed with full legal structural development and a stock offering. A steering committee worked with our California law firm and finally, by February 1995, Cardiology First of New Jersey, P. A. was born.

## LESSONS LEARNED

In retrospect, we were woefully undercapitalized, a shortcoming of most physician initiatives. Contrary to most industrial corporations in America, the cottage industry of medicine has always been cash poor, in part because of the desire of physicians to "zero out" their corporations each year, extracting the "profits" for their own personal use. It was clear that the undercapitalization of our venture had put us in a precarious position in terms of maintaining autonomy in a managed care environment that requires expensive information systems to manage capitation arrangements successfully.

To deal with the undercapitalization, many of the shareholders believed the cardiology network needed to co-opt market share to survive in a less collegial medical environment. But, with huge legal and consulting costs, the group could not expect to re-capitalize easily without some show of viability. Therefore, we were relentless in our efforts to secure contracts that could develop sufficient cash flow to pay the bills. Our commitment quickly "bore fruit" in the form of two noncapitated contracts. This gave our organization credibility and allowed us to separate ourselves from the more primitive efforts of two competitor networks that were developing.

It was critical to demonstrate success and justify to the membership that loyalty to this network was reasonable. No loose organization of this size (105 cardiologists working in more than 35 offices) could possibly be considered effective if the same cardiologists were identifiable in other similar networks. As such, we had originally developed an exclusivity clause that bound our members to only Cardiology First, prohibiting them from joining a similar statewide network. Although we were initially skeptical about the practical (and political) enforceability of this clause, it became apparent that this exclusivity was critical to the network achieving a distinctive identity and success in the managed care market.

## VISION

Our vision for the cardiology network was rooted in the geography of the area. Given the unique nature of the metropolitan New York area with three densely populated, contiguous states, the defined market areas for many MCOs encompassed portions of New York, New Jersey, and Connecticut. Moreover, the southern New Jersey market is considered a significant portion of the Philadelphia market. The concept of a "seamless" integrated cardiovascular organization was evolving. Such an integrated organization could include cardiologists, cardiac surgeons, vascular surgeons, and interventional vascular radiologists working in concert to provide "seamless" care in a regional setting across artificial state boundaries. Surely a regional delivery model based on the dynamics of the particular economic and geographic marketplace was much more likely to be successful than a statewide organization. This was a chance to have a hand in the re-engineering of cardiovascular care in the most populous area of the United States.

## MANAGEMENT AND ADMINISTRATIVE INFRASTRUCTURE

Armed with this new vision, we began selling the concept to other physician leaders who in turn organized similar networks in their respective states. Nearly two years after the initial establishment of Cardiology First, there are similarly constructed networks in New York, southeastern Pennsylvania, and Connecticut. A camaraderie has developed among the physician leaders and an infrastructure and the basic foundation of an integrated cardiovascular system has been formed.

It became obvious during this process that the commitment of member stockholders alone would not make the organization effective. To convert the developmental work into a viable entity that delivers value to the cardiovascular market, we needed to develop or acquire a sophisticated information system and management structure. After a long analysis, we determined that we lacked sufficient confidence in our ability to hire the correct people, make the proper decisions about sophisticated systems, and analyze the complex financial considerations. After a period of extensive review, we contracted with a physician practice management company that was making a major niche for itself in the northeastern cardiovascular marketplace. Through its cutting-edge information systems technology (based on hand-held computers) we are cautiously hopeful that we will be able to provide value to the marketplace. Developing a computerized medical outcomes database will give Cardiology First a superior market edge over the average cardiologist working in a small group or solo settings. Eventually, this technologic advantage will prevail in channeling a greater share of the market to a smaller number of highly qualified and efficient cardiology providers.

## CONCLUSION

Despite the frustration of dealing with MCOs that lack leadership, vacillate on contract negotiations, and cannot meet our aggressive timeline for reengineering cardiology care and garnering market share, we believe success is just around the corner. Cardiology First expects to execute two capitated contracts with approximately 260,000 lives by the second quarter of 1997. Our pending marketplace success is tarnished by the emergence of the "hired gun organization," a quasi–management services organization (MSO) that seeks simple across-the-board reductions in specialty reimbursement on behalf of MCOs. These entities try to exclude doctor-driven single specialty physician organizations from forging payer relationships (and from sharing risk pools with MCOs). This is a serious development for physician specialists and one that must be addressed collectively and immediately.

# 7

# Ambulatory and Ancillary Care Contracting

*Wendy Knight*
*Lisa A. Sansone*

Ancillary care are support services that are delivered in conjunction with primary or tertiary care services. These include radiology, laboratory, podiatry, physical and other rehabilitation therapy, home care, anesthesia, and diagnostic testing. Ambulatory care refers to medical services that are delivered to patients on an outpatient basis—a physician's office, hospital, patient's home, or other facility. In addition to many ancillary services, other types of care rendered on an outpatient basis include surgery, emergent and urgent care, home health care, and chemotherapy.

## AMBULATORY SURGICAL SERVICES

Hospital services account for nearly 50 percent of the medical costs of a managed care organization (MCO); therefore, contracting with a hospital's outpatient surgical department or a freestanding surgical center is one way for an MCO to reduce inpatient medical costs and expand its provider networks, both of which may improve its competitive advantage in the marketplace.

For the ambulatory care provider, contracting with an MCO is a way to obtain predictable income, guarantee payments for authorized services, maintain or increase its patient base, and remain a viable health care provider.

### The Shift to Outpatient Care

Advances in medical technologies have enabled physicians to perform an increasing array of surgical procedures on an outpatient basis.

As a result, more MCOs will reimburse certain routine surgical procedures only if they are performed in an ambulatory care setting. While some of these surgeries can be performed in a physician's office, most are scheduled as one-day surgeries in hospitals or freestanding surgical centers. Exhibit 7–1 is a sample list of surgical procedures that MCOs may require or advocate to be performed on an outpatient basis.

The shift to ambulatory care has created a conflicting dynamic for providers and MCOs. Initially, as MCOs have focused on reducing inpatient stays and their associated costs, they have negotiated vigorously for competitive per diem rates. Their success in having traditional inpatient surgical procedures performed in ambulatory care settings has had negative financial ramifications for providers and MCOs alike, however. As the surgeries performed on an outpatient basis increase in complexity, the costs of performing those surgeries also increase and hospitals increase their charges accordingly. MCOs have attempted to constrain these costs by limiting the contracted payment for outpatient surgeries to the average per diem rate or a percentage of the per diem. Pressured by declining revenues from inpatient stays, hospitals try to maximize their revenue from outpatient services by resisting attempts of MCOs to restrict payments for ambulatory services.

## Contractual Arrangements

Depending on the type of ambulatory care provider, the MCO may use a standard ancillary contract, a hospital contract, or a specific

---

**Exhibit 7–1** Sample Surgical Procedures Required On Outpatient Basis

Rhinoplasty
Tonsillectomy, with or without adenoidectomy
Colposcopy
Cone biopsy of cervix
Hysteroscopy
Laparoscopy
Extraction of cataracts, with or without insertion of intraocular lens
Laser traveculoplasty
Abdominal lipectomy
All endoscopies, with or without biopsies
Bone marrow biopsy
Cardiac catheterization

ambulatory surgery contract to outline the terms of the relationship. Reimbursement methodologies for outpatient surgeries are consistent with those of most physician services. The principal payment arrangements are fee-for-service (FFS), case rates, and capitation.

*Fee-for-Service*

An MCO and provider may negotiate one discount for all outpatient services, including surgeries, or multiple discounts for different categories of outpatient service. For example, an MCO may propose a 30 percent discount from the provider's usual and customary (U&C) charges for ambulatory surgeries, a 25 percent discount for radiology services, and a 20 percent discount for all other outpatient services.

Reimbursement based on a fee schedule for procedures identified by Current Procedural Terminology-4 (CPT-4) codes is for the professional component only. The provider will bill the MCO according to the CPT-4 codes that correspond with the appropriate surgical procedure and other services rendered, such as laboratory work. Most MCOs reimburse physicians for surgical assists one-quarter of the payment the principal surgeon receives.

*Case Rates*

Case rates for outpatient surgery are structured to achieve more predictability and control of surgical costs. Generally, case rates (also called flat rates, package pricing, or bundled charges) include all professional and technical components of the service, including preoperative laboratory work, anesthesia, and postoperative care. Case rates can be structured as single rates or sliding scale rates and can be based on U&C charges or type of surgical procedure.

Under a single case rate structure, the provider will receive one rate for all ambulatory surgery, that is, $1,200 per surgery. A sliding scale rate adjusts the payment according to billed charges. For example, surgeries with U&C charges of up to $1,000 may be paid a case rate of $750; surgeries between $1,001 and $1,499 may be paid $1,200, and so on. The Ambulatory Surgical Center (ASC) Groupers (developed for use by Medicare) divide outpatient surgical procedures into groups by surgical procedure. The MCO and provider negotiate varying payments for each surgical group. For example, the provider may receive $500 for each surgery in ASC Group I and $700 for those surgeries in ASC Group II. Anesthesia may be included in the ASC Group rate or billed separately. Some provider groups are contemplating the modification of inpatient Diagnostic Related Groupings (DRGs) to be used for ambulatory surgeries.

The MCO and provider may negotiate any number of combinations of financial arrangements. For example, a sliding scale case rate might be negotiated for ambulatory surgeries and a discount for all other outpatient procedures.

## Capitation

Capitation rates are also an option for MCOs and outpatient surgical departments or freestanding surgical centers. There are several considerations in developing such arrangements as outlined in Exhibit 7–2.

First, the ambulatory surgical center should know the scope of services it is expected to provide. This includes both the types of surgeries and the ancillary services associated with the surgical procedures. To protect the ambulatory care provider from unnecessary risk, the arrangement may contain a mechanism to adjust the capitation

---

**Exhibit 7–2** Questions to Consider in Negotiating a Capitated Ambulatory Surgical Contract

1. What specific services are covered under the capitation contract (i.e., preadmission testing, postoperative care, surgical assists, anesthesia)?
2. What specific surgeries are covered under the contract? Are pediatric surgeries included?
3. Does the contract identify surgeries required to be performed on an outpatient basis? Does the contract include a mechanism to modify the capitation payments if surgeries are added to or deleted from the list?
4. On what clinical criteria is the list based?
5. How does the contract address complicated surgeries? For example, what if a patient needs to be admitted for a surgical procedure that is identified on the list of required ambulatory surgeries?
6. What preauthorization policies exist for ambulatory surgeries? Does the referring physician need to obtain authorization from the health plan or are PCPs empowered to authorize referrals for certain surgeries?
7. On what treatment protocols, if any, are the referral authorization procedures based?
8. How are enrollees "assigned" to a surgical center? By PCPs? By geographic region?
9. How does the contract address leakage (i.e., referrals to noncapitated providers)? How does it handle payments when patients self-refer to nondesignated providers?
10. What are the existing and expected utilization rates of capitated surgical procedures?

payments for the severity and mix of the surgical cases. The contract should be structured to accommodate an expanded list of surgical procedures that are possible to be performed on an ambulatory basis as current medical technologies and treatments evolve.

The expected referral and utilization patterns (and consequences for deviations from these) should be identified in the contract. An improperly structured capitation contract for ambulatory surgery may encourage physicians to admit patients for procedures that might, under routine circumstances, be appropriate to perform on an ambulatory basis, or refer patients for services not covered under the capitation payment solely for the purposes of retaining capitation monies. Conversely, the existence of a capitated surgical contract might tempt primary care physicians (PCPs) to refer patients for minor surgeries that the physician could reasonably be expected to perform him- or herself. For these reasons, it is wise to structure capitation arrangements for ambulatory surgical services in combination with other risk-sharing arrangements, such as a hospital incentive bonus, or with expected utilization corridors. Furthermore, the authorization procedures for emergency care should be stated explicitly in the contract.

## EMERGENT AND URGENT CARE SERVICES

The provision of emergency services under a managed care contract has become controversial in recent years. Regulations developed to prevent for-profit hospitals from refusing to see uninsured patients and "dumping" them onto public hospitals have been transformed into challenges by hospitals to receive payment for all emergency care services rendered to a managed care member, irrespective of conformity to an MCO's authorization procedures.

### Defining Emergency Care

Definitions of emergent and urgent care are not as clear to members or providers as many managed care contracts assume. Most members in health maintenance organizations (HMOs) and similar plans are instructed to contact their PCP for medical advice in urgent medical situations or in the event of a perceived emergency and to seek care from the nearest emergency room facility immediately if the medical situation is life- or limb-threatening. However, in a real medical emergency the distinctions between emergent and urgent care become clouded and these instructions understandably irrelevant. All this leaves emergency care providers uncertain about when they should render services and if they will receive payment from the MCO.

Most managed care contracts do not recite a comprehensive list of procedures or services that are considered emergent, as this may vary by each patient's circumstances, but they usually include a provision that attempts to define emergency care. This might read, "Services that stem from symptoms that are severe, occurred suddenly and unexpectedly, and would have resulted in loss of limb or life if immediate care was not sought are considered emergency care."

## Emergency Care Provisions

The emergency care provider should have a clear understanding of the MCO's authorization procedures, contractual obligations of the PCP, and payment policies to ensure adequate payment and minimize the hassles of providing emergency care.

### PCP Responsibilities

Plans that require members to select a PCP usually obligate the PCP or affiliated medical group to provide, direct, or authorize a member's emergency care. The PCP or designee is contractually obligated to be on call 24 hours a day, 7 days a week, to assist members needing emergency services. The MCO may stipulate under what conditions a PCP should refer members for emergency treatment and often monitors emergency room referral patterns prospectively to determine if the PCP is in compliance with plan procedures.

### Care Outside the Service Area

If a member is injured or becomes ill while temporarily outside of the service area, the MCO will pay nonparticipating providers reasonable charges for emergency services rendered if they are required because of unforeseen illness or injury. Except in rare instances, the MCO does not pay for follow-up or continuing treatment provided by nonplan providers. Payment for covered services outside the service area is limited to treatment that is necessary before the member can reasonably be transported to a participating hospital or returned to the care of the PCP.

*Special Payment Provisions*

Providers should also understand the MCO's payment policies to ensure appropriate payment. Many managed care contracts include a provision that precludes payment for emergency care services rendered if the member is admitted immediately following an emergency room visit. Obstetrical observation rates are negotiated to compensate the provider for services provided to an obstetrical patient when she presents to the hospital with false labor and is monitored for a short time, not admitted, or sent home. Observation rates can be reimbursed at a discount off billed charges, a single flat rate, or an hourly rate.

## Contractual Arrangements

Most financial arrangements between MCOs and emergency departments are structured through the MCO's contract with the hospital. They may include both the technical and professional component of services rendered. Depending on the relationship between the hospital and its emergency care providers, MCOs may negotiate separate contracts with emergency care physicians, such as anesthesiologists or trauma surgeons. Payments for services rendered in the emergency room by participating primary or specialty care providers are covered in the applicable contract with that provider.

*Fee-for-Service*

Reimbursement for emergency room services can be negotiated as a single discount off U&C charges, such as a 20 percent discount per emergency room visit, or a discount with a maximum allowable charge, such as a 20 percent discount up to a maximum dollar amount of $150 per visit. To reduce the high costs associated with emergency care and to increase the practice options available to members, many MCOs contract with urgent or immediate care centers for the treatment of nonemergent care such as fever, minor wounds, and nausea.

*Flat Rates*

Flat rates pertaining to emergency care are structured as per visit fees, such as $150 per visit. Sliding scale rates based on U&C charges or diagnoses can also be structured. For example, the contract might reimburse the provider $150 for U&C charges up to $200, and $275 for U&C charges up to $400. As with ambulatory surgeries, flat rates for emergency care can include ancillary services, such as laboratory and radiology, and can include payments for the hospital-based physicians, as well.

*Capitation*

As with other specialty care capitation contracts, capitated arrangements for emergency care services must be structured to avoid the unintended effects of capitation, such as PCPs unnecessarily referring members for emergency treatment. As with any provider, the emergency care provider contemplating a capitation contract must have available to him or her the basic information needed to evaluate a proposed capitated arrangement, including the services covered under the capitation rate, the member demographics, the covered benefits and plan designs, and the historical utilization of the services. Other considerations are outlined in Exhibit 7–3.

## HOME HEALTH CARE

Home health care is administered to members in the home by themselves, a family member, or home care nurses or other trained health professionals. The availability of home health care services gives members and their physicians an alternative treatment setting

**Exhibit 7–3** Questions to Consider in Structuring a Capitated Emergency Care Contract

1. Are PCPs responsible for authorizing emergency care? How are they compensated?
2. Is there a hospital incentive bonus for PCPs?
3. What services are defined as emergency care? Are they clearly defined in the contract?
4. Does the contract cover both emergency and urgent care services?
5. What protocols are used for emergency referrals?
6. How does the contract address emergency visits that result in an admission?
7. How does the contract address out-of-area emergency care?
8. Are payments to hospital-based physicians included in the capitation payment?
9. Are emergency surgical procedures covered in the contract? How are they reimbursed?
10. How is the capitation payment adjusted for out-of-area emergency visits?

to hospitals. By arranging for home care services for the appropriate diagnoses and conditions, the MCO and physician can do the following:

- minimize the need for an unnecessary emergency room visit;
- prevent an unnecessary hospitalization;
- shorten a hospital length of stay;
- provide continuous monitored follow-up care;
- provide care to the member in the safety and comfort of his or her home; and
- facilitate the provision of vital nonmedical services, such as custodial or child care.

## Range of Services

In general, home health care services can be arranged for the treatment of any diagnosis that a physician determines can be managed effectively in the home with proper training and supervision. Patients suffering from asthma, diabetes, cancer, acquired immune deficiency syndrome (AIDS), and some neurological disorders often can be treated safely and effectively in the home. Postsurgical care, posttrauma care, high-risk maternity and prenatal care, postpartum care, and healthy newborn care are examples of other home care services.

Many MCOs are interested in contracting with home care agencies that can provide the full range of home care services, including skilled nursing care, physical therapy, durable medical equipment, infusion care, total parenteral nutrition, pharmaceuticals, and supplies. Home health care is provided by multiple health care professionals including registered nurses, licensed practical nurses, physical therapists, speech therapists, occupational therapists, respiratory therapists, and medical social workers.

In non-risk contracts, home health care services are generally coordinated and approved through the health services department of the MCO. When MCOs contract with provider organizations on a risk basis, they may transfer the responsibility for arranging home care and related services to the provider organization.

## Contractual Arrangements

There are a multitude of reimbursement arrangements for providers of home health care services, including discount from U&C charges, fee schedules, flat rates, and capitation. Home health care rates may also vary by level of care, such as adult or pediatric; or by day of the week, such as weekdays or weekends. Similar to physicians and other providers, home care providers can be reimbursed based on a single discount off U&C charges, such as a 20 percent discount for skilled nursing services, or multiple discounts according to type of care or service, such as a 20 percent discount for skilled nursing services and physical therapy and a 10 percent discount for durable medical equipment.

*Flat Rates*

Flat rates for home care services are set payments per visit or per day. These can fluctuate depending on the level of care or type of service provided. A home care service provided within two hours is usually considered a "visit" and paid accordingly. Services consuming more than two hours are paid according to a per diem rate schedule. For example, the MCO may reimburse the home care provider a flat rate for skilled nursing services as follows:

> *home health RN:*  *$50 per visit or $110 per diem*
> *home health LPN:* *$45 per visit or $90 per diem*
> *home infusion:*  *$75 per visit*

*Capitation*

Finally, some HMOs and gatekeeper preferred provider organizations (PPOs) are developing capitation rates for a single home care company to provide all required home care services to members. These arrangements generally encompass the full range of home care services and may include participation in the MCO's disease-management programs and health promotion activities. Home care companies interested in structuring capitated contracts with MCOs should:

- offer a broad spectrum of services, through alliances with other home care vendors if necessary;
- ensure high quality of care by using licensed providers and employed (vs. contracted) personnel, and offering continual staff education and training;
- acquire information systems that can track and monitor capitation payments and payments to subcontractors; and
- establish treatment protocols and other policies for continuity of care.

## SOLE-SOURCE CONTRACTING

In sole-source contracting an MCO negotiates a single contract with one company to provide a specific set of services to all or most of its members in defined markets. Generally, these arrangements are structured as capitated agreements and they can be national or regional in scope depending on the service area of the MCO. Most sole-source contracts involve laboratory, radiology, physical therapy, home care, or vision care services. Because of the size and complexity of the these arrangements, some MCOs will initiate the sole-source contracts on a pilot basis in selected markets and create a gradual implementation schedule for its remaining markets. MCOs are developing sole-source contracts with ancillary providers to

- achieve predictability of costs;
- reduce administrative expenses associated with receiving and paying claims;
- share the financial risk of delivering the services with providers;
- obtain more complete and uniform utilization and other data; and
- develop targeted disease management and other patient care programs.

### Criteria In Establishing A Sole-Source Relationship

The criteria an MCO uses in establishing a sole-source arrangement is usually specified in the request for proposal (RFP) that the MCO distributes to selected vendors. The MCO will request a comprehensive proposal from each vendor based on the parameters established in the RFP. The principal criteria for selection are as follows.

*Partnership*

Because the MCO is replacing multiple providers with one in a sole-source contract, it wants to ensure that the selected provider is suitable as a long-term partner. The MCO will look for the demonstrated ability of the provider to work collaboratively with the MCO, including modifying its systems and strategies to better align with those of managed care firms. In addition, the MCO wants assurance that the provider embraces the concept of managed care and has the clinical and administrative capacity to accommodate the expanded managed care business.

*Customer Service*

The MCO seeks a provider that can meet or exceed the service expectations of the MCO and its clients, contracted providers, and members alike. This would include the ability of the provider to solicit, respond, and track patient complaints or comments, staff customer service lines, prepare and distribute member education materials, and produce reports on various performance measures.

*Quality*

MCOs are very concerned about a provider's quality assurance activities, especially in a sole-source arrangement. This includes how a provider hires and trains its clinical staff, the extent to which it uses contracted personnel, its applicable accreditation status, its process for measuring quality, and the use of patient satisfaction surveys. In conjunction with affiliated providers, many MCOs are developing specific patient care programs based on evolving clinical practice guidelines and are interested in contracting with health care professionals that have the interest and capability of establishing clinically-based, patient-centered programs.

*Information Systems*

The key to successfully managing and administering a capitated arrangement is current data and sophisticated information technology. The prospective sole-source provider must have the sophisticated information systems necessary to obtain, input, track, and monitor capitation payments, enrollment data, claims payments, and related data. Moreover, the provider must acquire or possess the system infrastructure indispensable in capturing and analyzing physician referral patterns, utilization statistics, patient risk factors, and other essential clinical information. The provider's ability to manage a capitated contract of this size using compatible and sophisticated information systems is an important issue in sole-source contracting.

*Experience*

Providers considering sole-source arrangements should have significant experience in delivering the specified services, particularly in a managed care environment. MCOs will look for providers with an established track record in providing high-quality services and with experience in capitated contracts. Providers lacking considerable managed care experience should create alliances with providers more experienced in working under capitated contracts.

A sole-source contract is a major endeavor for the MCO and provider alike and involves a variety of contractual and operational issues that both should explore thoroughly. These include covered services, product lines, network development and subcontracting, reimbursement, utilization management, and reporting. Exhibit 7–4 outlines some of the numerous questions providers and MCOs should consider when structuring sole-source contracts.

## OTHER CAPITATED ANCILLARY PROGRAMS

In a similar vein as sole-source contracting, MCOs are creating other types of capitated programs for ancillary services such as physical therapy, radiology, and podiatry. These are developed as regional or market-specific capitation programs that involve several providers, rather than one, for a specific set of services. Capitated programs are

---

**Exhibit 7–4** Questions to Consider in Negotiating Sole-Source Contracts

1. What scope of services are included? Are ancillary services included?
2. What parameters exist for subcontractual arrangements?
3. Who is responsible for network development and provider relations?
4. What if the vendor doesn't service all the MCO markets?
5. How does the contract address future MCO expansions into new markets?
6. Does the contract cover all product lines?
7. How will payments for out-of-network benefits be handled?
8. Will some services be reimbursed FFS? Are these defined in the contract?
9. Who has responsibility to minimize out-of-network leakage? What are the penalties or incentives to reduce leakage?
10. Who has responsibility for managing client and member relations, including staffing member services telephone lines and developing member education materials?
11. How will the contract be administered in each market? What additional administrative and management services are necessary?
12. Is there an administrative fee for managing the network?
13. What utilization assumptions were used in developing the capitation rate? Do these mirror existing utilization rates for the services or are they lower than present utilization rates?
14. Does the contract include utilization (or risk) corridors?
15. What utilization and medical management reports will be provided and expected?

usually instituted after the provider network has been established and operational on a FFS basis for a period of time. This gives the provider and MCO concrete utilization and cost data on which to base the capitated contract. The re-contracting effort intends to select fewer providers that will provide a wider range of services at a fixed rate.

For example, an MCO developing a regional capitated program for imaging services wants to select six providers that can offer the full complement of imaging services, including contrast studies, CT scans, MRIs, echography, angiography, ultrasounds, and chest x-rays. The proposed capitation rate covers professional and technical services. Unless the single radiology provider offers all these services or can create a partnership with other providers, freestanding imaging centers or hospital radiology departments have an advantage. Questions the prospective radiology provider should consider when structuring such an arrangement are outlined in Exhibit 7–5.

## CONCLUSION

The intense price competition among MCOs forces them to focus on reducing or containing all medical and administrative costs. The availability of high-quality and well-organized ambulatory and ancillary care providers enables MCOs to continue to move more services to alternative care settings. This can have the dual result of reducing medical costs and improving patient health outcomes. Cost containment is further accomplished through the negotiation of package pricing and capitated arrangements. Moreover, contracting on a single-source basis for some of these services eases the administrative

---

**Exhibit 7–5** Questions to Consider When Negotiating a Capitated Ancillary Program

1. How are the PCPs aligned with the radiology provider? Can the PCP select his or her radiology provider or is one assigned?
2. What imaging services, if any, can be performed in the physician's office? How does the contract address emergency radiology care?
3. What are the referral protocols for radiology services? Are PCPs required to obtain authorization from the MCO or can they refer patients directly for radiology services?
4. How does the contract address payments to non-designated providers? Are the payments deducted from the capitation payments?
5. What is the expected utilization of radiological services? Does the contract include utilization corridors?

burden of managing multiple contracts, facilitates the capture of valuable data on patient risk factors, and shares the financial burden of delivering care between the MCO and provider. As with all providers, ambulatory and ancillary providers need to be skillful and savvy contract negotiators to maintain their valued status in the changing health care market.

# Ambulatory and Ancillary Care Contracting— Comments from the Field

*Beth Winter*

A case study of radiology services is an effective way to demonstrate the considerations and challenges of contracting for ancillary services on a "carve-in" capitation basis.

Green Health Plan (GHP) is a good-sized, multi-product, managed care organization (MCO) with a strong regional presence. Orange Radiology Services Network (ORSN) is a well-established radiology network that includes freestanding physician-owned imaging centers and some hospital outpatient departments. This case study presents an overview of the business relationship between the two entities through examination of several questions.

Why would GHP consider working with a network of radiologists? What guiding principles should be considered in maintaining the relationship? After two years of experience, what lessons are to be learned?

## ADVANTAGES OF A PHYSICIAN NETWORK

When developing a comprehensive provider network for all services necessary to care for a population, an MCO may assess the capabilities of individual providers or small groups and assemble the network on its own, or may use existing networks of providers who have already joined together to assume and manage risk. Within the array of ambulatory care services, the market for radiology services is among the most advanced in the organization of providers able to meet the geographic and service requirements of MCOs. These radiology networks are highly price competitive; the managed care portion of their business produces thin margins.

There were several advantages to GHP selecting ORSN to provide radiology services to members, including the following:

- Through a single signature, GHP could obtain commitment to rates and all other terms and conditions of the contract.

- Credentialing and other performance monitoring and reporting responsibilities could be partially shifted to the radiology network.
- GHP could shift a significant amount of utilization and business risk to the network.
- ORSN is well-positioned to assess and monitor changes in technology and clinical practice.
- ORSN can assume responsibility for providing additional geographic coverage as GHP expands its service area.

A well-managed network can use all of these attributes to gain leverage in negotiations with MCOs.

## LESSONS LEARNED

According to Boland, there are few guiding principles in a relationship between a provider network and an MCO.[1] When evaluating the success of the relationship, it is useful to compare the experience of the parties to the following guiding principles.

1. The network must represent an acceptable provider panel.
2. Reimbursement mechanisms should be reasonable and must support the features outlined previously.
3. The parties must share a cooperative operational commitment to support a long-term relationship.
4. Contract terms and conditions must be mutually beneficial and consistently honored.

## NATURE OF THE PROVIDER PANEL

ORSN represents a collection of high-quality providers who are fairly well distributed in relation to the membership and primary care physicians (PCPs). Radiology services present a great opportunity for competition between hospital and physicians; radiologists in single-specialty networks often are the same ones who manage the hospital's imaging department. ORSN has succeeded in overcoming this potential obstacle by incorporating certain hospitals into the network. Radiologists from the strongest freestanding centers are major players in these hospitals. Including both hospital-based and independent radiologists in the network encourages the efficient allocation of services among the sites and avoids duplication of high-tech equipment. Maintaining the delicate balance in the appropriate delivery of services requires frequent direct and open communication among institutional and freestanding center participants. Including hospitals in the network has allowed ORSN to incorporate professional and facility coverage for inpatient and emergency room imaging in its contract with GHP. This increases the value of the network to GHP.

## REASONABLE REIMBURSEMENT MECHANISMS

In the contract between ORSN and GHP, reimbursement for most outpatient radiology services is included in the base capitation rate. However, the following complicated exceptions have challenged the other guiding principles.

- Adjustments to the base capitation rate must be made for PCPs who provide flat film radiology studies in their own offices. A different set of adjustments must be made for Medicare-risk enrollees.
- Additional capitation payments are made for gadolinium (requiring an annual reconciliation to reflect actual utilization) and additional fee-for-service payments are made for nonionic contrast, inpatient and emergency room coverage, nuclear cardiology, and invasive procedures. This requires precise claims and administrative procedures, and frequent manual oversight.
- To encourage appropriate and efficient practice behavior of ORSN providers, GHP incorporated several performance measures as bonus compensation. Additional payments could be earned if goals were met for measures such as mammography screenings, appropriate access to services, member satisfaction, and satisfactory ratings from referring physicians.
- ORSN is not the sole provider of radiology services for GHP. Because most services are provided on an outpatient basis to a mobile population, considerable "inflow" and "outflow" of services occur. These require monitoring and reporting of enrollee utilization patterns, and additional adjustments to and reconciliations of the capitation payment.

## COOPERATIVE OPERATIONAL COMMITMENT

Management information, claims payment, and enrollment systems have not been adequate to support the creative nature of the contract. It has been necessary to implement manual administrative procedures and a costly and time-consuming survey process to assess eligibility for bonus payments. The parties are now in the process of evaluating base and bonus payments structures and incentives to make the contract more workable.

## CONTRACT TERMS AND CONDITIONS

After two years, both GHP and ORSN recognize that contract specifications and performance standards need to be reworked for the relationship to continue. The operational capabilities of the parties have not matched the sophistication of the reimbursement mechanisms. Because there are significant advantages to the arrangement with the radiology network, the parties are committed to an ongoing process of modifications so that a successful partnership will result for the long term.

GHP and ORSN developed a creative and unique contractual arrangement containing many features designed to contain costs and ensure quality. Both parties will need to devote time and resources to improve systems that measure up to that creativity, and continue to monitor progress by referring to these basic principles.

---

**NOTE**

1. Boland, P., ed. 1993. Delivery systems. In *Making managed healthcare work*. Gaithersburg, Md: Aspen Publishers, Inc.

# 8

# Managed Prescription Drug Programs

*Kenneth W. Schafermeyer*

Managed care has affected pharmacy practice in the United States profoundly and permanently. Although payment to pharmacies through public and private health insurance plans accounted for less than 12 percent of all retail prescriptions before 1970, by 1995 they accounted for more than 62 percent of all retail prescriptions.[1] By 1993, almost all health maintenance organizations (HMOs) included an outpatient prescription benefit whereas 57 percent of preferred provider organizations (PPOs) covered prescription drugs.[2]

Although retail prescription prices have increased significantly during the last decade, managed care reimbursement rates for prescriptions have decreased. Consequently, gross margin (that is, retail price minus wholesale cost for the product) for the average pharmacy has decreased from 32.6 percent of sales in 1985 to 28.1 percent of sales in 1994.[3] Successful pharmacies have adjusted by decreasing expenses and becoming more efficient, primarily through computerization and the use of pharmacy technicians. Pharmacists' future professional and economic success depends on demonstrating how pharmaceutical care services (which constitute less than 10 percent of most plans' health care expenses) can reduce the other 90 percent of health care costs while improving patient outcomes.

*Source:* Portions of the material and the figures in this chapter were adapted from Schafermeyer, K.W. Overview of Pharmacy in Managed Health Care. In: *A Pharmacist's Guide to Principles and Practices of Managed Care Pharmacy.* Alexandria, VA: Academy of Managed Care Pharmacy; 1995.

## ADMINISTRATION OF MANAGED CARE
## PRESCRIPTION CONTRACTS

Because the administration of managed care pharmacy programs is rather complex and requires a large prescription volume to be conducted efficiently, managed care organizations (MCOs) often "carve out" prescription benefits and contract with pharmacy benefits managers (PBMs) to manage these services. Using a PBM isolates cost centers and concentrates a workforce of prescription benefit experts to manage the prescription program. The administrative services provided by PBMs include the following:

- contracting with pharmacies to provide specified services;
- communicating with both patients and providers to explain and update administrative policies;
- providing reports to plan sponsors;
- identifying eligible beneficiaries;
- processing claims submitted by pharmacies;
- reimbursing pharmacies;
- auditing pharmacies;
- controlling utilization; and
- ensuring program quality.

Figure 8–1 shows the typical relationships in which PBMs and other participants operate. As indicated, a major function of PBMs is obtaining discounts from both pharmacy providers and from pharmaceutical manufacturers. In exchange for these services, PBMs may receive a percentage of manufacturer rebates or a fee per prescription. Contact between PBMs and patients has usually been limited to providing general information explaining program benefits and issuing identification cards to document patient eligibility.

In carved-out programs, the extent to which MCOs can integrate prescription data with data for medical, hospital, and other health care services is often limited. Unless all medical data are integrated, it is difficult to assess the impact of pharmacy services on overall health care costs.[4]

Managed care contracts for prescription drugs can be on either a fee-for-service or capitation basis. Payers generally dislike fee-for-service reimbursement because of the inherent conflict of interest that occurs when providers have the ability and incentive to increase the demand for their services. Although pharmacists do not initiate prescriptions, they can influence the utilization of prescription drugs.

The PBM Network

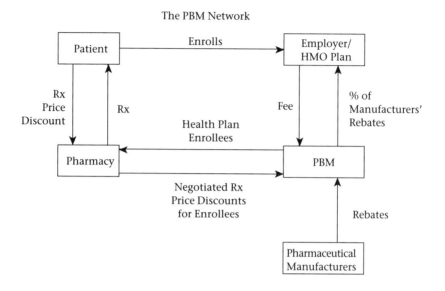

**Figure 8–1** Relationship of Pharmacy Benefit Managers with other Managed Care Program Participants. *Source:* Reprinted from *Pharmacy Benefit Managers: Early Results on Ventures with Drug Manufacturers*, p. 6, November 9, 1995, United States General Accounting Office, Health, Education and Human Services Division.

Because pharmacies are paid for dispensing prescriptions, fee-for-service reimbursement offers little financial incentive to control prescription utilization, reduce costs, or provide nondispensing services.

### Capitated Plans

Figure 8–2 shows that pharmacy income from a capitated program comes from the following two sources: (1) the capitation fees paid by the MCO at the beginning of each month for patients assigned to receive services from that pharmacy; and (2) the co-payments patients pay when they receive prescriptions. Because the greatest portion of reimbursement is fixed, capitation offers pharmacists incentives to reduce unnecessary prescription utilization and offer nondispensing services.

Despite its theoretical advantages, capitated reimbursement for pharmacies is not used often today. Just 6 percent of HMOs used capitation to reimburse pharmacies in 1993, down from 11 percent in

$$\begin{matrix} \text{Total Rx} \\ \text{Program} \\ \text{Income} \end{matrix} = \left( \begin{matrix} \text{Capitation} \\ \text{Fee} \end{matrix} \times \begin{matrix} \text{No. of Patients} \\ \text{Enrolled} \end{matrix} \right) + \left( \begin{matrix} \text{Amount of} \\ \text{Co-payment} \end{matrix} \times \begin{matrix} \text{No. of Rxs} \\ \text{Dispensed} \end{matrix} \right)$$

**Figure 8–2** Components of Pharmacy Income Under Capitation Reimbursement.

1991 and 17 percent in 1989.[5] The problem with capitating pharmacies is that physicians, not pharmacists, have the most influence over prescription utilization and costs. Therefore, physicians are more likely to be responsible for prescription costs. The most common way of giving physicians incentive to control drug costs is to include prescription costs in the physician's capitation rate. In 1995, approximately 39 percent of all HMOs used financial withholding, risk pools, or other capitation arrangements in which physicians assumed financial liability for drug utilization budgets.[6] Pharmacy capitation may work best when pharmacists and physicians participate in the same risk pool and share responsibilities for controlling prescription utilization and costs.

## Fee-For-Service Plans

As illustrated in Figure 8–3, costs for fee-for-service prescription benefit plans can be grouped into the following three main categories: (1) unit costs; (2) utilization rate; and (3) administrative costs.

*Unit Costs*

Unit costs, the average amount paid by the MCO for each prescription, consists of the following two components: the cost of drug ingredients and a professional dispensing fee. Although the amount that the patient is required to pay out-of-pocket (that is, patient cost sharing) reduces unit costs, it is used primarily to control utilization. Most MCOs will not reimburse the pharmacy more than the pharmacy's usual and customary (U&C) price—the price charged most commonly to private-paying patients. Therefore, if a pharmacy maintains a competitive prescription pricing system by charging a low markup on selected "fast-movers," it cannot charge more to the MCO. Figure 8–4 illustrates the unit cost for a fee-for-service prescription program in more detail.

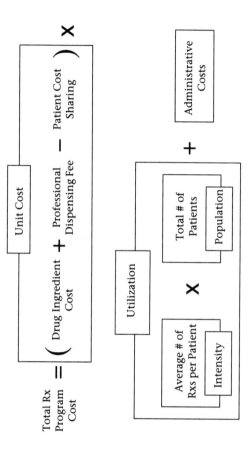

**Figure 8-3** Components of Managed Care Organizations' Prescription Costs Under Fee-for-Service Reimbursement.

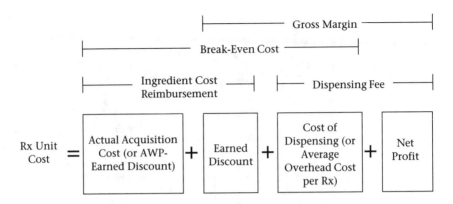

**Figure 8–4** Components of Unit Costs Under Fee-for-Service Reimbursement.

*Drug Ingredient Costs.* Drug ingredients represent approximately 72 percent of an average prescription's cost.[7] Traditionally, reimbursement for drug ingredient costs was based on the "average wholesale price" (AWP)—an artificial "list price" approximately 15 percent higher than the actual acquisition cost (AAC) that pharmacies pay for prescription drugs. Because AAC is so variable and difficult to determine, prescription benefit programs usually reimburse pharmacies an estimated acquisition cost (EAC). EAC is calculated as a percentage of AWP (for example, 90 percent of AWP). The difference between AAC and AWP is usually greater for pharmacies that buy larger volumes and have more efficient purchasing practices. This difference, known as the "earned discount," should be considered a part of the pharmacy's average gross margin. This relationship is shown in Figure 8–4. By supplementing low dispensing fees, earned discounts have allowed pharmacies to participate in MCOs that would otherwise be unprofitable.

To reduce ingredient costs, prescription benefit managers establish formularies—lists of drug products that are covered (that is, a positive formulary) or excluded from coverage (that is, a negative formulary). Formularies were used by nearly all HMOs in 1995; about 47 percent were closed formularies with tight management and high compliance rates.[8] Financial incentives to physicians and pharmacists (through reimbursement) and patients (through co-payment incentives) are used to encourage formulary compliance. Public and private prescription benefit plans commonly exclude certain classes of drugs such as oral contraceptives, products used primarily for cosmetic purposes, weight control products, experimental drugs, parenteral drugs (other than insulin), and certain compounded drugs.[9]

Another way of controlling drug product costs is to encourage the use of generic drugs. In 1994, about 38 percent of all prescriptions filled under a managed care plan were for generics.[10] Payers often limit reimbursement to a generic price level when a multiple-source drug is prescribed—regardless of whether the brand name drug is actually dispensed. This is known as a "maximum allowable cost" (MAC) provision. Some programs have "dispense as written" (DAW) provisions for overriding MAC prices when physicians indicate that brand-name drugs are medically necessary. For other prescription benefit plans, if the patient insists on receiving a brand-name drug, the payer will reimburse the pharmacy at the generic price and require the patient to pay the pharmacy the additional cost of the brand-name drug. Another incentive encouraging patients to accept generic substitution is a differential co-payment, which requires patients to pay a larger share of the costs when insisting that brand-name, rather than generic, medications be dispensed.

Some MCOs have gone beyond generic selection to encourage therapeutic selection—the substitution of therapeutically equivalent drugs in place of originally prescribed drug products. Selected drugs may be given preferred status by PBMs in return for cash rebates offered by pharmaceutical manufacturers.[11] Therapeutic selection works more efficiently in a closed panel program that has more control over physician prescribing.

*Dispensing Fee.* The second component of unit costs—the professional dispensing fee—is designed to cover the pharmacy's overhead expenses (that is, the "cost of dispensing") plus provide a reasonable net profit. This is a much smaller portion of the unit cost than the ingredient cost—only about 28 percent of the average pharmacy's prescription price.

Usually, PBMs do not decide on the amount that pharmacies will be reimbursed. The dispensing fee received by the pharmacy is ultimately determined by program sponsors (that is, employer groups). Employer groups obviously have strong incentives to minimize their health benefit costs, including prescription dispensing fees for pharmacists.

Although many community pharmacy managers may think that dispensing fees are too low, MCOs are not likely to increase fees significantly as long as there is an adequate network of participating pharmacies. It is often assumed that if fees were inadequate, pharmacies would not accept them. However, pharmacies choose to participate in managed care programs to cover a portion of the pharmacy's fixed costs or because they are reluctant to lose customers who may also buy non-prescription goods.

## Utilization

Another component of fee-for-service prescription drug costs is utilization. As shown in Figure 8–3, utilization is the product of "intensity" (that is, the average number of prescriptions per patient) multiplied by the "population" (that is, the total number of patients enrolled in the program). The program intensity is an important benchmark used to compare managed prescription drug plans. For example, prescription intensity is 5.8 prescriptions per person per year for HMO patients under the age of 65.[12] The utilization multiplied by the average unit cost is the total program reimbursement for prescription drugs. Controlling program intensity (or the average number of prescriptions per patient) can save more money than restricting expenditures for drug ingredients or dispensing fees.

*Drug Utilization Review.* To control intensity, most MCOs monitor drug utilization and establish program limits to reduce what they consider to be unnecessary expenditures. The process of monitoring the frequency and usage of prescription medications is known as drug utilization review (DUR). Traditional DUR programs attempt to control unnecessary overutilization of prescription drugs by avoiding duplication of therapy and reducing drug misuse and drug abuse. More advanced DUR programs use drug-specific therapeutic criteria to detect drug therapy problems such as underutilization, contraindications, and refill compliance, as well as overutilization. Review based on claims data for prescriptions that have already been dispensed is known as retrospective DUR. The primary goal of retrospective DUR is educational—to find ways in which drug therapy could be improved and to inform prescribers and dispensers accordingly.

Another type of utilization review, known as prospective DUR (pro-DUR), is conducted at the time the prescription is dispensed. Under a pro-DUR program, patients' medication records are reviewed during the dispensing process to determine the following: (1) whether the prescriptions are appropriate; (2) whether patients are taking medications properly; and (3) whether there are any drug therapy problems. Unlike retrospective DUR, a pro-DUR program is designed to prevent the misprescribing and misusage of drugs. Pro-DUR programs require electronic claims processing systems in which participating pharmacies submit claims via computers at the time prescriptions are dispensed.

*Counterdetailing.* Some MCOs participate in "counterdetailing" or "academic detailing." In this case, plans monitor physician prescribing patterns to identify those physicians who are high prescribers of costly drugs. An MCO representative (or the contracting PBM) visits targeted physicians to provide information regarding the most cost-effective use of selected drugs and to encourage physicians to prescribe in ways that will reduce overall costs while maintaining program quality.

*Patient Cost-Sharing.* Another method used to control utilization is patient cost-sharing in the form of co-payments, deductibles, or coinsurance. A co-payment is the most common form of patient cost-sharing for prescription benefits. This mechanism requires patients to pay a specified dollar amount for every prescription received (for example, $5.00 per prescription). Deductibles require patients to pay for all of their prescription expenses until a specified dollar amount has been paid out-of-pocket. For example, the prescription plan may cover prescriptions only after the patient has paid the first $200 of prescription expenses. With the expansion of on-line computerized claims processing, more programs are including deductibles. Coinsurance requires patients to pay a specified percentage (usually 20 percent) of the prescription cost whereas the MCO or PBM covers the remainder.

PBMs also provide a number of management reports to help employers analyze their costs. By examining prescribing, dispensing, and drug usage patterns, the managed care programs attempt to identify cases of unnecessary utilization or outright fraud.

### Administrative Costs

More than 95 percent of nonstaff model HMOs reduce administrative costs by requiring pharmacies to submit claims electronically.[13] By linking plans to pharmacies at the time a prescription is dispensed, these point-of-sale (POS) systems help enforce formulary compliance, prevent overutilization, and accumulate data needed for studies of plan effectiveness. Pharmacies usually incur nominal costs for each claim sent electronically. However, these costs are exceeded by the savings that result from fewer claims processing errors and bad debts, and faster payment. PMBs also save money by reducing data entry time, resulting in fewer claims processing errors.[14]

MCOs can simultaneously reduce administrative expenses and pharmacy reimbursement by contracting with fewer providers. These "closed panels" not only reduce administrative costs, but they enable the program to negotiate greater fee reductions by guaranteeing participating pharmacies increased prescription volume. Closed panels may be limited to one pharmacy, a small group of pharmacies, a chain pharmacy, a mail order pharmacy, or an HMO-owned pharmacy.

Some pharmacy organizations have developed "pharmacy services administrative organizations" (PSAOs) to make it easier for MCOs to contract with community pharmacies. PSAOs are pharmacy-sponsored PPOs that can negotiate contracts on behalf of pharmacy members. PSAOs can decrease an MCO's administrative cost by assuming responsibilities for maintaining pharmacy provider networks, processing claims, preparing management reports, and controlling drug utilization.

*Limitations of Cost Controls*

The discussion about cost controls has focused primarily on minimizing costs—dispensing fees, drug ingredient costs, administrative expenses, and utilization. However, programs that concentrate solely on reducing costs are controlling or restricting care—not managing it. On the other hand, managing the prescription benefit to optimize patient outcomes may increase drug expenditures while reducing total health expenses. Consequently, MCOs are beginning to expect pharmacists to counsel patients, monitor drug therapy, ensure proper drug utilization and, as a result, achieve positive patient outcomes. Although minimizing costs is important, the ultimate goal of MCOs should be maximizing cost-effectiveness or cost-benefit.

## EVALUATING MANAGED CARE PRESCRIPTION CONTRACTS

For pharmacy managers, the most important consideration in the evaluation of managed prescription drug programs is to determine whether the level of reimbursement is adequate. There are two ways to do this. First, the pharmacy can compare its U&C charges for a sample of private-pay prescriptions to the reimbursement that would have been received for the same prescriptions under the managed care plan. By extrapolating the sample to the expected number of managed care prescriptions, the manager can get a crude estimate of the financial impact of the managed care plan. Second, the pharmacy manager can conduct a differential analysis to determine the actual impact of the managed care plan on pharmacy profits. A differential analysis involves the following several steps: (1) calculating additional revenue (that is, differential revenue) that will accrue from participation in the managed care plan; (2) calculating additional expenses (that is, differential costs); and (3) calculating the contribution margin (that is, differential revenue minus differential costs).[15] The contribution margin is the amount of additional net profit resulting from participation in the managed care plan (or the amount that decreases the pharmacy's net loss if it has not reached its break-even point). If the contribution margin is positive, participation in the managed care plan will be profitable for the pharmacist; if it is negative, the pharmacist's participation will not be profitable.

### New Versus Established Patients

The differential costs and revenues will vary depending upon the proportion of the managed care program's beneficiaries that are new customers versus the proportion that were private-pay customers but converted to the plan. Current patients who are converted from private-pay to managed care will result in a loss of revenue (the difference between the private-pay and managed care reimbursement). This loss of revenue should be added to the additional costs incurred in dispensing the managed care prescriptions to determine the total differential cost of converting these patients from private pay to managed care.

New patients, on the other hand, will result in both additional revenue and additional expenses. When prescription volume increases, some expenses, such as bad debts and prescription vials and labels, will also increase, but to a lesser extent. The expenses that increase with additional prescription volume are known as variable costs; those that do not increase with prescription volume, such as utilities and license fees, are called fixed costs. Although most variable costs are differential costs, most fixed costs are not.

Another factor to consider is the additional over-the-counter (OTC) sales to new patients. The contribution margin from OTC sales would be the OTC sales revenue (the differential revenue) minus the sum of the cost of OTC goods sold and the variable costs incurred in selling OTCs (the differential costs). The pharmacy manager should include the contribution margin from OTC sales when determining the feasibility of participating in the managed care plan.

The pharmacy manager must consider the financial impact of not participating in the managed care plan. If the pharmacy does not participate, some current customers will be lost to competitors. The contribution margin from prescription sales and OTC sales to these patients will also be lost.

**Contract Terms**

If reimbursement is adequate, the pharmacy manager should then review the other terms of the participating pharmacy contract to determine whether they are fair. Other important factors that the manager should check include the following:

- how often the PBM pays claims;
- how often and by what method the PBM updates drug cost information in its computers;
- how program beneficiaries are identified;
- the method by which claims are submitted (that is, paper or electronic claims);
- how the PBM will audit the pharmacy's records; and
- what types of services are excluded from coverage.

Pharmacy managers must be both good managers and good clinicians to survive or prosper in the managed care environment. Increased competition requires pharmacists to know their costs and to lower them to the extent possible by managing costs and utilization efficiently. Managed care reimbursement may look more attractive if the pharmacy can reduce its costs. Computerization enhances efficiency and also makes maximum use of available patient information so that pharmacists can provide patient case management. Pharmacy managers must also reduce cost of goods sold by purchasing inventory as efficiently as possible (usually through large volume purchasing cooperatives) and by using generics as much as possible. Eventually, groups of community pharmacies, in collaborative arrangements with physicians, will establish community formularies in order to select therapeutic equivalents and alter therapeutic regimens.

**THE EVOLVING ROLE OF THE PHARMACIST**

Pharmacists must demonstrate that pharmaceutical care services have value. For example, patient counseling can improve patient compliance, which results in more favorable patient outcomes as determined by cure, alleviation of symptoms, avoidance of relapse, or decreased use and expense for other health care services. Pharmacies that provide pharmaceutical care services affecting patient outcomes (and document this value) will make themselves indispensable to MCOs.

Pharmacy managers must know their local managed care markets—especially the major employer groups and proposed changes in prescription benefit programs. They should also be prepared to document the value of their services and market these services to local employer groups (and perhaps labor unions representing employees).

Pharmacies' survival and prosperity in the managed care environment depend in part on obtaining reimbursement for cognitive services. According to Rupp, the steps involved in developing a reimbursement strategy for cognitive services include the following: (1) identifying key participants in the reimbursement decision; (2) demonstrating patient need for the service; (3) marketing to establish payer demand; (4) documenting the service-outcome link; and (5) setting prices to reflect value to the payer.[16] Reimbursement may not be easy to achieve as MCOs will pay for these services only if they are convinced that doing so is in their best interest. Several pharmacy organizations, computer companies, and managed care programs are currently attempting to develop standardized methods to pay for pharmacy interventions.[17] Providing cognitive services requires that pharmacists excel at counseling patients, monitoring therapy, conducting utilization review, ensuring compliance, and maximizing therapeutic outcomes.

## CONCLUSION

Ultimately, pharmacists will provide disease-state management, focusing first on those disease states that are most susceptible to improvement through pharmacists' interventions—such as diabetes and asthma. Pharmacies concentrating on managing one or more of these diseases are already creating market niches.[18] Later opportunities may involve disease states such as cancer, hypertension, depression, digestive diseases, and respiratory, cardiac, or circulatory problems. Greater focus on patient outcomes and cost-effectiveness will encourage pharmacists, physicians, and other health care providers to collaborate for the benefit of the patient. Hopefully, the result will be realization of the goal of optimally managed health care.

**NOTES**

1. Marion Merrell Dow, Inc. 1994. *Managed care digest.* HMO Edition. Kansas City, Mo.: Marion Merrell Dow, Inc., 33.
2. Marion Merrell Dow, Inc. 1994. *Managed care digest.* HMO Edition. Kansas City, Mo.: Marion Merrell Dow, Inc., 5.
3. Huffman, D.C. Jr. 1995. *National association of retail druggists–Lilly digest.* Alexandria, Va.: National Association of Retail Druggists, 34.
4. Cohen, K.R., and R.A. Levy. 1992. Pharmaceutical benefits: To carve or not to carve. *Journal of the American Association of Preferred Provider Organizations.* December/January, 33–35.
5. Marion Merrell Dow, Inc. 1994. *Managed care digest.* HMO Edition. Kansas City, Mo.: Marion Merrell Dow, Inc., 45.
6. Navarro, R.P. 1996. *CibaGeneva Pharmacy benefit report.* Summit, N.J.: Ciba-Giegy Corporation, 22.
7. Huffman, D.C. Jr. 1995. *National association of retail druggists–Lilly digest.* Alexandria, Va.: National Association of Retail Druggists, 39.
8. Navarro, R.P. 1994. *CibaGeneva Pharmacy benefit report.* Summit, N.J.: Ciba-Giegy Corporation, 4–5.
9. Schafermeyer, K.W., and S.D. McCann. 1992. Medicaid Task Force recommends policies on prior authorization. *Missouri Pharmacist,* 66 (January): 7–9.
10. Managed pharmacy drug expenditures. 1994. *Weekly Pharmacy Reports* 43 (October 17): 3.
11. United States General Accounting Office, Health, Education, and Human Services Division, 1995. *Pharmacy benefit managers: Early results on ventures with drug manufacturers.* Washington, D.C.: United States General Accounting Office, Health, Education, and Human Services Division, 5.
12. Marion Merrell Dow, Inc. 1995. *Managed care digest.* HMO Edition. Kansas City, Mo.: Marion Merrell Dow, Inc., 5.
13. Navarro, R.P. 1994. *CibaGeneva Pharmacy benefit report.* Summit, N.J.: Ciba-Giegy Corporation, 8.
14. Schafermeyer, K.W. 1995. Basics of managed care claims processing: From claims payment to outcomes management. *Journal of Managed Care Pharmacy* 1 (November/December): 200–205.
15. Carroll, N.V. 1991. *Financial management for pharmacists: A decision-making approach.* Philadelphia, Pa.: Lea & Febiger, 146–156.
16. Rupp, M.T. 1992. Strategies for reimbursement. *American Pharmacy* 32 (April): 79–85.
17. Winkler, C. 1994. Closer to pay day? *American Druggist* 37 (February): 37–38, 40.
18. Meade, V. 1994. Pharmaceutical care in a changing health care system. *American Pharmacy* 34 (August): 43.

# Managed Prescription Drug Benefits— Comments from the Field

*Eric Sorkin*

---

Contracting with pharmacies to develop a pharmacy network has changed dramatically over the years. Pharmacy networks have grown rapidly from their initial charter of simplifying claims administration through the submission of a common paper claim form to using computer systems to receive, track, and analyze claims, and exchange pertinent pharmaceutical care information on-line. Today's networks have a direct impact on the cost and quality of pharmaceutical care. These changes have also made the development and management of pharmacy provider networks and the overall management of pharmaceutical care more complex.

## NETWORK CONSIDERATIONS

The specific needs of the client drive the construction of the pharmacy network. The size of and access to the network usually drive the price of purchasing managed prescription drug benefits. The larger the network, the less opportunity individual pharmacy providers have in obtaining a large share of the managed care membership and the less flexible they will be on price. Conversely, the smaller the network, the greater the opportunity pharmacies will have in gaining market share and the more flexible they will be on price. Sufficient access to a network is usually measured by ZIP code density and the average member proximity to a pharmacy provider. Acceptable access standards will vary based on geographic region. For example, in urban areas, the average acceptable distance to a pharmacy provider is approximately three miles and in rural areas it is ten miles. When quantifying accessibility, one must take into account whether there is a licensed pharmacy in good standing within the required geographic area.

## KEY CONTRACT ISSUES

Among other things, pharmacies contemplating participation in a managed care program must be concerned with price, administrative procedures, and clinical guidelines.

Pricing in a fee-for-service contract arrangement is usually based on a discount from average wholesale price (AWP) for brand drugs and maximum allowable cost (MAC) for generic drugs. If a MAC price is not assigned to a specific generic chemical entity, the default price is usually a discount from AWP or the baseline price (BLP). BLP is a calculated average AWP based on a market "basket" of manufacturers. AWP and BLP are published by national sources and updated on a regular basis.

Most contracts include "lower of" language, where the price of the drug is the "lower of" the calculated price (based on the contract pricing formula) or the pharmacy's usual and customary (U&C) price to the cash-paying public. This ensures that the maximum price charged to the pharmacy benefit manager (PBM) or client is the price charged to the cash-paying consumer.

The discount from U&C price is not the main determinant in controlling costs, but rather the mix of products dispensed. Therefore, it is extremely important to structure the benefit design to maximize use of generic drugs and a drug formulary, control overall utilization, and promote member cost-sharing. For example, if the average AWP for a multi-source drug is $32.00; the ingredient cost at AWP less a 10-percent discount would be $28.80. If the discount was increased to 12-percent, the same drug would be reimbursed at $28.16. The additional 2-percent discount reduced the ingredient cost by $0.64. On the other hand, if the generic was dispensed at a MAC price of $15.60, the client would save $13.20 more than if it had been reimbursed at AWP less a 10-percent discount ($28.80 − $15.60). If the program included a $5.00 co-pay differential (lower co-pay) for the generic, the client would still have a net savings of $8.30 ($13.30 − $5.00).

Pharmacy providers differ in their ability to encourage or enforce the use of generic drugs and formularies, largely because of differences in in-house technology and training of personnel. PBMs also differ in their designation of pharmaceutical drugs as "preferred" that are used in specific therapeutic classes when there are clinically similar single-source brand products with different costs (AWPs) to choose from. The difference in the AWP between the preferred and nonpreferred products can easily offset differences in AWP discount offerings.

Beyond dispensing prescription drugs, managed care contracts usually require pharmacies to provide other services. These include verifying the eligibility of the member through the PBMs on-line adjudication system or toll-free help line, submitting all claims on-line using mutually approved standards, participating in the plan's utilization review and other programs, and complying with the drug formulary and agreements with manufacturers.

Through a drug utilization review (DUR) program or other messaging mechanism, rejected and paid claim messages will be transmitted on-line from a central database. Using the database of drugs, drug interactions, and other clinical information, the PBM can send on-line messages to the dispensing pharmacists to assist them in making professional decisions on appropriate pharmaceutical care.

## PARTNERS IN THE DELIVERY OF PHARMACY SERVICES

When providing quality pharmaceutical care through a contracted network, it is important to meet the needs of each partner in the delivery system. This includes clients, members, pharmacy providers, physicians, and pharmaceutical manufacturers. The partners may expand to include other ancillary health care professionals, such as laboratories and emergency departments.

As more data are integrated into an accessible health care database, the database can be used to assist managed care organizations and providers in the delivery and management of overall health care. There are great challenges to creating this database, including how to collect the data in a timely manner, how to verify the accuracy of the data, how to make the data available at the point of service, and how to ensure its confidentiality.

### Clients

It is extremely important that the PBM work closely with clients to identify their top priorities and goals for delivering pharmaceutical care to their members. The PBM should offer valuable and affordable products, programs, and services that assist clients in achieving these goals.

### Members

Members need to know how their pharmacy drug benefit package is structured and how to use these benefits cost-effectively. In addition, members should be able to resolve coverage and payment issues

246 OF CARE CONTRACTING

expeditiously, have questions answered timely and accurately, and locate quality, convenient pharmacy providers.

## Pharmacy Providers

Communication to the pharmacy provider explaining the structure of the benefit, what information is to be transmitted on-line, where to find the appropriate information on the member's card, and how to resolve eligibility and benefit questions is essential to quality service. This step is important to prevent a member problem at the point of sale, and to help simplify the handling of the claim for the provider, therefore limiting any unnecessary impact on the provider's cost of filling the prescription.

## Physicians

Diligent physician education on the importance of prescribing generics, formulary drugs, and preferred products is a critical step in promoting these cost-containment opportunities. Depending on the prescription drug program, either prospective, concurrent, or retrospective physician communication and education can be utilized.

## Pharmaceutical Manufacturer

Involving pharmaceutical manufacturers in physician- and member-education efforts and disease-management initiatives can be useful in better managing diseases, improving patient health outcomes, and promoting overall patient wellness.

The pharmacist is the most readily available professional on the health care team; therefore, he or she can play an integral role in the future of managed health care. With limited health care dollars, it is imperative that the pharmacist use technology and professional support to lower prescription filling costs so that he or she can perform other important professional activities at little or no additional cost.

# 9

# Dental Managed Care

*Peggy M. Vargas*
*Richard B. Ryan*

Over the last decade, the dental profession, like the medical profession ten years earlier, has experienced the emergence and rapid growth of managed dental programs. Managed dental programs now represent an all-encompassing term to define the wide variety of cost-saving alternative dental benefit products beyond indemnity or traditional fee-for-service insurance.

Managed care product designs vary widely. Each new plan design is an attempt to attract the employer, employee, patient, or purchaser of benefits. At the same time, the dental plan must offer sufficient provider compensation to attract a competent provider network. This tug of war between plan benefits and adequate provider compensation to deliver quality care has caused much emotional and heated debate.

## TYPES OF MANAGED DENTAL PROGRAMS

Although new dental benefit products emerge every week, the following represents those most commonly found in the marketplace.

### Fee-For-Service Payment

This type of program is a professional relationship between a doctor and a patient without dental benefits. A private-pay patient pays the doctor for dental services. No outside party is involved in the financing of the patients' dental care.

## Direct Reimbursement

Direct reimbursement is not an insurance product, but is a self-funding strategy that allows employers to pay dental benefits to employees by reimbursing them directly, thus eliminating insurance involvement.

## Indemnity Insurance

Presently, the most common type of dental insurance is indemnity insurance. Under this dental benefit program, the insurance plan compensates the dentist at a percentage of his or her usual and customary (U&C) fees (generally ranging from 100 to 50 percent depending upon the type of services provided). Some insurance plans pay the percentage of the customary fee to a maximum allowable for the area or region. In other words, a dental office whose fee is higher than the allowable for the area will receive the area fee percentage. The patient is responsible for the difference between the office's customary charge and the payment from the insurance plan. The percentage of coverage may vary depending upon the type of dental services, and the benefit design may include an annual maximum or patient deductibles. A patient with indemnity insurance can select any practicing dentist for his or her dental care.

## Preferred Provider Organization

In a preferred provider organization (PPO) benefit product, a dental plan (traditional insurance company or managed dental plan) negotiates discounted fees with a network of dental providers in exchange for promoting that network to the insured population of patients. Generally, these networks have some type of quality assurance or membership screening protocols. The patient has a more limited selection of dentists to select from than with the complete and total freedom of choice allowed with traditional insurance. However, PPOs often allow the patient to use nonparticipating or nonpanel dentists with some type of financial disincentive (that is, a deductible when a nonpanel dentist's services are used). As with indemnity plans, the dental office is paid by procedure at a percentage of the total fee. However, under a PPO, the plan will pay a percentage of its established fee schedule rather than a percentage of the doctor's customary fee.

## Exclusive Provider Organization

An exclusive provider organization (EPO) is similar in design to that of a PPO. The dental plan contracts with a network of dental providers at some discounted fee schedule in return for the marketing of the network to employees and insured patients. Contrary to a PPO, an EPO patient does not receive coverage for services obtained from a nonparticipating dentist. Similar to a dental HMO or capitation plan, this plan design may require the member (and member's family) to receive all his or her dental services from a selected provider office.

## Dental HMO

Also referred to as a prepaid or capitated dental program, a dental HMO compensates the dentist based on a fixed monthly fee for each member who has selected him or her as participating provider. Payment is made to the office regardless of whether the member actually seeks dental care. Generally, these programs have some requirement for patient cost-sharing including co-payments for designated dental procedures. In a dental HMO, specialists are not typically paid a capitation rate, but according to a fee schedule or a percentage of their normal fee schedule. As a general rule, there is an inverse relationship between the level of capitation and co-payments, that is, the higher the capitation rate, the lower the patient co-payments (and vice versa).

## CONSIDERATIONS FOR PARTICIPATION IN A MANAGED DENTAL NETWORK

A practitioner may decide to participate in a managed dental network if a local employer, affecting a large patient population, makes the decision to replace its indemnity insurance program with a managed care plan. Facing a potential mass exodus of existing patients, a dentist will often decide to participate in a dental network. As more employers in a geographic region offer managed dental products to employees and their dependents, more dentists will join such networks. As a result, dental networks will improve in both the quality of care delivered and the composition and size of the dental network.

A dentist should know why he or she is considering participation in a managed dental network. The following may be some of the questions to ask oneself:

- Is my fee-for-service business shrinking?
- Am I looking to expand my practice?
- Do I have empty-chair time or open-appointment time?
- Do I want new sources of patients and referrals?
- Are local employer groups shifting to managed care?

It is extremely important to understand why managed care is being considered as a practice option. Too often, a dentist will make a hasty decision to join a managed dental network because he or she thinks the practice needs to be busier. As a result, a dentist might agree to participate in a managed dental program without much thought to the specific plan design, contract terms, or compensation structure of the program. A dentist must understand that the decision to participate can represent a contractual obligation to provide patient care for up to 18 months initially. A dentist should make a decision to participate in a managed dental network based on a thoughtful evaluation of both the dental practice and the managed dental care programs under consideration.

### Excess Capacity

If the doctor's decision to integrate managed care is based upon unused or open-chair time, or the practice has decided to add an associate dentist, then the evaluation of the managed dental programs (and the associated compensation) should be based upon the ability of the dental plan to generate the highest compensation level possible for the practice. This will maximize the use of the facility and appointment schedules beyond the practice's "marginal" or "variable" costs to deliver such care.

Dentists often make the erroneous conclusion that if they are presently operating a practice at an overhead of 75 percent and they contract with a managed care program for 75 percent of their U&C fees, they will not make any money. Unfortunately, this misinformation has often been perpetuated by dental organizations. What is missing from this thinking is a common business understanding of fixed and variable costs.

### Fixed Versus Variable Costs

As in any business, there is a fixed (or defined) cost of operating a dental practice. Fixed costs, such as rent, equipment lease, and professional liability insurance are present regardless of patient volume.

Variable costs are those associated with patient volume. As the number of patients increases, these costs also increase. Variable costs include laboratory fees and dental supplies.

If a dental practice has a private patient base that fills 80 percent of the available appointment time, it has 20-percent excess capacity. The dentist does not incur additional fixed costs to fill the remaining 20 percent, unless the fixed costs consume 100 percent of his or her practice. Adding a handful of new patients a week does not require the dental office (with excess capacity) to add another treatment room or obtain a new equipment lease. The additional patient flow contributes only to the variable costs associated with the increased patient care.

The challenge to the dentist is to fill his or her office with the most profitable patient source at the lowest cost of acquisition. It is essential that today's practitioner know the cost of delivery. More specifically, he or she must be able to calculate both the fixed and variable cost of delivery. Typically, a general dentist can expect fixed expenses to consume roughly 75 percent of the total overhead, with variable expenses consisting of the remaining expenses. Specialists will generally have a lower percent of variable expense relative to total expenses.

## Differences in Managed Care Products

Capitation compensation programs differ vastly from indemnity programs, PPOs, or EPOs. Therefore, capitation plans require the consideration of other unique factors and variables when assessing the potential financial benefit (or detriment) to the dental practice.

## Patient Cost-Sharing

Originally, when dental capitation plans first emerged in the 1960s and 1970s, capitation programs included a monthly per member per month (PMPM) reimbursement or capitation, but involved little or no patient co-payments, provisions for specialty referrals, or contained provisions to exclude or limit patient benefits. In more recent years, as employers have resisted increases in their health care premiums, capitation plans have shifted more financial responsibility to patients. There has been a steady increase in co-payments as well as an expanded listing of services to which a patient co-payment applies (that is, office visit, amalgam restorations, and cleanings).

Dental HMOs are generally more competitively priced for the employer or purchaser than are PPOs. For this reason, dental HMOs have been a more attractive product purchase to employer groups historically. Therefore, capitation plans will generally produce significantly more patient volume in the dental office than PPOs or other managed dental programs. This knowledge is important for the dentist in deciding what programs he or she should be considering for their practice.

For example, a larger practice with more chairs and appointment schedules to fill may be a more suitable candidate for a capitation contract than a solo practitioner. Because these practices can accommodate a larger patient flow, capitation programs can be profitable. As in medicine, many dental group practices under capitated arrangements are beginning to look at patient care as population-based health management. Again, it is important to evaluate every program and its unique plan design carefully.

On the other hand, the more traditional solo practitioner with much less patient capacity and an existing healthy private patient base is generally not a good candidate for a dental HMO. Smaller offices are often better suited for PPO or EPO contracts. Deciding which programs are more appropriate for the practice should be best based on a review of the PPO fee schedules, how these fees compare to the office's full fees, the office's excess capacity level, and the existing variable costs of the practice.

## CAPITATION PAYMENT ISSUES

The provider contract should state that the provider will be paid by a specific date of the month for all eligible members enrolled with the dental office. There are other issues to consider with capitation payments.

### Initiation of Capitation

Does the plan pay capitation monies for all members when they enroll with the office or when the member accesses the dental office (and therefore becomes a patient)? Capitation programs should compensate the provider for all eligible members regardless of when members seek care. A capitation rate is based on the provider's assumed risk for members enrolled in the practice, regardless of whenever or even if members seek care.

## Member Eligibility

Does the plan pay capitation money after or during the month in which the patients first become eligible for treatment? Capitation plans represent pre-payments because the providers assume the risk of patient care before actual patient care. In general, a dentist should receive capitaton payment before or during the same month that care is rendered.

## Employee Premiums

Dental plans receive premium payments from employers or purchasers and, in turn, pay dentists. Some dental plans indicate that if the employer fails to make their premium payment, capitation payments to providers will be withheld for those affected members until such time that premiums are received. The dentist should either not participate in such programs or define contractually, and in advance, his or her clinical obligation to these "unpaid" members.

## PARTICIPATION GUIDELINES

Although different programs have varying participation guidelines, there are basic similarities in criteria for provider participation.

## Regulation

Managed care programs are regulated by a state insurance department or similar agency. States also have widely varying levels of regulatory scrutiny and compliance standards. Check your local state requirements and license verification before contracting with any dental program(s). Because many states do have dental plan licensing requirements, the plans, in turn, monitor the quality of care delivered by each dental provider. In many states, and under many programs, providers of managed care programs are closely scrutinized, more so than any other private dental practitioner.

## Office Reviews

Although the review process for PPOs and EPOs may vary, many do not require an on-site review of the office. Instead, they often use utilization review strategies to monitor appropriateness of care. For example, a PPO may accept only those dentists who have utilization ratios with a standard range (for example, the number of crowns to multi-surface restorations or the number of cleanings to root plannings). These utilization review organizations develop accepted community standards for utilization patterns, and then determine if significant deviations from these norms exist. Such deviations may be due to overtreatment, inaccurate billing codes, fraud, and abuse. The review is done to ensure quality of the dental care provided and to reduce costs for the purchaser.

Most capitation programs require an on-site review of the practice before they will accept the provider for participation. A typical review of a dental HMO assesses the administration, aesthetics, and management of the practice. Either as part of this initial review or in a second appointment, some plans will perform a clinical evaluation of the office, using a dentist or hygienist. This review will typically include an assessment of sterilization, Occupational Safety and Hazard Authority (OSHA) compliance, and patient charts. The reviews are called quality assurance reviews. Exhibit 9–1 illustrates a sample audit of a dental office.

The auditor will review the office to ensure that the following guidelines are met:

- facility regulatory compliance with the state or federal requirements;
- proper sterilization;
- employee and patient safety standards;
- cleanliness of practice; and
- proper and adequate level of care being both provided and documented (determined through patient chart review).

An audit can be done using a point system or a checklist (yes or no) format. During the review, any areas of concern are usually addressed with the dentist directly. The dentist will be asked to comply with the plan's recommendations for improvement. Generally, the dental program will give a practice 90 days to make the recommended changes.

**Exhibit 9–1** Sample Office Review Checklist

| **Facility Appearance** | **Findings** | |
|---|---|---|
| Cleanliness | | |
| Accessibility | | |
| Available seating | | |
| Handicap accessible | ❏ Yes | ❏ No |
| Computer system | ❏ Yes | ❏ No |
| Exit signs visible | ❏ Yes | ❏ No |
| Number of operatories—doctor, hygiene, & x-ray | | |
| Type of x-ray equipment | | |
| Ability to expand | ❏ Yes | ❏ No |
| Laboratory on the premises | ❏ Yes | ❏ No |
| After hours emergency system—answering service, machine pager, etc. | ❏ Yes | ❏ No |

| **Clinical Review** | **Findings** | |
|---|---|---|
| Sterilization | | |
| Type of sterilization procedures utilized | | |
| Storage of instruments after sterilization | | |
| Type of sterilizer | | |
| Cold sterile—How often is solution changed? | | |
| Is there a written protocol for sterilization procedures? | ❏ Yes | ❏ No |
| Are instruments cleaned prior to sterilization? | ❏ Yes | ❏ No |
| Are all instruments bagged? | ❏ Yes | ❏ No |
| Is there a monitoring system for sterilization? | ❏ Yes | ❏ No |
| Are masks and gloves worn by all clinical staff? | ❏ Yes | ❏ No |
| Is protective eyewear worn by all clinical staff? | ❏ Yes | ❏ No |

| **Radiation/X-ray** | **Findings** | |
|---|---|---|
| Are lead aprons worn? | ❏ Yes | ❏ No |
| Are cervical collars used? | ❏ Yes | ❏ No |
| Does the staff wear x-ray headgear? | ❏ Yes | ❏ No |
| How is radiation monitored? | | |
| When was equipment last serviced and/or checked? | | |

| **Mercury** | **Findings** | |
|---|---|---|
| Are premixed capsules and/or covered amalgamators used? | ❏ Yes | ❏ No |
| How is used amalgam stored (used fixer, glycerin, or commercial product)? | | |
| Does the office have nitrous and oxygen tanks? | ❏ Yes | ❏ No |
| Does the nitrous have a recovery system? | ❏ Yes | ❏ No |

*continues*

**Exhibit 9–1** *continued*

| Medical Emergencies | Findings | |
|---|---|---|
| Is there written protocol for medical emergencies? | ❏ Yes | ❏ No |
| Have all staff members been instructed in the office's emergency protocol? | ❏ Yes | ❏ No |
| Does the office have a medical emergency kit? | ❏ Yes | ❏ No |
| If yes, what is included in the kit? | | |
| Is oxygen readily available? | ❏ Yes | ❏ No |
| Are emergency phone numbers posted at all stations? | ❏ Yes | ❏ No |

| Chart Review | Findings | |
|---|---|---|
| Is medical/dental history signed by patient and treating dentist? | ❏ Yes | ❏ No |
| Is medical history comprehensive and inclusive of all required medical questions and issues? | ❏ Yes | ❏ No |
| Are medical alerts indicated on the inside and the outside of charts? | ❏ Yes | ❏ No |
| Is there a place for signature/initial for health history reviews at appropriate intervals? | ❏ Yes | ❏ No |
| Are prescriptions documented? | ❏ Yes | ❏ No |
| Are base medication and materials documented? | ❏ Yes | ❏ No |
| Are specialty referrals documented? | ❏ Yes | ❏ No |

*Source:* Courtesy of Dental Management Decisions, Lake Forest, California.

The dental practice facility should be accessible to patients and patients should be able to make office appointments easily. There should be an adequate number of incoming phone lines and parking spaces. Entrances and exits should be clearly marked and parking and ramps for handicapped patients should be in a proper location to accommodate these patients.

The office appearance will also be evaluated. It should be neat and clean in appearance. The reception area should accommodate existing and anticipated patients. The business area should be organized with adequate storage.

## Dental Provider Credentialing

As part of the review of dental providers, the dental plan will require a number of documents from each prospective dentist. This will include a current copy of the following documents:

- declaration page of the professional liability insurance;
- dental license with an expiration date;

- license through the Drug Enforcement Agency (DEA);
- specialty education certification from an accredited school (if a specialist); and
- board certification or board eligibility verification (if a specialist).

The requirements for general and professional liability insurance coverage may vary by program; however, the most commonly required coverage limits are not less than $200,000 per incident and not less than $600,000 in the aggregate. A copy of the evidence of coverage form with the effective dates and coverage amounts is also requested by the dental plan. This form should be provided throughout the term of the agreement at each renewal period of the coverage.

Increasingly, state regulators and private accrediting bodies are establishing rigid guidelines for the credentialing of health care providers. In addition, to the standard verification of credentials, dental plans are querying the National Practitioner Data Bank for any negative reports, suspensions, or malpractice suits; contacting state boards of dental examiners for any sanctions, suspensions, or a revocation of licensure; and contacting the dental schools to verify that specialty training was completed.

## Access Standards

A managed dental program will also scrutinize the dental practice's ability to service the enrolled members. Appointment availability and patient capacity are both reviewed before accepting the provider into the network. The agreement will usually stipulate appointment access standards the office must meet.

Although appointment accessibility requirements may vary by plan, it is generally acceptable for offices to accommodate patients requiring routine dental care within two to four weeks, and to provide emergency care within twenty-four hours of the initial request. The appointment availability is based on the office appointment schedule, not necessarily the patient's availability. The dental practice is also required to have twenty-four–hour telephone emergency service, such as an answering service or pager system.

## Specialty Care Guidelines

A dental specialist must have a certificate from an accredited dental school and may be either board certified or board eligible in his or her specialty. A general dentist does not typically qualify as a specialty provider, even if he or she has additional training.

Because capitation plans withhold a percentage of the premium dollar (not paid to the general dentists in capitation) to cover the cost of specialty referrals, they monitor and control specialty care costs carefully. Consequently, capitation programs specify those services that should be referred to specialists and those that fall within the scope of general dentistry (for example, a certain basic level of oral surgery, endodontics, and preliminary periodontal care). The general dentist is contractually obligated to comply with the referral guidelines of the plan. If the guidelines are not followed, the general dentist may incur financial responsibility for the care rendered. A prospective provider should review carefully the specialty referral guidelines in a capitated program to ensure that he or she is comfortable with the services considered within the scope of general dentistry.

Generally, PPO programs have less restrictive specialty referral protocols. A participating specialist in a PPO or EPO network is usually paid at a reduced "specialty fee schedule," a percentage of his or her U&C fees, or according to the same fee schedule of the participating or general dentist. A patient may seek the care of a participating or nonparticipating specialist without prior approval from a general dentist or dental program. The dental program may require a prior treatment authorization, and/or impose limitations of dental benefits, as is typically the procedure for indemnity plans.

## THE DENTAL PROVIDER CONTRACT

When a dentist makes the decision to become a contracted provider for any type of managed dental program, the contract should be reviewed carefully. The contracting dentist must understand what his or her obligations are as a participating provider. There are termination clauses, hold-harmless clauses, specialty referral guidelines, appointment accessibility requirements, as well as an outline of fee schedules and dental plan products the dentist is obligated to accept. Exhibit 9–2 outlines some questions dentists should ask when reviewing provider contracts.

### Termination Provisions

In any provider contract, there is specific language concerning the termination of the contract by the parties. These provisions outline

**Exhibit 9-2** Ten Questions To Ask In Reviewing A Dental Contract

1. What is the termination notification period? Is there a one year waiting period before contract termination is permitted?
2. Does the dental plan allow the provider to close the practice to new enrollment? If so, what is the notification period?
3. Is there a "hold-harmless" clause? If so, how is it structured?
4. Are there state licensing requirements for managed dental programs or dental insurance programs? If so, does the plan under consideration meet those requirements?
5. Does the provider contract allow the plan to add new programs without the prior approval of the dental provider?
6. What are the required insurance liability coverage amounts? Does the practice meet these requirements?
7. Can the practice refer patients for specialty care without additional financial obligation or penalty?
8. Can the practice meet the appointment accessibility requirements of the plan?
9. If a capitation program, what are the specific terms of the capitation arrangements?
10. Is there a provider income guarantee or stop-loss protection included in the provider agreement?

how, under what conditions, and with what specific notification period the parties may terminate association with each other. Some dental plans have termination clauses that require a dentist to participate as a provider for a minimum of one year before he or she may terminate the contract. More commonly, contracts specify that either party may terminate without cause upon advanced written notice of some designated period. The termination notification period will vary from contract to contract, but is often 60 to 90 days.

The advance notice allows the dental plan sufficient time to remove the name of the dentist(s) from the existing provider listings, and when necessary, to transfer enrolled members to another dental provider office. During the interim termination period, the dental office remains responsible for the treatment of existing members enrolled in the practice, as well as any new members who may be assigned or become eligible for care during the transition period. (As a general rule, most dental plans will attempt to prevent any new members from enrolling into the terminating [or terminated] practice.) The dental office should notify the patient of the pending termination so that the patient can transfer to another provider for care.

## Hold-Harmless Clause

Initially, when dental managed care provider agreements were drafted, many contained language that was favorable for the dental plan. Such language usually held the dental provider responsible for the care of the member and the dental plan was "held harmless" for any acts, omissions, or errors that the plan made.

Today, most of these hold-harmless clauses have been modified to make each party responsible for its own actions; or, in other contracts, these hold-harmless clauses have been entirely removed from the provider contracts.

## Benefit Plan Design

In addition to reviewing the contract language carefully, a dentist should evaluate the benefit plan design. The plan design includes the fee schedules; patient co-payment, coinsurance, and deductible requirements; capitation rates (when applicable); program exclusions and limitations; anticipated membership and patient bases; and program underwriting guidelines.

A recent phenomenon is a plan design structure for capitation plans that is commonly referred to as LEPEAT. A LEPEAT benefit structure stands for the least expensive, professionally ethical, acceptable treatment. This plan benefit is not intended to limit the doctor's professional obligation to diagnose and treat members comprehensively. In an attempt to offer employers competitive premiums, some plans are limiting and defining the scope of coverage to deliver a reasonable level of compensation to the provider dentist. An example of payment under a LEPEAT benefit design is illustrated in Exhibit 9–3. The patient accesses the dental office for care, and the doctor diagnoses the need for a five-unit fixed bridge. In the opinion of the dentist, this is the ideal (or optimum) level of care. However, under the LEPEAT definition of the patient's coverage, the plan will cover a partial denture. The partial denture will address the patient's present condition and restore him or her to good health.

If the member opts for the covered treatment, his or her financial responsibility is the co-payment amount of $210. If the member opts for the optimal treatment, his or her financial obligation increases to $1,985. Whatever the decision by the doctor and patient, the dental plan's obligation remains simply the monthly capitation payment for this and all other enrolled members.

**Exhibit 9–3** Payment for Optimal and Covered Treatments

| | |
|---|---:|
| Optimal Treatment-UCR Fee for 5-Unit Fixed Bridge | $2,750.00 |
| Covered Treatment-UCR Fee for Partial Denture | – 975.00 |
| Difference | 1,775.00 |
| Patient Co-payment for Covered Treatment | + 210.00 |
| Total Fee for Optimal Treatment (Difference + Copayment) | $1,985.00 |

*Source:* Courtesy of Dental Management Decisions, Lake Forest, California.

## Underwriting Guidelines

The underwriting guidelines of the dental plan are another important variable when considering the potential financial benefit of a capitation plan. These guidelines establish to whom, under what circumstances, and at what premium level a dental plan will be sold. These guidelines can work to the benefit or detriment of the participating provider.

For example, some dental HMOs will sell their capitation programs only to employer groups that have had previous dental coverage. This protects the provider from the high costs of treating patients with extreme dental needs. This is under a fixed income capitation program. More patients in a better state of oral health will lessen the provider's risk of maintaining the total patient population's oral health.

Some plans will sell their capitation plan only to employer groups that cover 100 percent of the premium, and all employees participate. Again, this type of employer coverage lessens the financial risk for the capitated provider dentist.

Many dental programs are now selling HMO plans to individuals directly, including those who do not have dental care coverage through an employer. In many cases, these individuals are purchasing HMO coverage because of an existing need for dental services. This type of patient typically requires the most care. Moreover, because they have paid for such coverage out of their own pockets, these patients are frequently demanding. Considering such guidelines is probably one of the most significant issues surrounding an evaluation of a capitation program.

### Enrollment

Another area that is important in the evaluation of a dental HMO program is the potential membership the plan will generate for the practice. If the program is assuming dental coverage for a local employer group that represents a significant share of the practice's patient base, the practice may decide to participate in the plan to keep these existing patients.

A plan with no current patient enrollment poses a much higher financial risk for the dental provider. Under a capitated program, any patient utilization for a practice with a small enrollment can be costly, relative to the limited income (that is, capitation) that the office is receiving. In situations like this, the office should negotiate with the plan for some type of "safety net" or guarantee. (Safety net reimbursement is discussed in the supplemental payment section of this chapter.)

A dental plan may want to transfer or assign a block of patients to the dental practice. This is sometimes the most desirable option for the provider. It gives the dentist a patient base and a reasonable capitation payment to offset patient care costs. It is important for the dental office to accommodate the anticipated increase in patient flow without displacing their existing patient population. Assuming that the transferred block of patients has not been without access to dental care and does not have excessive dental needs as a result, the dental office can anticipate that approximately 10 percent of the enrolled population will seek dental care services per month. For example, if the office accepted a transfer of approximately 1,000 eligible members, the dental office might expect 100 to 120 additional appointment visits per month.

## CONTRACT NEGOTIATIONS

Can a dentist negotiate with a dental plan for higher compensation? Maybe. Depending on the dental plan's need for providers in specific geographic areas, the dentist may be able to negotiate supplemental (or safety net) payments.

The ability of a dentist to negotiate such arrangements has little to do with the specifics of the dental practice, but everything to do with basic supply and demand. As with any business, the higher the demand, and the more limited the supply, the higher the price. If a dentist is located in a marketplace with few or no competitors, he or she is likely to negotiate favorable compensation terms. Conversely, if there is an ample pool of available providers in the dental community, it is possible that no supplemental payments can be negotiated.

## Safety Net Payments

In certain geographic locations, dental programs have agreed to compensate the dentist at a higher rate to secure a strong provider network for members. A safety net is offered by some dental plans that think there is a temporary (or longer) need to assist the office financially. A safety net is a guarantee not to let the office compensation fall below a previously agreed-upon compensation level.

Safety net payments can be defined loosely as a minimum provider income guarantee paid in a variety of forms, including the following: monthly, relative value unit (RVU), or hourly guarantees; a minimum capitation payment at a higher-than-standard capitation rate; supplemental payments; or a guaranteed reimbursement level (usually equal to or greater than a percentage of the doctor's U&C fee level). Safety nets are offered by dental HMOs principally, because in PPOs or EPOs, the dentist is accepting little financial risk.

## Relative Value Unit or Hourly Guarantees

In the last few years, managed care organizations (MCOs) have attempted to move away from fee-for-service reimbursement (or fee-for-disease) toward compensating doctors based on the time required to deliver patient care. RVUs, or hourly doctor compensation, have become an accepted formula for this type of reimbursement.

An RVU represents 15 minutes of a doctor's time to deliver patient care. Four RVUs are worth one hour of doctor time. This form of compensation is an effective way for dentists to compare income from a variety of referral sources. For example, regardless of the patient dental program, a crown may be worth seven RVUs, a one-surface amalgam one and a half RVUs, and a denture twelve RVUs.

As a safety net payment, dental plans more frequently now offer a guarantee of a specified RVU value (or doctor hourly income level). An example of this type of RVU guarantee calculation is illustrated in Exhibit 9–4. The plan may guarantee $20 per RVU or $80 per doctor hour. If a dentist's income falls below this guarantee level, the plan will pay a "supplemental check" or safety net to cover the difference and the provider's financial risk.

## Minimum Monthly Guarantees

A second type of HMO provider compensation is the monthly income guarantee. This type of arrangement is seen often when a

**Exhibit 9–4** RVU Guarantee

| | |
|---|---:|
| Total Monthly Capitation Payments | $6,550.00 |
| Total Patient Payments | 2,900.00 |
| Supplement Payments | 235.00 |
| Total Office Income | $9,685.00 |
| Total Chair Hours of Reported Treatment | 178 |
| Total Dollars per Chair Hour Received | $54.41 |
| Plan Guarantee=$80 per Chair Hour | |

Guaranteed chair hour compensation is $80.00 per chair hour. In this example, the difference between the income received and the guaranteed income is $25.59 per chair hour. The difference ($25.59) multiplied by the number of chair hours reported (178) results in an additional payment of $4,555.02 from the plan.

This is a typical formula used to determine any additional payments due from a plan to cover the chair hour guarantee negotiated. The chair hours are determined from the number of relative value units (RVUs) reported to the plan. RVU values vary from 10–15 minutes per unit. In this example, the units are based on 15 minutes of provider time, using a total of 712 reported units.

*Source:* Courtesy of Dental Management Decisions, Lake Forest, California.

dental program has no enrollment but needs providers to market their dental program. Moreover, this type of compensation is popular because it is easy for both parties to administer. The plan will pay a flat monthly fee or capitation check to the dentist regardless of his or her membership enrollment. The fee is paid monthly until the enrollment grows to where the capitation rates for the actual membership exceed the monthly guarantee. An office agreeing to a monthly guarantee is then protected with the additional capitation from the financial risk if those few enrolled members do access the office and have any significant level of dental care need. The guaranteed amount will be negotiated based on the plan's need in the area. The monthly guarantee will usually be offered for a limited period. For instance, the plan may agree to pay the dentist a flat fee of $1,000 to $2,500 a month for six months or until enrollment exceeds the guaranteed capitation payment level. This agreement will terminate at the end of six months or may be renegotiated at that time.

## Adjusted Capitation Rates

A third type of compensation is an upward adjustment to the member capitation rates. For example, if the dental provider expects to receive low initial membership enrollment (that is, less than 100 insured members), then the dental plan may agree (rather than to pay the standard product capitation rate, a rate that may range from $5 to $7 PMPM) to pay $10 PMPM.

The purpose is again to offset some of the provider risk. For example, if the provider had only 50 members and, in the first month, ten of these show up for dental care, the dentist under a standard capitation rate of $5.50 per month would receive only $275 (plus patient co-pays) for the treatment of these patients. This would equal a per-appointment income level of just $27.50 (plus co-pays). If a $10 adjusted capitation rate per member were in place, the total capitation would equal $500 and $50 per visit.

This compensation formula is a good tool for a dental office that has some membership enrollment but needs additional compensation to make the program economically viable. With this type of agreement, as the plan membership slowly grows within the dental office, so does the capitation income at a higher level than the standard product capitation rate.

This type of provider negotiation is frequently used for an office that has been a provider with the plan for some limited time period, and is renegotiating their contract because of the financial risk (or loss) that they have experienced.

## Supplemental Payments

Supplemental payments are payments made by the dental plan for specific procedures in addition to a patient's fees or co-payments. The dental office would charge the patient only the designated co-payment fee; however, in addition to, for example, a $180 patient co-payment for a crown, the dental plan would agree to pay the dental office an additional or supplemental co-payment of $120. The dental office then would effectively receive $300 for the delivery of any crown.

This type of compensation arrangement is often more popular with dentists than that of a flat or upgraded capitation rate. Dentists still frequently feel more comfortable regarding their reimbursement as on a fee-for-service or per-procedure basis. Many dentists have been slow to understand or digest an income evaluation based upon time (that is, capitation reimbursement) and feel much more comfortable negotiating procedure fee rates. This type of compensation is more closely aligned with the traditional indemnity compensation structure.

It should be pointed out that although supplemental plan co-payments are popular with dentists, these arrangements are not necessarily the best or most lucrative for the dentist. Such agreements depend upon which procedures include supplemental compensation, what the utilization rate of these procedures are, and the level of compensation "supplement" for such procedures. For instance, dental plans will frequently offer reimbursement for laboratory costs on all prosthetics. This is, of course, reasonable as long as the co-payments and the dental program as a whole are profitable. However, an office frequently does much fewer lab processed procedures than they do diagnostic, preventive, or basic restorative procedures. So, if the dental plan cannot or is not covering this type of dentistry profitably, then an additional supplemental lab payment on prosthetics is not going to make the plan any more viable for the dental practice.

If, on the other hand, the supplemental payments are set to cover other more common procedures, this would have a much more positive financial benefit to the dental provider office. For example, there are plans that may pay a supplemental $6 per patient visit fee for sterilization and OSHA compliance costs. Other programs may have guaranteed supplemental reimbursement for periodontal care, endodontics, and even prosthetic care. These latter examples are often more beneficial because of the frequency with which such procedures are typically performed in the dental office.

Again, such income-versus-frequency calculations are important and should not be considered half-heartedly. These are important business considerations. The office should be computerized and able to track their procedure utilization so as to accurately evaluate the impact of these reimbursement formulas.

## Percent of UCR Agreements

Another contract negotiation option that is often used in dental communities where there is less managed care and therefore less experience with evaluating these compensation formulas is that of a simple agreement to guarantee the dentist income of at least a certain percentage of his or her UCR fees. It is much like a guarantee of a PPO or fixed-fee level. Simply put, the dentist and dental plan are agreeing to an acceptable per-procedure discount to his or her U&C fees.

This type of arrangement is frequently more palatable for dentists unfamiliar with managed care because they have worked with and understand payment by insurance companies at percentage of UCR fees for many years. The percentage of full fee (or percentage of discount) is negotiated and the plan will frequently factor into these negotiations the additional administrative work required to track and reimburse these payment claims for services. This PPO type of reimbursement arrangement is not affected by membership enrollment. Income is solely based upon utilization of dental care services. If the dental office has no patient utilization, the dentist will not receive any income (this is, of course, different from a capitation plan design).

As managed care grows in a community, more dentists are impacted, and, as the patient bases in these practices are impacted, more dentists become interested in participating. For example, in Los Angeles County where nearly 40 percent of the dental coverage is now managed care, there are as many as 1,200 dentists on a "waiting list" to become a provider. Obviously, in this situation, provider contract negotiations are not possible.

## CONCLUSION

Managed care is not a disease, but a symptom of a changing and competitive health care environment. And dentistry, like medicine, has been forever changed in the process. The integration of managed care into the dental practice can be a successful and profitable endeavor if done with knowledge of the available options. If and when dentists make the decision to participate with managed dental plans, it is vital that they continually monitor the effects such programs have on the practice's profitablity and ability to deliver quality care. If dentists do not monitor their managed care programs, they cannot be managing their patients and profitability appropriately. A dental practice should manage managed care.

# Dental Managed Care—
# Comments from the Field

*Ross Wetsel*

---

Contracting with managed care organizations (MCOs) has been an evolving project for our seven-doctor group. Although we have learned a great deal, we know we will need to master new skills in the years to come. We believe dentistry is undergoing dramatic and irreversible change that will cause great pain for those who are unable to adapt.

## SOLO VERSUS GROUP PRACTICE

Before we heard the term "managed care," we had already committed to the concept of a group dental practice because we believed a great deal of inefficiency existed in solo practices, especially in the area of cost containment. Seven dentists do not need seven x-ray developers, seven copiers, seven computer systems, or seven separate staffs. One of each is sufficient, provided we can learn to work together successfully. There are more than 40 dentists within a two-mile area around our office, all operating independently. Although this is the traditional structure for dental practices, it is not efficient. There is tremendous duplication of resources, as well as underutilization of facilities, equipment, and personnel.

Our traditional dental culture is responsible for the belief held by many dentists that practicing solo affords us the most freedom, power, and control. However, if we examine the situation honestly we will find this interpretation to be a myth. Unfortunately, it is the inability of dentists to work together that will cause their loss of power and income more than the method of reimbursement they receive for their services.

## OUR PHILOSOPHY

We do not think all dentists should practice in groups, any more than all physicians, attorneys, or accountants should; however, we believe working as an organization is an excellent way to meet the challenges of a competitive marketplace. In the past, dentists who owned and operated solo practices could sustain a healthy revenue. Today, the system favors organizations.

We are better able to control our destiny as a group. It enables us to take action, rather than be acted upon. If we did not develop our own successful organization, we feared we might end up working for an organization that would dictate our financial future, or worse, determine the quality and nature of our work.

When our group was formed in 1984, we went to work on the issue of cost containment immediately. In working together, we each gave up a degree of autonomy, but collectively we are more insightful and more intelligent than we could possibly be individually. The results have been exceptional.

It has been our experience that fee-for-service dentistry is not the only way to deliver quality care. There is absolutely no difference in the level of care we provide to our patients, regardless of the method of payment we receive. We would consider it immoral to sign a contract to provide dental care to a group of patients, then give them less than our highest level of care. This is a core value of the organization and a shared vision to which we are all committed.

## BUSINESS STRATEGY

We attribute our current professional achievements to our decision, several years ago, to work toward containing our costs, improving our efficiency, and developing a sophisticated computer system to monitor our results. Today, understanding how to operate effectively is as important as negotiating a favorable contract.

The main interest of an MCO is to offer a health care product employers will purchase. The dentist, not the MCO, is responsible for the success of his or her practice. The successful practitioner of the future must be more than a good clinician. In years past, dentists did not have to operate in a highly competitive business environment. Certainly, our training in dental school has done little to develop strong management skills. In today's changing market, we need to acquire these abilities ourselves or hire an individual or organization to supplement our skills.

Along with cost containment and quality improvement, an equally important part of our strategy has been the creation of a position known as "owner-administrator." Physician groups and hospitals have relied on qualified executives to manage their organizations for years. In dentistry, the administrative responsibility is usually handled by the dentist, with help from a dental assistant. Today, there are excellent dental administrators who have received formal education and training. This is a valuable new asset to our profession. Even though our group has developed confidence and experience in managed care contracting and have established a proven track record, we are more successful in achieving favorable contract terms when using the services of a professional consultant, our administrator, or, ideally, both.

Another important responsibility of our administrator is to maintain open channels of communication with the MCOs with whom we have chosen to work. This does not come naturally. Historically, dentists have regarded MCOs and health plans as a mortal enemy.

Our administrator has helped move us toward successful integration with the MCOs and health plans. We believe collaboration is critical to the future of our practice.

## CHALLENGES

Dentists who cannot operate a highly efficient and profitable fee-for-service practice should not attempt to enter into managed care contracts. If a dentist does not have the necessary business skills to succeed in a fee-for-service environment, he or she will not be able to manage the unfamiliar risks associated with managed care.

We believe both the dentists and MCOs need to move away from a "command and control" attitude. Collectively, we should strive to achieve cost savings for those paying the premiums, satisfaction for dental practitioners, and improved quality of care for patients.

Strategic partnerships with MCOs are the essence of the contracting process. We have succeeded in developing successful partnerships with certain MCOs because we have demonstrated that we are capable of delivering the level of care we have promised, and have fulfilled our contractual obligations with integrity and clinical efficiency. As a result, we have developed a mutual trust and an acceptance from the MCOs that we are a valuable partner. Once we proved ourselves and established a track record, it has not been difficult to develop additional relationships with MCOs willing to treat us fairly and with respect. As we continue to evolve as an organization with more dentists joining us, we will become more skillful in developing these important partnerships.

# 10

# Regulation of Managed Care Contracting

*John Hoff*

The contractual arrangements between a managed care organiza-tion (MCO) and providers are affected by a complex overlay of regulatory controls. These are imposed by the federal government and by state governments. The regulations vary greatly among the states, and different regulations are applicable to different types of plans. Therefore, rather than describe what regulations are relevant to a specific plan, this chapter will describe the kinds of government regulation that may affect negotiations between MCOs and their providers. This will serve as a notice of potential issues that should be examined in more depth in the context of a particular plan.

## SOURCES OF REGULATION

Federally qualified health maintenance organizations (HMOs), "com-petitive medical plans" that have a contract with the U.S. Department of Health and Human Services (DHHS) to provide care to Medicare beneficiaries, MCOs that serve Medicaid recipients, and plans pro-vided to employees by their employers are subject to regulation by the federal government and state governments. The relationship between federal regulation and the regulation of any state is complicated. In some cases, both sets of regulations apply; in others, only the federal regulation (or certain parts of the federal regulation) applies. The applicable regulation and the identity of the regulator depend on the type of MCO, the nature of its sponsor, whether it is exempt from taxation, and whether it assumes the financial risk for providing covered care.

Managed care plans that are provided by employers (other than governments) are subject to federal law in the form of the Employee Retirement Income Security Act (ERISA). ERISA regulation is limited to reporting and disclosure requirements, fiduciary obligations, denials of claims, and certain narrowly targeted requirements concerning benefits and continuation of coverage. At the same time, ERISA preempts—and thus makes ineffective—any state law that "relates to" the employer's health benefit plan (even if there is no comparable federal regulation). This preemption does not apply to state laws that "regulate insurance." In general, a state law has been found to regulate insurance if it is limited to insurance and does not apply to other financing and delivery mechanisms. In addition to whatever federal regulation is applicable, a state law that "regulates insurance" applies to the plan.

A two-step analysis is necessary to determine whether a state regulatory requirement governs the plan that an employer offers: Does the state law relate to a health benefit plan? If it does, is it a law that (exclusively) regulates insurance? The answer to these questions in most cases is not clear, and the issue is the subject of frequent litigation. Therefore, it often is not possible to know whether a plan will be subject to a particular state regulation. In general, employer "self-insured" plans are free of state regulation.

If an employer operates its own plan or pays an MCO for the health care costs of its employees as they are incurred, the plan is self-insured. But if the employer's plan capitates the providers or otherwise puts them at financial risk, the state could regulate the plan as insurance. If the employer "rents" a plan by paying it to provide care to its employees, it may be a self-insured plan, depending on how the employer's payment to the plan is determined: Is it based on the employer's prior year's experience, or is it based on current costs? The latter is more likely to be considered self-insurance. But, if the plan also serves other enrollees on a prepayment basis, it will be at least to that extent an insured plan and subject to applicable state law.

A separate question is whether a plan that purchases stop loss coverage can be considered a self-insured plan. This question has not been resolved. Stop loss coverage does not insure the beneficiaries; it limits the exposure of the plan sponsor. Therefore, according to one theory, stop loss protection may not constitute insurance; however, according to another theory, it is insurance.

This combination of factors will determine what regulation affects a plan's agreements with its providers.

## ANY WILLING PROVIDER LAWS

Various state laws determine whom an MCO must include in its panel of participating providers. There is no federal law mandating that particular types of providers be included in managed care networks.

A plan providing services to Medicaid beneficiaries will be subject to requirements in state Medicaid law, the terms of a federal waiver, or the agreement between the state and the MCO to include certain types of providers. Typically, these do not require that all providers be included, but may require that certain types needed by Medicaid beneficiaries be included, such as substance abuse providers.

States have enacted a wide variety of Any Willing Provider (AWP) laws. These require the MCO to permit any facility or provider that meets the standards of the MCO to participate on the same terms as others. Some AWP laws apply only to certain types of providers and facilities or only to certain types of MCOs (for instance, preferred provider organizations [PPOs] or, even more specifically, insurer-sponsored PPOs). Or the law may apply only if the MCO captures more than a specified share of the market (leaving what is thought to be an insufficient amount of potential business for the providers who are not included in the MCO).

A 1996 survey conducted by the American Association of Health Plans (AAHP) found that 24 states had enacted AWP requirements. Figure 10–1 profiles AWP laws on a state-by-state basis. Twenty-two of these states applied the AWP requirement only to PPO or insurer-based provider networks, and seventeen applied them to HMOs (in some cases, with exceptions for certain types of HMOs, staff or group model HMOs, or HMOs that are federally qualified).

A variant of AWP legislation is freedom of choice (direct access) laws. These are designed to make it possible for enrollees to go outside the network and choose their own physician (often these laws apply only to particular types of providers, such as obstetricians and gynecologists). The laws limit the ability of an MCO to have financial or other barriers (such as requiring higher co-payments) for a member who obtains care from nonplan providers. In another approach, at least one state protects existing patient-physician relationships for a period even if the physician has joined a different MCO.

AWP legislation straddles the fault line of managed care. MCOs often limit the number of providers who can participate and then channel members to these select number of providers. AWP legisla-

| STATE | AWP PROVISION | STATE | AWP PROVISION |
|---|---|---|---|
| Alabama | ●❑ | Montana | |
| Alaska | | Nebraska | |
| Arizona | | Nevada | |
| Arkansas | ○●❑■ | New Hampshire | ○❑ |
| California | | New Jersey | ○●❑ |
| Colorado | | New Mexico | |
| Connecticut | | New York | |
| Delaware | ○●❑ | North Carolina | ○●❑ |
| District of Columbia | | North Dakota | ●❑ |
| Florida | ‡ | Ohio | |
| Georgia | ●■/‡ | Oklahoma | |
| Hawaii | | Oregon | |
| Idaho | ○●❑■ | Pennsylvania | |
| Illinois | ●■ | Rhode Island | |
| Indiana | ●❑■ | South Carolina | ○●❑ |
| Iowa | | South Dakota | ○●❑ |
| Kansas | | Tennessee | |
| Kentucky | ○●❑■ | Texas | ○●❑/●■ |
| Louisiana | ○●❑/●■ | Utah | ●■ |
| Maine | | Vermont | |
| Maryland | | Virginia | ●■ |
| Massachusetts | ○●❑ | Washington | |
| Michigan | | West Virginia | |
| Minnesota | ○●❑■ | Wisconsin | ○●❑ |
| Mississippi | ○●❑ | Wyoming | ○●❑■ |
| Missouri | | | |

**Figure 10–1** State "Any Willing Provider" (AWP) Laws. *Note:* This chart is intended only to provide a brief overview of state laws, and is not intended as a substitute for review of the actual laws. *Source:* Courtesy of American Association of Health Plans, Washington, D.C.

Key: ○ = Law applies to HMOs
● = Law applies to PPOs and other similar networks
❑ = Law affects pharmacy/pharmacists
■ = Law affects entities other than pharmacy
‡ = AWP law does not fit into above categories
/ = In states with more than one AWP law, a "slash" is used to separate them

tion limits a plan's ability to choose its panel of providers by preventing it from controlling the number or composition of participating providers. AWP laws also impact an MCO's ability to negotiate discounts with providers; if the MCO has an excessive number of providers, it cannot guarantee each one the number of patient visits necessary for the provider to grant a discount. At the same time, AWP laws also limit the need for a provider to negotiate fees or conditions of utilization because he or she is guaranteed inclusion in the provider network by the law. And AWP legislation impedes MCOs' efforts to differentiate themselves on the basis of their participating providers; the nature of the MCO is determined by the providers that present themselves for inclusion, rather than the decisions of the plan.

There is significant uncertainty regarding whether an AWP or similar laws are legally effective when applied to an employer-provided plan. Depending on the nature of the plan to which it applies, the AWP law may be preempted by ERISA. If the plan is provided by a nongovernmental employer and is self-insured, the AWP law is almost certain to be preempted by federal law. If the plan is not self-insured, the issue is more complex; preemption, as discussed before, is determined by whether the state law regulates insurance. If it does, the state law is saved from the federal preemption. Finally, an AWP requirement may be preempted by federal law if the plan is a federally qualified HMO.

## GAG RULE

MCOs often include in their agreements with providers language that prohibits the provider from communicating with patients in a way that could undermine confidence in the MCO. This may include requiring the participating provider to maintain the confidentiality of plan guidelines, procedures, and compensation arrangements. These contractual provisions have been generically characterized as "gag rules." Generally, the MCOs' contractual demands for physician confidentiality are limited to matters the MCO deems proprietary. They are not intended to prevent physicians from discussing treatment procedures the physician believes are appropriate for patients.

A number of states are considering or have enacted "anti-gag rule" legislation. These laws prevent the MCO from including such a provision in its contract with providers or from terminating a provider who violates it. In one state, for instance, the law provides that an MCO "shall not refuse to contract with or compensate for covered services an otherwise eligible provider or nonparticipating provider solely because such provider has in good faith communicated with one or more of his or her current, former, or prospective patients regarding the plan." Another state forbids a plan to include a provision that prohibits a provider from discussing treatment alternatives with enrollees, and other issues that pertain to the provider-patient relationship, appeals, coverage determinations, and public policy issues.

The AAHP itself has issued guidelines for MCOs that discourage the inclusion of gag rules in provider contracts. "Health plans encourage full and open communication between physicians and patients about patients' health care. Health plans, by contract and policy, will not prohibit physicians from communicating with patients concerning medical care, medically appropriate treatment options (whether covered or not), or from making factual and nonproprietary statements regarding the plan."

The federal government is also considering its own form of anti-gag rule legislation. In 1996, Congress considered a bill that would prevent a plan, in its contract with a provider or by written or oral communications, from restricting any "medical communication" by the provider. A "medical communication" in the proposed bill was defined as a communication between the provider and patient "with respect to the patient's physical or mental condition or treatment options." Thus, a plan would have been prohibited from preventing a physician from discussing a possible treatment with a patient even if the plan did not consider the treatment appropriate and would not pay for it. The bill contained one limited exception. A plan could prevent a provider from recommending another plan if the sole purpose of the communication would be to financially benefit the provider. The bill provided civil money penalties for violations. More importantly, any contractual provision (or communication) that violated the bill would be null and void, and thus the plan could not sanction the provider for not heeding it. The federal legislation would not have interfered with state laws. A state could impose restrictions that were more protective of medical communications. This provision was not enacted in the last Congress, but will be considered again in 1997.

Even without federal legislation, steps have been taken by the federal government to restrict the application of gag rules. In December 1996, the Health Care Financing Administration (HCFA) announced its position that existing federal law makes it unlawful for managed care plans providing care to Medicare beneficiaries to "prevent physicians from providing information to patients regarding all medically necessary treatment plans." This position was based on the law governing managed care plans under Medicare. According to HCFA, this provides that Medicare beneficiaries of managed care plans "are entitled to the same benefits that they would be entitled to under standard fee-for-service Medicare." HCFA has issued a similar interpretation of the law governing MCOs that provide care under Medicaid.

## CRITERIA AND PROCESS FOR SELECTION AND DE-SELECTION

The "due process" system that has developed to govern physician membership on hospital medical staffs generally does not apply to contractual relationships between MCOs and participating providers, although some states may enact legislation requiring certain processes. Federal law provides one exception. An HMO can be exempt from liability for damages (other than for civil rights violations) resulting from a peer review action against one of its participating physicians on the basis of his or her professional competence if it applies a process similar to hospital medical staff due process hearings.

Contracts between providers and MCOs typically provide for termination with or without cause. This is standard in contracts in other sectors of the economy. However, in a few instances, courts have refused to enforce the clause permitting termination without cause. In one case, the court held that the clause must be applied with good faith and fair dealing. It said that the relationship between plan and physician deserves the "same sort of special consideration as those between husbands and wives, lawyers and clients, and clergy and parishioners." Other courts have rejected this approach.

The National Association of Insurance Commissioners (NAIC) has adopted a Health Care Professional Credentialing Verification Model Act for consideration by the individual states. This would set standards for plans' credentialing activities. In any state that adopted it, MCOs would be required to do the following:

- establish policies and procedures for verifying the credentialing of participating providers before contracting with them (and every three years thereafter);
- make those policies available for review by health care professionals applying to participate in the plan; and

- establish a committee of health care professionals to make decisions regarding verification of credentials.

The plan would also be required to obtain primary verification of a number of credentialing facts, including the following:

- current license and certificate authority;
- current level of liability insurance coverage; and
- status of hospital privileges.

In addition, MCOs could obtain verification of the applicant's license, and malpractice and professional history. MCOs would be required to give the health care professional an opportunity to review and correct credentialing verification information.

## PROVIDER COMPENSATION

Regulatory requirements affect the way MCOs may compensate their providers. Generally, these regulations attempt to prevent compensation arrangements from influencing how and when physicians refer patients to specialists.

### Underutilization of Specialists

Some states have imposed regulations to restrict compensation arrangements that they fear give plan physicians an incentive to refer to specialists less than is considered appropriate. For instance, they may prohibit certain MCOs from varying compensation to providers based on the MCO's ability to meet certain financial goals (either by withhold mechanisms or bonuses). Other states require that incentive compensation arrangements be disclosed to patients. In addition, guidelines issued by the AAHP suggest that MCOs should, on request, give members a "summary description of how participating physicians are paid, including financial incentives (disclosure of specific details of financial arrangements should not be required)."

The most detailed regulation of providers' compensation arrangements with MCOs is the federal law prohibiting MCOs from operating physician incentive plans (PIPs) unless they meet certain standards. This law applies to compensation arrangements of federally qualified

HMOs and prepaid health care organizations providing care to Medicare or Medicaid beneficiaries if the PIP may "directly or indirectly have the effect of reducing or limiting services provided."

The law prohibits an MCO from giving a financial inducement to a physician to limit or reduce medically necessary services for any individual enrollee. Further, the MCO must disclose to HCFA or to the state Medicaid agency information about its physician incentive arrangements to enable the agencies to monitor MCO compliance with the law.

If the PIP puts physicians at financial risk for referral services, it is subject to a number of further requirements. The MCO must conduct annual surveys of enrollees and people who have disenrolled to determine the level of their satisfaction with the quality of and access to services provided by the plan. In addition, the MCO must ensure that adequate stop loss protection is in place for the physicians who are put at substantial financial risk for referral services.

DHHS has issued regulations explaining these requirements, particularly the definition of substantial financial risk and of adequate stop loss protection. In general terms, "substantial financial risk" is defined as occurring if the physician's compensation can be increased 33 percent or more by bonuses or decreased by 25 percent or more by withholds (or can be affected 25 percent or more by a combination of bonuses and withholds) based on the cost of referral services. However, there is no requirement for stop loss protection for physician groups that are at risk for 25,000 or more patients (including Medicare, Medicaid, and commercial patients). The regulations also require the MCO to disclose information about the PIP to an enrollee who requests the information. A Medicare or Medicaid beneficiary may request information about the physician incentive arrangements, including the results of any patient satisfaction surveys that must be conducted if the PIP puts physicians at substantial financial risk for the cost of referrals.

## Overutilization of Specialists

The laws of a number of states prohibit payment for referrals. The scope and applicability of these laws vary greatly. In addition, physicians providing care to Medicare or Medicaid beneficiaries or those participating in other federal health programs (other than the one providing insurance to federal employees) are subject to the provisions of federal law, prohibiting a physician from accepting payment in exchange for referrals. In those cases, it is unlawful for a provider to receive or give "directly or indirectly any remuneration in return for the referral of patients." A physician who grants a discount to a patient or a payer to receive more patients is likely to be found to violate the law.

Yet MCOs negotiate with providers for reduced fees with the understanding that the MCO will channel patients to them. This process could violate the anti-referral law. To avoid this result, "safe harbor" regulations have been promulgated under the federal law for physicians negotiating with MCOs. Providers may negotiate a discount with the MCO if the MCO is at risk and has a contract with HCFA or a state Medicaid agency, and if the provider does not recoup the discount from Medicare or Medicaid. A further exemption was provided in 1996 by the Health Insurance Portability and Accountability Act. Remuneration "between" an MCO and a participating provider does not violate the federal anti-referral prohibition if there is a written agreement and the plan has a contract to provide services to Medicare beneficiaries or the provider is at "substantial financial risk" for the cost of services provided to the MCO.

## CONCLUSION

Americans' attitudes toward managed care are ambivalent, and even incongruous. People want the benefits of lower cost, comprehensive and coordinated care, and less paperwork, but are wary of the restrictions necessary to provide these benefits. Consumers and providers turn to government to protect them from the restrictions inherent in managed care. But the political process is not well positioned to strike the proper balance between the benefits and restrictions of managed care. There is no answer to how closely government should control the contractual relationships an MCO has with its members and participating providers. Therefore, the nature of the regulation is determined by the relative political strengths of different interests in a state. The ambiguities of the regulations reflect the policy uncertainties. Various states have different rules, and the rules are often ambiguous and frequently changing. Moreover, managed care is regulated in the context of a federal system. The boundaries between federal and state regulation (which generally are unclear) are particularly difficult to determine in the context of health care. They are under continual scrutiny and change by the courts. The combination of these and other confounding factors creates a regulatory structure that is varied and variable, ambiguous and complex, yet of increasing importance in the relationship between MCOs and providers.

# Regulation of Managed Care Contracting— Comments from the Field

*Edward P. Potanka*

Before the introduction of managed care, payers (that is, insurers and self-insured plans) acted as passive indemnitors with no contractual relationship with health care providers. To combine the financing and the provision of health care services, most managed care organizations (MCOs) establish a contractual relationship with health care providers. This relationship is between parties that are not natural allies. It is a fragile foundation upon which to build a business.

The provision and financing of health care are a complex undertaking that is becoming more complex. New relationships and contractual arrangements involving different forms of compensation and the performance of different services are being constructed on a daily basis. There is considerable truth in the maxim "when you've seen one managed care contracting arrangement you've seen one managed care contracting arrangement." MCOs want as much flexibility as possible in contracting with health care providers.

The need for flexibility in contracting with health care providers is in obvious conflict with attempts to regulate the relationship between MCOs and health care providers. Laws or regulations perceived by MCOs as "anti-managed care" are those that impair the ability of MCOs to selectively contract (any willing provider [AWP] laws), that mandate the inclusion of certain types of providers in managed care networks, that dictate the criteria for selection and de-selection of providers, that prohibit certain forms of compensation, or that dictate the exclusion or inclusion of particular provider contract provisions. However, attempts to regulate the contractual relationship between MCOs and health care providers should be viewed from a broader perspective.

MCOs can rightly complain that they are being singled out. What other private business has its contracts with independent contractors scrutinized and regulated so closely? Do legislators or regulators attempt to dictate to any other private business organizations the

The statements and opinions expressed are those of the author and do not necessarily reflect the views of CIGNA Corporation or its affiliated companies.

parties with which they must contract or how their subcontractors can be compensated or offered incentives? Few, if any, examples come to mind. In fact, the very notion of regulating agreements between independent contractors engaged in private business strikes one as alien to the American free enterprise system. The fact that legislators and regulators have taken the remarkable step of attempting to regulate private contracts in the health care business is simply evidence that the health care business is peculiarly identified with the public interest.

Health care is not just another business. It is a very important and personal aspect of people's lives. Accordingly, MCOs must expect that their contractual arrangements will continue to receive disproportionate scrutiny by legislators and regulators. Because the business is unusually affected by the public interest, those engaged in contracting on behalf of MCOs must wear two hats. Not only must they act in the best interests of their organization, they must also ask whether a particular arrangement is the right thing to do for a health care system in which we all participate. The use of so-called "gag clauses" (which I define narrowly to mean provisions prohibiting a provider from discussing medical treatment options with a patient) are a good example. They have no place in our health care system nor in our provider contracts. To the extent that regulation of our contracts reminds us of how influenced our business is by the public interest, it can have a salutary effect.

Regulation of provider agreements can benefit managed care and MCOs in other important ways. Managed care is about change and MCOs are the chief agents of that change. Change is naturally received with skepticism. Regulation has the unique ability to legitimize change. To the extent that contracts between MCOs and health care providers become "regulated," they are legitimized in the process. As a rule, the public feels much more comfortable with and accepting of contractual arrangements if they know that those contracts are somehow "regulated."

Regulation can also have the salutary effect of forcing MCOs to see things through others' eyes. Our perspective can, at times, be narrower than we care to admit. Legislators and regulators may approach an issue from an entirely different perspective. Normally, those who "regulate" us place the consumer's interests first. (AWP laws are a notable exception because they advance the selfish pecuniary interests of a few.) In so doing, issues with which we need to concern ourselves are given center stage. If anything we do in our provider contracting is a problem for consumers, it's a business problem for us because managed care is a consumer business. Managed care and MCOs are the winners when consumer issues are identified and properly addressed.

With the notable exception of AWP laws, MCOs have not suffered much under the weight of regulation of provider contracting arrangements to date. To the contrary, MCOs may owe much of their success to such regulation. State licensing laws have effectively preserved a "level playing field" despite attempts by providers to contract directly with employers in ways that would allow them to unfairly compete with MCOs. So too, state and federal anti-trust laws have held in check potentially destructive anti-competitive contracting practices by competing MCOs.

In summary, the appropriate "regulation" of managed care contracting is not necessarily something to which MCOs should object. MCOs do need considerable flexibility in their contracting if they are to succeed in making high quality and reasonably priced health care accessible to the majority of Americans. Anti-managed care regulation such as AWP laws that the Federal Trade Commission has characterized as being anti-competitive and anti-consumer should and will continue to be opposed by MCOs. Reasonable regulation of provider contracting, on the other hand, can have advantageous effects that promote the continued development and acceptance of managed care.

# 11

# Antitrust and Managed Care

## C. Joël Van Over

The shift from traditional fee-for-service reimbursement to managed care prospective payment has sparked consolidations and restructurings among providers to create delivery systems that are responsive to managed care needs. That initial spark has become a firestorm. This continuing trend of consolidations, including mergers, acquisitions, joint ventures, and the integration of delivery systems represents a fundamental restructuring of health care financing and provider markets.

Any organization contemplating changes in its structure or relationships with providers or managed care organizations (MCOs) must have a basic understanding of the antitrust laws.[1] By understanding the purpose of the antitrust laws and their application to certain areas of conduct, health care professionals will be in a position to assess when they should seek antitrust counseling and to better understand the counseling they receive.

The antitrust laws are concerned with competition and, more specifically, with preventing anti-competitive conduct. The antitrust laws themselves give little guidance concerning how this is to be achieved. The courts, the Department of Justice (DOJ), and the Federal Trade Commission (FTC) have woven a complex web of antitrust rules and regulations to implement the antitrust laws. Fortunately, experience gleaned from court opinions, actions of the DOJ and FTC, and publications provide guidelines for determining acceptable competitive conduct.

## UNDERSTANDING ANTITRUST CONCEPTS

The antitrust laws favor a free market paradigm in which consumers can choose among competing products and services based upon their respective prices, quality, and convenience. In a perfectly competitive health care market, MCOs could choose among competing providers, negotiating provider contracts that paid providers amounts for their services close to the provider's marginal costs.[2] Providers that were efficient and provided a quality service would obtain managed care contracts and make a reasonable profit. Providers that were not efficient and thus could not offer their services at a reasonable price, would not be as successful in obtaining managed care contracts and would lose patients to more efficient competitors. MCOs that were successful in negotiating competitive types of contracts would be in a position to offer lower premiums to subscribers and thus would themselves be more competitive.

Thus, antitrust laws are designed to foster an environment that encourages the success of the cost-efficient, quality MCOs and providers, and implicitly to discourage economic inefficiency and excessive profits. The antitrust laws operate under the principle that it takes several competitors to create the incentives necessary to maintain the ideal competitive balance in the health care marketplace. For example, three competing acute care hospitals would be better than one because only through competition will each hospital strive to operate efficiently while offering quality and innovative services to attract more patients and MCOs. One hospital may not have the incentive to operate efficiently and to charge less for its services without the competitive pressure of another competing hospital. This same principle operates at every level of the health care delivery system.

In theory at least, competition tames the profit motive by forcing organizations and providers to find efficient ways of operating (lowering costs) so that they may price services at a competitive level while maintaining quality.

## Unlawful Agreements

Section one of the Sherman Act makes unlawful any contract, combination, or conspiracy that substantially lessens competition. This section recognizes that even when there are multiple competitors, certain types of agreements or joint conduct by those competitors may stifle competition.

Section one pertains to all joint conduct by two or more independent business entities. Joint conduct includes joint ventures, formal or informal agreements, or a course of conduct that implies an agreement to act in concert. If the joint activity has the effect of substantially lessening competition in a relevant product and geographic market, it may violate section one. However, not all joint conduct is unlawful. If joint conduct produces procompetitive efficiencies, some lessening of competition may be justified.

Measuring the potential anti-competitive effects of joint activity is the critical element in a section one analysis. Potential anti-competitive effects are measured in a relevant product and geographic market. Thus, the first step is to determine the relevant markets by asking the following questions: (1) What products and services are covered by the joint conduct (the product market)? (2) What is the geographic area in which the parties to the joint conduct actually compete (the geographic market)?

In the health care marketplace, identifying relevant markets is complicated by the fact that joint conduct inevitably impacts several markets. For example, if several physician-hospital organizations (PHOs) join together through a network or alliance for the purpose of negotiating managed care contracts, the PHOs may not be direct competitors if they are distributed throughout a multi-county or state region (they do not compete in the same geographic markets); but, managed care plans operating throughout that region might argue that the network adversely affects competition in the managed care market by limiting contracting opportunities. Thus, while the PHO alliance may not reduce competition among the member providers in their respective local markets, the alliance may adversely affect the managed care market operating on a broader, perhaps regional, level.

Measuring potential anti-competitive effects of joint conduct in a relevant market or markets is an attempt to assess whether the participants to the joint conduct will have the power to increase prices or control the terms of sale as a result of the joint conduct.

There are four basic means to achieve this market power: One is almost always unlawful; two may be unlawful, depending upon other factors; and the fourth is almost always lawful.

First, the nature of the joint conduct itself may be synonymous with an intent and ability to exercise unlawful market power. These types of agreements are unlawful per se (on their face). Second, even if the nature of the agreement is not unlawful per se, it may not be justified unless it achieves legitimate pro-competitive cost efficiencies or enables the participants to offer new products or services each could not economically offer independently. Third, if the participants enjoy market dominance by virtue of their joint activity because of size, the risk of increasing their market power through control of a large share of the market may be considered too great. Finally, market dominance achieved independently based upon competitive prices, quality products and services, and innovation is almost always lawful. Thus, a joint venture that is not dominant at its inception, but grows because of its success in the marketplace, should not be a target of antitrust laws by virtue of its size alone.

Certain types of joint conduct among providers or MCOs are considered unlawful per se. These types of conduct may arise from improperly structured joint ventures, or properly structured joint ventures that are operated without proper safeguards, or from a misunderstanding of the impact of agreements not intended to result in per se violations of the antitrust laws.

*Price Fixing*

It is always unlawful for two or more independent competitors to agree on the prices or fees they will charge. For example, independent physicians, hospitals, or other health care providers may not agree on the fees they will individually charge managed care providers. Nor may they agree on other practices that influence price. For example, it would be unlawful for two or more providers or groups of providers (whether independent practice associations [IPAs], preferred provider organizations [PPOs], physician networks, PHOs, or hospitals) to get together and agree among themselves that each will do business with managed care providers only on a fee-for-service basis. This agreement would restrict the manner in which competitors compete on the basis of price or fees and would have the same effect on competition as an agreement on particular prices or fees. Nor may MCOs agree among themselves to accept only capitated contracts, or a certain level of reimbursement.

The principle here is that, for competition to work, buyers and sellers (providers and MCOs) must each bargain freely and independently based upon the particular merits of the goods and services involved, and the economic needs of both parties.

*Boycotts*

It is almost always unlawful for two competitors to agree not to do business with another competitor or purchaser. For example, two MCOs may not agree to each refuse to do business with a particular nonprofit hospital until that hospital ceases merger talks with a private hospital corporation. Nor may a PHO deny membership to a physician solely because that physician has admitting privileges at a competing hospital. This type of joint pressure reduces the free market choices or disadvantages a competitor.

*Tying*

In most cases, it is unlawful for a competitor to condition the sale of one of its products or services upon the purchase of a second. This would force the purchaser to purchase an unwanted product or service to obtain the desired product or service. For example, an MCO may not require its contracting providers to offer its managed care product to the provider's employees as a condition of contracting with that provider. Each product or service must be permitted to compete on its own merits. Likewise, a provider-owned integrated delivery system (IDS) controlling most or all providers in a particular specialty, for example, oncology services, will be vulnerable to an unlawful tying claim if it refuses to reasonably contract (or to permit the specialty providers themselves to contract) with competing provider networks or MCOs that need the oncology services, but not all of the services provided by the IDS.[3]

*Division of Markets*

It is unlawful for two or more independent competitors to agree not to compete by dividing (a) the geographic areas in which each will market and sell its products, (b) the products that each will offer, or (c) the customers that each will service. For example, two competing PHOs may not split the geographic areas in which they will market their services to MCOs. Nor may two MCOs split large employer subscribers by agreeing that one will market to certain employers and the second will market to different employers. Division of markets represents an agreement not to compete and is thus anti-competitive, by definition.

## Agreements That Lessen Competition

Agreements or other joint activities that are not unlawful per se are analyzed to determine whether they are designed to achieve pro-competitive goals that justify some lessening of competition between the participants. This evaluation determines whether the joint conduct is, on balance, reasonable. This analysis is termed a "rule of reason" analysis.

All joint conduct that does not run afoul of the antitrust laws by violating one of the per se rules is evaluated under the rule of reason. A properly structured joint venture falls within this category. To be properly structured, joint venture participants must share financial risk. This means that each participant provides capital or contributes something else of value so that the venture may operate successfully. This contribution is at risk—the contributions of the participants will be lost if the venture fails, and each participant will enjoy a return on their investment if the venture succeeds.

The parties to a joint venture may act as one economic unit to the extent that they pool their resources and share risks. However, they may act as one economic unit only regarding those activities that fall within the scope of the joint venture. For example, if two providers create a joint venture to purchase expensive high technology equipment that neither could afford separately, or could not fully use alone, the participants may agree on the fees the joint venture will charge for using that equipment. However, the participants may not agree on the fees each will charge for other services or procedures, such as office visits or routine radiographs because these fees would not fall within the scope of the joint venture.

Assuming that the joint venture is properly structured, the antitrust laws look to the purpose of the joint venture to determine whether it has been created to further pro-competitive goals or whether its purpose is merely a vehicle to permit competitors to engage in price fixing or other anti-competitive conduct.

Provider joint ventures are typically created to provide an efficient means for contracting with MCOs and to provide the internal structure for controlling costs: efficient case management, utilization review, and treatment protocols, for example. Additionally, these provider joint ventures may offer a fuller range of services and the ability to enter into capitated contracting arrangements. All of these purposes are pro-competitive and justify some lessening of competition among the joint venture participants. It is important to note, however, that a provider joint venture created for these purposes must operate to achieve these purposes. Any lessening of competition is justified only insofar as it is necessary to achieve these pro-competitive goals. Thus, if the joint venture, once created, refuses to entertain capitation or discounted fee arrangements, refuses to provide prospective or concurrent utilization review, or refuses to cooperate in developing reasonable treatment protocols, the joint venture would likely be viewed as a sham, especially if it seeks to negotiate fees on behalf of its members.

Likewise, an MCO alliance created to offer a unified product to large multistate corporations must operate under analogous antitrust constraints. The individual MCOs may not set joint subscriber fees unless they create a true joint venture, or use a model that prevents price fixing.

### Size of the Parties

The antitrust laws prefer that companies grow because they are efficient and successful competitors offering quality products and innovation at competitive prices. Large competitors involved in joint ventures, including networks or alliances that include a substantial percentage of providers or payers in the relevant market, must evaluate whether their joint arrangement is more likely to be challenged because of its size.

In general terms, exclusive arrangements are more likely to be challenged because they tend to foreclose competition to a greater degree than nonexclusive arrangements. An exclusive arrangement requires the participants to act solely through the joint venture for those activities within the scope of the venture. On the other hand, a nonexclusive arrangement permits joint venture participants to join other competing joint ventures and even to compete independently with the joint venture.

For example, if a hospital-based IPA and the hospital create a properly structured PHO that requires its physician and hospital members to contract with MCOs exclusively through the PHO, this exclusive arrangement may substantially lessen competition if (a) more than 20 to 30 percent of the physicians in the market join the exclusive PHO, or (b) if the hospital has a market share exceeding 20 to 30 percent of the relevant patient market. It is important to note that this PHO does not necessarily violate the antitrust laws, but the exclusive nature of the member arrangement, coupled with its size and any initial market success of the PHO, make it more likely that the arrangement may be challenged. Additionally, if the operation of the PHO runs afoul of the per se limitations on conduct, a challenge would be likely.

It is important to note that a joint venture will not necessarily violate the antitrust laws if, at its inception, it includes more than 30 percent of competitors in the relevant market. However, when the joint venture approaches or exceeds this size at its inception, it will likely be scrutinized more closely. If a provider joint venture exceeds 50 percent of the market participants, a challenge by the DOJ, the

FTC, another competitor, or an MCO becomes more likely. At this level, it may be generally presumed that the joint venture possesses market power, and is likely to substantially lessen competition, especially if the joint venture is exclusive. However, a joint venture, even if it approached 50 percent of the providers in the market, should not necessarily signal market dominance if the provider relationships are not in fact exclusive. For example, if 50 percent or more of providers join a network, joint venture, IPA, or PPO, and also participate in other networks, IPAs, or PPOs, as well as maintain independent fee-for-service practices, there is arguably little, if any, lessening of competition. In other words, MCOs seeking providers would not be limited, at least in theory, in their efforts to contract with a sufficient number of providers to compete effectively. In this case, the better assessment of the new joint venture's market power would be to evaluate the degree to which the providers act as if their relationship with the new venture is exclusive. For example, if the member providers refuse to join competing networks, PPOs, IPAs, or other provider organizations, or if the majority of their practices is dedicated to the new joint venture, it may be that the new joint venture functions as an exclusive joint venture. In this case, the joint venture may in fact unduly foreclose opportunities for both MCOs (wishing to contract with other networks or physician groups) and competing networks (unable to find a sufficient number of providers to join them). Alternatively, if the member providers serve many MCOs through other networks or physician groups, there should be virtually no competitive impact based simply upon the size of the new joint venture.

Finally, it is important to note that the analysis of a joint venture's size must be reviewed in two distinct steps: first, at its inception, and second, as it grows. Creating market power by consolidating otherwise independent competitors through a joint venture (or other type of consolidation) is viewed as an intentional consolidation of market power that may substantially lessen competition and create an unlawful monopoly.

In contrast, a joint venture that grows because it offers competitive fees, quality services, and other features that make it attractive to MCOs would not be unlawful. It would simply be a successful competitor. In summary, a properly structured joint venture that operates in a lawful manner and is not established at its inception in an unlawful manner, will not violate the antitrust laws solely because it becomes a dominant competitor.

Consolidations, especially mergers or acquisitions, that eliminate a competitor (creating a single larger and perhaps more dominant competitor) should always be reviewed for compliance with the antitrust laws. Guidelines have developed to assist in determining compliance, but each merger or acquisition must be judged in its own unique context. Guidelines focus upon market concentration—comparing competition before and after the merger in the relevant geographic area and the overall market share and size of the merged entity.

*Monopolizing Markets*

Section two of the Sherman Act makes it unlawful for health care providers or MCOs to monopolize or attempt to monopolize the market or markets in which they compete. A related Clayton Act provision prohibits mergers if the effect may be to lessen competition substantially or tend to create a monopoly. The monopoly provisions of the antitrust laws are concerned with (1) consolidations, including mergers, acquisitions, and creation of exclusive joint ventures, especially when the effect is to eliminate a competitor in a relevant market; and (2) conduct by a large health care organization that is anti-competitive.

The Sherman and Clayton Acts' monopoly provisions focus on the following three elements: (1) identifying the markets in which the health care organizations compete; (2) identifying the size and market share of the organization; and (3) identifying the factors that contribute to the health care organization enjoying this size or market share. If two health care organizations are contemplating a merger, acquisition, or joint venture, each of these issues must be reviewed for both entities separately and for the newly formed organization.

Exhibit 11–1 illustrates an analysis for a theoretical hospital merger or acquisition. The first step in evaluating the likely competitive impact of this merger is to determine whether Hospital A and B are competitors. If they are, the merger would likely be challenged, or at least closely scrutinized, by the FTC or DOJ.[4] If they are not, it is much less likely that the merger would be challenged. If the hospitals are not competitors, the notion is that they would not be in a position to adversely affect competition in their respective markets.

**Exhibit 11–1** A Theoretical Hospital Merger

---

**Hospital A:**
150-bed community-based, acute care hospital.
Located in Anytown, population 100,000 (Anytown has one other 100-bed hospital).
85 percent of its patients come from Anytown and neighboring rural areas in the Main County.

**Hospital B:**
200-bed acute care hospital; offers tertiary care in several specialties.
Located in Everycity, twenty-five miles away, population 300,000 (Everycity has three other hospitals.)
70 percent of its patients from Everycity.
30 percent of its patients, mostly those seeking its tertiary care services, come from Main County.

Hospital A and Hospital B wish to merge. Both hospitals will continue operating after the merger, but Hospital B would lose its neonatal intensive care unit. All billing and purchasing would be centralized, as would certain other administrative functions. Hospital A and B have managed care contracts with many of the same MCOs.

---

To determine whether Hospital A and B are competitors, it is necessary to look at the type of services each offers (the relevant product markets) as well as the geographic area (the relevant geographic markets) in which each compete. Each hospital may compete in the same geographic market regarding certain services but not others. It is likely that the FTC and DOJ would take the position that Hospitals A and B are competitors even though it appears that currently Hospital A draws its patients from a narrow geographic area that does not overlap with the geographic area from which Hospital B draws its patients (except regarding tertiary care services, for which the hospitals are not competitors). These agencies would argue that the close proximity of the two hospitals makes them potential competitors. From this perspective, if Hospital A lowered its prices (or Hospital B raised its prices), consumers would consider the hospital offering the lowest prices and would be willing to travel some extra distance to obtain those lower prices.

Hospitals A and B could counter this argument by showing that historical pricing information did not show this to be the case. They could also show that physicians with admitting privileges at Hospital A did not have admitting privileges at Hospital B.

Based upon guidelines adopted by the FTC and DOJ, the *1992 Department of Justice and Federal Trade Commission Horizontal Merger*

*Guidelines*, the determination concerning whether Hospitals A and B compete in the same geographic market would play a key role in determining whether these agencies challenged the merger. The DOJ and FTC use a threshold calculation to determine the effect of a merger (or acquisition) on market concentration. This calculation, the Herfindahl–Hirschman Index (HHI) measures market concentration based upon the number of hospitals in the relevant markets and their relative market shares, before and after the merger.

Unless Hospitals A and B were both small hospitals and each of the remaining hospitals had approximately the same market shares, showing that there were no dominant hospitals before or after the merger, the HHI for the merger of Hospitals A and B would show that the six-hospital market was concentrated before the merger and would be significantly more concentrated after the merger.[5] The DOJ and FTC would likely conclude that the merger would adversely affect competition unless other market factors indicated otherwise.

These other factors include the following: (1) the financial health of the merging hospitals—because a failing hospital may not be an effective competitor; (2) whether the remaining four competing hospitals had excess capacity that could respond to price increases by the merging hospitals; (3) whether hospital alliances exist that might indicate a lack of vigorous competition or opportunities for price collusion; (4) whether MCOs supported or opposed the merger; (5) whether services sold by the remaining hospitals are perceived to be the same or somewhat different (for example, do all hospitals provide basic acute care services, or does one or more specialize in a particular service, for example, cardiac surgery, or women's services?); and (6) whether new hospital competitors are likely to enter the market.[6]

Similar market concentration issues arise when competitors enter into joint ventures, including multi-provider networks. For example, the FTC and DOJ statements of *Antitrust Enforcement Policy in Health Care* issued August 28, 1996 (from the *1996 Guidelines*), established safe harbors for certain properly structured physician-network joint ventures, based upon the percentage of physicians that join them. An appropriately structured physician-network joint venture will fall within a safe harbor if it comprises no more than (a) 30 percent of all primary care physicians and no more than 30 percent of any particular specialty within the geographic area in which these physicians compete, as long as network members are free to join other networks or contract with managed care plans independently, and actually do so (a nonexclusive network); or (b) 20 percent of all primary care physicians and no more than 20 percent of those practicing in any particular specialty, if the network members are restricted to dealing with MCOs only through the network (an exclusive network).

It is important to note, regarding all provider networks, that the *1996 Guidelines'* safe harbor provisions do not preclude a private antitrust suit by a competing network, an MCO, an excluded physician, or a consumer. Private suits are typically filed by a competitor believing its business will be diminished because of the new venture or by a purchaser believing that competition will be substantially reduced and prices raised because of the venture. Therefore, it is important to review the likely impact of a new venture upon the other key players in the geographic and product markets in which the venture competes. If prices are likely to rise, the choice of providers is likely to shrink, or a particular segment of the market is likely to be (or perceived to be) adversely affected, those involved in the venture should be particularly careful to undertake a review of its antitrust implications.

## ANTITRUST ISSUES IN THE MANAGED CARE MARKETPLACE

To successfully compete in the evolving managed care marketplace, most providers must join a network, an IDS, or some form of joint venture to increase efficiency and maximize negotiating leverage. Likewise, non-provider MCOs must be large and efficient enough to attract contracting partners for provider organizations, and be able to spread risk over a sufficiently large and diverse subscriber base. Arguably, these MCOs must compensate providers at a level sufficient to discourage providers from creating their own IDSs that compete directly with MCOs.

Coming full circle, multi-provider networks and IDSs are themselves entering the managed care financing market, through management services organizations (MSOs) or by merging with (or acquiring) MCOs. All of these changes have antitrust implications.

### Provider Networks

Provider joint venture networks come in every size, shape, and intention. Providers have created joint ventures for several principle reasons, including the following: (a) to share costly new technology or services; (b) to reduce the drain of existing unprofitable services; (c) to reduce operating overhead; and (d) to become a more desirable contracting partner through size or geographic and product diversification. Although each of these goals may be considered pro-competitive (increasing purchasers' choices or the opportunity to lower costs and therefore fees), the antitrust laws seek to ensure that these joint ventures are not implemented in a manner that substantially lessens competition.

Some provider joint ventures do not provide for a sufficient sharing of financial risk to justify joint fee setting by their members. For example, most providers join networks and alliances for the purpose of negotiating contracts with MCOs, while retaining their independent practices or businesses. Networks in their most basic form typically conduct negotiations with MCOs, provide billing services, and coordinate or perform utilization review. These functions are funded by their members in some fashion depending upon their organizational form, for example, separate not-for-profit or for-profit corporation, association, partnership, and so forth.[7]

These types of limited-purpose joint ventures have not generally been considered as providing sufficient financial integration in the provision of medical services to permit joint fee setting. Therefore, they must create a mechanism for sharing financial risk through the nature of the managed care contracts themselves—capitated contracts; case rate contracts; fees that are dependent upon the overall performance of the network; and fees that are based upon managed care plan revenues or premiums. Each of these contract types place the network and its members at financial risk for the medical services provided to the managed care members. Even when the managed care contracts themselves do not impose financial risk, it may be possible for the network to adopt internal fee arrangements that introduce financial risk by withholding a portion of each physician's "fee," tying further distributions to utilization or some other cost-containment target.

Because most networks and alliances do not integrate provider services to a sufficient degree to permit joint fee setting, negotiating on a fee-for-service basis (or a discount from usual and customary fees) raises significant antitrust risks. For this reason, networks that wish to contract on this basis must ensure that fee-related information is not shared with or among member providers. In most cases, it is not permissible for a board or committee made up of providers to negotiate on a fee-for-service basis on behalf of member providers. These providers would be viewed as a conduit for price fixing—they would set fees for themselves and their competitors.[8]

The network illustrated in Exhibit 11–2 is unlikely to be challenged by the FTC or DOJ as long as the structure of the network itself includes appropriate safeguards to ensure that individual cost and fee information is not shared with other members. Significantly, this network provides the mechanism for physicians to share financial risk through capitated contracting. Because of this, the physicians may jointly negotiate all aspects of the capitation arrangement, decide the manner in which payments will be made and risk allocated to individual member physicians.

Although the fee-for-service contracting provides no means for risk sharing, physicians do not jointly set fees. Rather, the MCO negotiates fees with each physician individually through the messenger. Moreover, because the network is not exclusive, each member is free to contract with any MCO, to join other networks, and to provide services to other private or self-pay patients; the network is unlikely to reduce competition among physicians or to limit managed care plan contracting opportunities.

An analysis of a network that comprises the same physicians but contracts only on a fee-for-service model is illustrated in Exhibit 11–3.

The network structure illustrated in Exhibit 11–3 no doubt violates the price-fixing prohibitions of the antitrust laws. The network provides a mechanism for its members to agree on price without any true financial integration. Because each member knows how the board sets fees, those physicians charging under the average fees will likely raise their fees to or somewhat above the average on the theory that they will still be competitive. Over time, the average will become a floor (that is, no fees will be lower than the average) and overall prices will rise.

## Messenger Model Networks

The most recognized model for negotiating on a fee-for-service basis is the messenger model. Physician or other provider networks

---

**Exhibit 11–2** A Provider Network Unlikely To Be Challenged

35 percent of the primary care physicians (PCPs) and between 20 and 30 percent of physicians in each particular specialty decide to join together through a network for the purpose of contracting with MCOs. They agree that membership in the network is not exclusive. They also agree to utilization review for all managed care patients and to accept capitated payment if the managed care plan has at least 10,000 subscribers in the network's geographic market. It will contract only on a fee-for-service basis if there are fewer than 10,000 subscribers, and uses a messenger model to establish the fees each managed care plan will pay each physician.

**Exhibit 11–3** A Provider Network Likely To Be Challenged

35 percent of the primary care physicians (PCPs) and between 20 and 30 percent of physicians in each particular specialty decide to join together through a network for the purpose of contracting with MCOs. The network sets its fees as follows: The board of directors, which comprises physicians, surveys each physician's fee-for-service structure. The board then averages these fees for the five most common charges for each specialty and primary care practice and arrives at fixed standard charges for certain commonly used services. Although the network attempts to negotiate contract rates higher than the average, in no event does it contract rates below the average. The balance of each physician's charges are based upon their usual and customary (U&C) fees. This network provides for no financial integration, but fixes certain fees for each of its members to charge. The board, which comprises physicians, is not an independent messenger.

that operate on the messenger model and that are nonexclusive will rarely be challenged. In a messenger model network, the members do not communicate with each other concerning the fees each charges MCOs and other health plans, or contractual provisions that affect fees, such as discount rates or most-favored-nations (MFN) clauses. Nor do they communicate with MCOs directly. Rather, they use an independent messenger. The messenger solicits fee information from each member and communicates this information to a particular MCO. The messenger does not "negotiate" fees but communicates offers and counteroffers, acting only as a messenger of information. The messenger also negotiates non–fee-related provisions on behalf of all provider members.

As long as members do not share fee information among themselves, this model provides MCOs the advantages associated with negotiating through a single messenger while preserving price competition among the providers. However, for large provider networks, the messenger model is cumbersome, involving the communication of offers and counteroffers on behalf of hundreds of providers.

Several variations on the pure messenger model have developed in an effort to streamline the otherwise time-consuming communication of information on behalf of provider members. The extent to which these variations may be challenged remains unclear. In one variation, an independent messenger surveys fees charged in the community and develops an initial fee schedule for negotiating purposes based upon these usual and customary (U&C) fees. The provider members may either agree in advance to authorize negotiation within a range up to a certain percent discount or, in other cases, may opt in (or opt out) of an agreement negotiated by the messenger.

The DOJ has challenged these messenger model variations in at least two instances when PHOs had market power in their relevant markets. The first instance involved the only hospital in the community, and in both cases the PHOs included more than 80 percent of the physicians practicing in their respective communities.

## Integrated Delivery Systems

IDSs bring together a range of health care services and products designed to meet a substantial portion of a community's health care needs. An IDS may contract with an MCO or compete directly with MCOs by creating its own managed care plan (for example, a health maintenance organization [HMO] or PPO).

As discussed previously, competitors may not jointly agree upon the fees they will charge. However, to the extent that two competitors financially integrate their practices (share substantial financial risk), they are no longer competitors and thus they may set prices for their new venture. However, they may not agree on prices for any services that are not financially integrated.

Depending upon the extent to which they are financially integrated, IDSs are subject to the same price and fee setting constraints as are joint ventures. They are also evaluated on the basis of their size and market share in each of their product and service lines—hospital services, physician services, home health products and services, outpatient and specialty clinics, and other products and services included within the IDS.

The hallmark of a true IDS is common ownership. A completely integrated system often involves a parent company, perhaps acting as an MSO, with wholly owned subsidiaries operating various component businesses. Because a parent and its subsidiary corporations are considered one economic entity, no price fixing issues arise in this model. However, to the extent that certain IDS services are not offered through a common ownership umbrella, joint fee or price setting by independent competitors remains unlawful.

For example, a regional multi-hospital system desires to establish an IDS. To implement this goal it may purchase specialty and general outpatient clinics, employ physicians to serve these clinics, and create a separate MSO that forms a joint venture with a physician network. Several antitrust issues may arise.

First, if the IDS refuses to enter into a contract with an MCO on less than a full-service basis, the MCO may take the position that the IDS is unlawfully tying desired services with services that the MCO wishes to purchase from a competitor. Second, to the extent that the IDS does not contract on a full capitated basis, or some other risk-sharing method, the IDS must assure itself that its physician networks are using a fee-setting method that avoids price fixing. If the physician network prices unlawfully, the IDS could be considered a co-conspirator to the network's unlawful conduct. Third, if an MCO wishes to contract with the IDS but wishes to use another physician network, and the IDS refuses, the MCO may argue that this constitutes a boycott by the IDS and its physician network. Fourth, if the hospitals in the IDS are the only hospitals and clinics in the relevant market offering a particular specialty, an MCO may argue that the IDS has monopoly market power because it controls an essential ingredient to competition in the managed care market. An MCO wishing to purchase only this service, perhaps on a case-rate basis, may argue that the IDS is unlawfully using its monopoly power in this specialty if the IDS refuses to contract on this basis, alleging unlawful tying and unlawful monopolization.

The merits of any of these claims depend upon the particular facts, including the extent to which the providers own the components of the system and are thus financially integrated, and upon the market power of the IDS itself or the components of that system separately.

Finally, it should be noted that regional or statewide alliances among multi-provider networks or PHOs (super PHOs) are not true IDSs because they typically lack the requisite degree of financial integration or common ownership. They are properly evaluated under the antitrust rules that apply to provider network joint ventures. Although a properly structured nonexclusive alliance or super PHO should not run afoul of the antitrust laws, federal and state antitrust enforcement agencies have viewed these entities with some skepticism. They have been viewed as providing the vehicle for the unlawful sharing of price and fee information, especially when they will contract with MCOs only on a fee-for-service basis. Accordingly, these alliances must be carefully structured and operated with appropriate safeguards to ensure that they are not subject to a price fixing challenge.

## Managed Care Organizations

MCOs that attempt to contain health care costs through capitated contracting, case-rate contracting, discounted fee arrangements, utilization review, and treatment protocols are considered organizations serving pro-competitive goals. However, antitrust issues may arise from an MCO's contracting practices, from agreements with competing MCOs that violate per se restrictions on conduct (for example, division of markets), and, to a lesser extent, from an MCO's size or market power.

It is generally recognized that MCOs may enter into exclusive contractual relationships with provider groups without violating the antitrust laws. For example, the MCO may select only one hospital and physician network or IPA (or one PHO) in a particular geographic area to the exclusion of other providers. This is justified by the nature of capitated contracting or the likelihood that it will be able to negotiate better rates and fees if it commits all of its patient volume to those providers. As long as the contracting providers are not also required to contract exclusively with the particular MCO, no anti-competitive effects are likely. However, if the providers are required to contract only with one MCO, this could be construed as an attempt to monopolize the managed care market unless there are sufficient alternative providers in that market to serve competing MCOs.

An important antitrust case, decided last year, illustrates this point.[9] In that case, an HMO owned virtually all of the clinics in the relevant market, employing the physicians operating those clinics. It also contracted with a large number of physicians in that area to provide additional physician services. It served 90 percent of the HMO subscribers in the area. However, none of its physician contracts were exclusive. Moreover, only 6 percent of contracting physicians' income was derived from the HMO. These facts, coupled with the fact that the HMO employed less than 50 percent of the area's physicians, led the court to conclude that the HMO was not unlawfully monopolizing the managed care market in the area because another competitor (for example, a PPO) could enter the market by contracting with the same physicians with which the HMO contracted. The court rejected the argument that the HMO was an unlawful monopolist because it charged prices that were higher than average and enjoyed a higher rate of return than other HMOs. As the court concluded, a lawful monopolist, one that has achieved its size through lawful means, can charge whatever it wants to charge.

The court also addressed another significant antitrust issue facing MCOs: the use of MFN clauses in provider contracts. MFN clauses typically provide that the MCO will pay the provider no more than the provider charges other patients or MCOs. The court found that an

MFN clause reflects no more than a buyer's efforts to bargain for low prices, asking the seller to agree to treat them as favorably as any other customer. The court refused to find that the use of the MFN clause was unlawful.

Despite some courts' view that the practice of using MFN clauses in provider contracts is a legitimate means of controlling provider fees, the DOJ and the FTC continue to challenge MFN clauses as anti-competitive in many cases. The federal government argues that MFN clauses often result in higher prices to consumers (rather than lower prices), because providers subject to these clauses may refuse to negotiate with other MCOs offering lower fees or may withdraw from arrangements with other plans or insist that these competing plans raise their fees to the level of those subject to the MFN clause. The federal government argues that MFN clauses often decrease competition and, over time, raise all prices to the level of the MFN contracts. The federal government has also attempted to show that any savings supposedly gained from the use of an MFN clause are not passed on to the consumer in the form of lower subscriber rates.

Although the federal government has settled many of its challenges to MFN clauses (MCOs have agreed to cease their use of MFN clauses), one key case is currently pending. Therefore, any MCO using MFN clauses must evaluate the impact of these clauses carefully. Although it is less likely that an MCO with a small market share will be challenged, those MCOs enjoying a larger market share, exceeding 20 to 30 percent of the relevant market, should understand that MFN clauses subject them to the risk of an antitrust challenge by the federal government or a competitor.

## CONCLUSION

It is often difficult to rationalize basic antitrust principles with the operational decisions providers and MCOs must make daily. However, it is important for providers and MCO decision makers to understand the areas of their respective businesses that implicate antitrust concerns. With a sensitivity to these areas, decision makers will be better equipped to seek antitrust counseling when it is needed and to use these counselors effectively to achieve their competitive goals. Without this understanding, the complexities inherent in the antitrust laws may threaten the very competition these laws were designed to foster.

**NOTES**

1. The basic federal antitrust statutes are the Sherman Act, 15 U.S.C. §§ 1-7, and the Clayton Act, 15 U.S.C. §§ 12-27. Private parties, state attorneys general, and federal agencies may bring actions to enforce the antitrust laws. The Federal Trade Commission has authority to prevent "unfair methods of competition" and "unfair or deceptive acts or practices," 15 U.S.C. § 45. Anticompetitive conduct may also be subject to criminal prosecution, 15 U.S.C. §§ 1-2; 15 U.S.C. §13a. Moreover, certain health care professional review activities are governed by the Health Care Quality Improvements Act, 42 U.S.C. §§ 11101-11152, and may be protected from antitrust damages. In addition to federal laws, each state has enacted its own antitrust laws which are generally consistent with federal law.

2. Fundamental antitrust economics assume that a supplier of goods and services in a competitive market will, "in the long run, earn no profits above the return necessary to keep his or her productive resources employed," Areeda and Turner, Antitrust Law, Vol. I at ¶ 108 (1978). A firm may earn higher profits in the short run, but only until another competitor expands, or a new competitor enters the market. Id.

3. Many courts evaluating the lawfulness of a tying arrangement focus on the competitor's market power in the tying product. In other words, if the purchaser has a significant need for the tying product (oncology services in our example) then the provider will be in a position to "force" the purchase of the unwanted or tied product.

4. Many hospital or other health care mergers or acquisitions are subject to premerger filing requirements under the Hart-Scott-Rodino Antitrust Improvements Act, 15 U.S.C. § 18a. The rules for this premerger notice filing program are technical and complex. Although a discussion of this program is beyond the scope of this article, it is important to determine whether these rules apply to a proposed transaction.

5. The HHI index for this theoretical merger shows a premerger market concentration index of 1750, a moderately concentrated market. The postmerger concentrated index of 2350 is considered a highly concentrated market. The increase of 600 points is considered significant and raises significant concerns of potential adverse effects unless other market features suggest otherwise.

Premerger HHI

| Hospital | Market Share | HHI Value | | |
|----------|--------------|-----------|---|-----|
| A | 15% | $15^2$ | = | 225 |
| B | 20% | $20^2$ | = | 400 |
| C | 15% | $15^2$ | = | 225 |
| D | 10% | $10^2$ | = | 100 |
| E | 20% | $20^2$ | = | 400 |
| F | 20% | $20^2$ | = | 400 |

Postmerger HHI

| Hospital | Market Share | HHI Value | | |
|----------|--------------|-----------|---|------|
| A, B | 35% | $35^2$ | = | 1225 |
| C | 15% | $15^2$ | = | 225 |
| D | 10% | $10^2$ | = | 100 |
| E | 20% | $20^2$ | = | 400 |
| F | 20% | $20^2$ | = | 400 |
| Total (high concentration above 1,800) | | | | 2350 |

6. The likelihood that a new competitor may enter the market is a significant factor for certain types of mergers. For example, some antitrust courts have found this element persuasive when dealing with MCO consolidations because MCOs can enter a new market without a significant outlay of capital. New hospital entrants are not as likely because of the significant capital outlay and licensing requirements associated with opening a new hospital.

7. Specialty networks are also emerging on a regional and national level. Under a typical framework, an MSO is created to undertake MCO contracting activities and utilization review, develop practice protocols, implement billing, and provide other management services. Some of these networks financially integrate key specialty practice groups in strategic regional or national markets, especially where MCOs control a large share of those markets. Specialty networks achieve financial integration by operating all management functions, from purchasing, practice management, and billing to marketing and strategic planning. To achieve full integration, the MSO may lease physician group practices or purchase these practices, both in exchange for long-term physician employment contracts, stock in the MSO corporation, and cash compensation. This specialty network model has avoided antitrust scrutiny largely by limiting the number of physician practices to 20 percent of the relevant specialty physicians in any single market, and by creating a structure to accommodate true financial risk sharing. By doing so, these specialty activities are well positioned to create independent delivery systems by developing, purchasing, or joint venturing with specialty outpatient clinics and specialty hospitals. As these networks and IDSs gain market success, they will no doubt be scrutinized more closely by antitrust enforcement agencies, their competitors, and MCOs.

8. The newly adopted FTC/DOJ *Antitrust Enforcement Policy in Health Care* (the "1996 Guidelines") recognize that provider networks that do not involve substantial financial risk may be sufficiently integrated to produce significant efficiencies and thus agreements on price reasonably necessary to accomplish pro-competitive benefits will be evaluated under a rule of reason analysis. The contours of this analysis remain uncertain and network structures that depart from the requirements for financial risk sharing should be carefully evaluated by antitrust counsel.

9. Blue Cross Blue Shield United of Wisconsin v. Marshfield Clinic, 65 F.3d 1406 (7th Cir.) cert. denied, 166 S.Ct. 1288 (1966).

# Antitrust and Managed Care— Comments from the Field

*Philip A. Shelton*

---

Traditionally, health care providers, particularly physicians, have not viewed their practices as business entities subject to competitive and market forces that govern other enterprises. The formal training of most practitioners does not include the business aspects of medicine, and providers are collegial, not competitive, in training and practice. Although large multispecialty groups and many allied health professionals (for example, chiropractic physicians and physical therapists) have integrated business planning and marketing into their operations for years, other providers are just now recognizing the need to treat their practices like a business. In large part, this is due to the competition among providers that managed care has fostered.

## CURRENT ENVIRONMENT

Although managed care has played an increasingly important role in generating patients and income for most private practitioners over the past ten to fifteen years, the demands of managed care have not been particularly intense in most markets until recently. Over the past five years, numerous factors have forced providers to rethink their practice model. These include the following:

- the implementation of Resource-Based Relative Unit Scale (RBRVS) reimbursement fee schedules, which has reduced revenues for many specialists and made contracting with managed care organizations (MCOs) on a fee-for-service basis considerably less attractive;
- the growth of Medicare risk contracting and resultant demand for specialty or global capitation arrangements;
- the growing sophistication of many providers about the financial underpinnings of MCOs and the recognition that savings generated by providers are returned in large part to shareholders' profits and reserves;
- the emergence of multispecialty and single-specialty provider groups of various types and levels of integration sponsored by

forward-thinking and entrepreneurial providers and health care administrators; and

- a refocusing of cost containment on outpatient and ambulatory services and a recognition, albeit reluctantly, by many MCOs that providers are in a better position to determine how to control these costs.

Collectively, these factors signal the end of the solo and small group practice. Traditional provider organizations, particularly the inclusive multispecialty independent practice associations (IPAs) formed in the 1980s, are either transforming themselves into leaner, more efficient groups or are withering away. Solo practitioners have been forming group practices, or joining single- and multispecialty IPAs and physician-hospital organizations (PHOs) to form larger, more influential groups at a rapid rate. This accelerating trend toward group formation has significant antitrust implications.

## Antitrust Implications for Developing Provider Organizations

The fee-for-service, third party payer environment that dominated the landscape during the past few decades encouraged individual providers to become entrepreneurs and led to an expansion of capacity in the health care delivery system over multiple fronts. Growth in managed care has resulted in a flattening or decline in the demand for specialty, inpatient, and other services. The development of group practices, merging of hospitals, and the relocation of specialists are, in part, a response to this trend. Although this consolidation and redistribution are appropriate in the context of declining demand, they risk crossing antitrust boundaries, at least as these boundaries have been defined historically.

Antitrust laws presume multiple competitors in any given market; but, in many health care markets, two or three groups or hospital systems are likely to dominate over time. Inevitably, many of these groups will exceed the 20-percent safe harbor threshold. The Department of Justice (DOJ) is recognizing a need for the relaxation of traditional antitrust benchmarks based on efficiency and broader definitions of the market. Oligopolistic or monopolistic consolidation reduces excess capacity in the delivery system, but can breed complacency and inefficiency over the long term. Enforcement agencies must assess the balance of these conflicting issues in their evaluation of provider organizations.

Groups that form as integrated economic entities to reduce over-head, manage risk, and return at least a portion of these cost savings to the market should survive most antitrust tests. Businesses that achieve market dominance through some mixture of aggressive marketing, favorable pricing, and quality product delivery do not generally violate antitrust guidelines. This is an important lesson for many emerging provider groups. Provider organizations who achieve a dominant market position by competing more effectively may have more flexibility in pricing once they achieve dominance.

## Antitrust Guidelines for Provider Organization Development

The following are specific recommendations for the development, financing, and operations of provider organizations (POs) that may lessen the risk of antitrust actions.

### Organizational Structure

POs should be incorporated. A "C" corporation or limited liability corporation (LLC) are two viable options. The group should develop articles and bylaws and follow the organizational procedures established in the bylaws.

### Market Definition

The more expansive the market for the PO, the more difficult it will be for the group to define its market. Provider groups who develop a minor presence (for example, through a satellite location or agreement with another provider) in a contiguous market can expand their market effectively.

### Financial Risk

The definition of risk is multifaceted. At the outset, participating providers should capitalize the venture with money rather than sweat equity alone. This initial capital should be sufficient to cover development and pre-operational costs including those associated with establishing the infrastructure necessary to acquire and manage risk contracts. POs should seek risk contracts preferentially over fee-for-service agreements. Risk contracts are viewed as evidence of true financial integration and are generally exempt from cumbersome communications mechanisms like the "messenger model."

## Operational Integration

Providers who integrate operationally are better insulated from antitrust challenges. Single-specialty, multispecialty, and primary care group practices represent a clear expression of complete economic integration. Most POs including IPAs, groups without walls, and PHOs are only partially integrated. Emerging POs often are developed solely for the purpose of securing payer contracts. The more that these organizations integrate other functions (for example, billing, equipment and supplies purchasing, staffing, etc.), the better they are protected from antitrust actions. The ability to consolidate these other functions depends largely on the quality of the management infrastructure. This infrastructure may be internally developed or subcontracted to a management company. A provider organization that is staffed primarily through the part-time efforts of participating providers is unlikely to achieve true integration and may have to resort to a messenger model to operate. Newly formed groups should establish an integration plan and adhere to the principles and timeline.

## Protective Measures

POs should engage a qualified health care attorney to assist them with the organizational process and guide them through the antitrust maze. Additionally, the group should purchase Directors and Officers and Errors and Omissions Insurance specific to MCOs from an established carrier.

In summary, the health care delivery system is undergoing a rationalization process driven primarily by the growth of managed care. POs of various types are developing, reorganizing, or expanding to compete for covered lives in the managed care marketplace. Antitrust concerns must be considered by these organizations both structurally and operationally. Insulation from antitrust challenges is linked to the degree of economic integration exhibited by the group. Groups that integrate economically and compete successfully for managed care market share through efficiency and aggressive marketing are reasonably protected. POs are wise to seek good legal advice during the formative stage, develop a management infrastructure, and plan for operational integration.

# Appendix A _____
## Resources

**Academy of Managed Care Pharmacy**
4435 Waterfront Drive
Suite 101
Glen Allen, VA 23060
(804) 527–1905

**American Academy of Family Physicians**
8880 Ward Parkway
Kansas City, MO 64114
(816) 333–9700

**American Academy of Orthopaedic Surgeons**
6300 North River Road
Rosemont, IL 60018
(847) 384-4322

**American Association of Health Plans**
1129 20th Street, NW
Suite 600
Washington, DC 20036
(202) 778–3200

**American College of Cardiology**
9111 Old Georgetown Road
Bethesda, MD 20814–1699
(301) 897–5400

**American College of Surgeons**
1640 Wisconsin Avenue, NW
Washington, DC 20007
(202) 337–2701

**American Medical Association**
515 North State Street
Chicago, IL 60610
(312) 464–5000

**American Medical Association Solutions, Inc.**
200 North LaSalle, Suite 500
Chicago, IL 60601
(800) 366-6968

**American Medical Group Association**
1422 Duke Street
Alexandria, VA 22314–3430
(703) 838–0033

**American Society of Internal Medicine**
2011 Pennsylvania Avenue, NW
Suite 800
Washington, DC 20006–1808
(202) 835–2746

**Association of Managed
Healthcare Organizations**
555 13th Street, NW
Suite 600 E
Washington, DC 20004
(202) 824–1770

**The Association of
Physician Hospital
Organizations/Integrated
Delivery Systems**
4435 Waterfront Drive
Suite 101
Glen Allen, VA 23060
(804) 747–5823

**Blue Cross Blue Shield
Association**
676 North St. Clair Street
Chicago, IL 60601
312-440-5955

**The IPA Association**
330 Hegenberger Road
Suite 305
Oakland, CA 94621
(510) 569-6561

**Medical Group
Management Association**
104 Inverness Terrace East
Englewood, CO 80112–5306
(303) 799–1111

**National Association of
Dental Plans**
5001 LBJ Freeway
Suite 375
Dallas, TX 75244
(214) 458–6998

**National Association of
Insurance Commissioners**
120 West 12th Street
Suite 1100
Kansas City, MO 64105
(816) 842–3600

**National Association of
Managed Care Physicians**
4435 Waterfront Drive
Suite 101
Glen Allen, VA 23060
(804) 527–1905

**National Committee for
Quality Assurance**
2000 L Street, NW
Suite 500
Washington, DC 20036
(202) 955–3500

**National Health Lawyers
Association**
1120 Connecticut Avenue, NW
Suite 950
Washington, DC 20036
(202) 833–1100

**National IPA Coalition**
1999 Harrison Street
Suite 2750
Oakland, CA 94612
(510) 267–1999

# Appendix B

## Glossary

### A

**Actuary**—An employee within the insurance industry or related field who is trained and recognized as an accredited insurance mathematician who calculates premium rates, reserves, and dividends within a given plan and who prepares statistical studies, reports, and projections based on the experience of given populations or plans.

**Adverse selection**—A phenomenon that occurs within the mix of covered lives for a plan when patients with high health care utilization habits select a particular plan in greater numbers than are otherwise representative of the population as a whole.

**Affiliated health care provider**—Any hospital, clinic, outpatient services facility, or individual physician or surgeon listed under the definition of provider, or groups of physicians or surgeons that may be affiliated with a particular insurer, and that by contract provide professional health care services to patients and others in support of the mission and stated initiatives of the named insurer; *see also* participating provider.

**Age/sex factor**—Within the discipline of health care insurance underwriting, this factor accounts for the age and sex risk of medical costs for a given population, regarding the likely medical claims or health care utilization from such a group.

**Ambulatory care**—Health care services that are rendered on an outpatient basis or to patients who are not confined overnight in a

*Source:* Some of the terms have been adapted from R. Rognehaugh, *The Managed Health Care Dictionary*, © 1996, Aspen Publishers, Inc.

health care institution; outpatient care; may be provided in a doctor's office, a medical clinic, an acute hospital, or a freestanding facility.

**Ancillary**—Outpatient or auxiliary services to support diagnostic workup of the patient, or supplemental services needed as part of providing other care; ancillary services include anesthesia, lab, radiology, or pharmacy; other than room, board, medical, and nursing services.

**APG**—Ambulatory patient groups are a modification of ambulatory visit groups (AVGs), developed as an outpatient classification scheme for Health Care Financing Administration (HCFA); APGs are the reimbursement methodology for outpatient procedures as diagnosis-related groups (DRGs) are for inpatient days; APGs provide for a fixed reimbursement to an institution for outpatient procedures or visits and incorporate data regarding the reason for the visit and patient data; they prevent unbundling of ancillary services.

**ASO**—Administrative services only; typically, a portion of the per member per month rate which is performed either by a payer or provider; a contract between an insurance company and a self-funded plan when the insurance company performs administrative services only and does not assume any risk; services usually include claims processing but may include other services such as actuarial analysis, utilization review, etc.; *see also* ERISA.

**Average wholesale price**—The standard charge for a pharmacy item; derived by computing the average cost of the item to a pharmacy as charged by a large representation of pharmacy wholesale suppliers (for items not otherwise being sold at a discount).

**AWP laws**—Any willing provider laws; multiple state laws that challenge and establish policy governing managed care organizations; requires the granting of network enrollment to any provider who is willing to join, as long as they meet provisions outlined in the plan; the central issue is the fairness of physician de-selection by a plan, and conversely, the plan's ability to reduce medical costs by eliminating overutilizing physicians.

# B

**Beneficiary**—Person or persons specified by a policyholder as eligible to receive insurance policy proceeds (private or government).

**Benefit**—Amount payable by the insurance company to a claimant, assignee, or beneficiary when the insured suffers a loss covered by the policy.

**Benefit levels**—The degree to which a person is entitled to receive services based on his or her contract with a plan or insurer.

**Benefit package**—The health care services or supplies provided to an individual or group and specified within a contract with a carrier or federal agency.

**Billed charges with maximum**—Hospital charges that are billed to the health maintenance organization (HMO), up to a ceiling or cap that has been agreed upon by the hospital and HMO.

**Board certified**—A physician or other health professional who has passed an exam from a medical specialty board and is thereby certified to provide care within that specialty.

**Board eligible**—A designation of caliber applied to participating providers by some health plans, expressed as a percentage of those eligible to take the specialty board exam (as opposed to the number of providers who have actually passed the exam—board-certified); graduates from an approved medical college or university after completion of the required training and practical experience.

**Bundled case rate**—A single charge or reimbursement mechanism that includes the institutional and professional charges.

## C

**Capitated payment**—A contractually agreed fee (monthly, bimonthly, or annual) paid by an HMO or competitive medical plan (CMP) to an IDN, hospital, physician, or group practice, in exchange for health care services to enrolled members.

**Capitation rate**—Providers and HMOs (and other "customer-supplier" entities) negotiate a rate per enrollee, per period (often monthly); the provider renders all contracted care and services to members for a prospective payment with retroactive adjustments, taking the risk that the capitation rate will be sufficient to cover all of the costs of care to members; similar agreements can be made between the hospital and delivery system, and physician groups, for either primary care physicians (PCPs) or specialists; *see also* capitated payment and per member per month (PMPM).

**Carve out**—A category of health care not covered as a benefit within the contract (thus, carved out of the pricing structure), usually an area of high cost or requiring special expertise (for example, behavioral, subacute, podiatry, chiropractic, radiographic, and transplant areas) that is not subject to discretionary utilization and not included within the capitation rate.

**Case mix**—The frequency and intensity of hospital admissions or services reflecting different needs and uses of hospital resources; case mix can be measured based on patients' diagnoses or the severity of their illnesses, the utilization of services, and the characteristics of a hospital; case mix influences average length of stay (ALOS), cost, and scope of services provided by a hospital.

**Case rate**—A reimbursement model used by hospitals to establish a flat rate per admission based on an assumed average length of stay per admission; the HMO is charged this rate for each member admitted; unique rates may be set or grouped by diagnosis type or categories of medical and surgical, obstetric, critical care, cardiac, etc.; other elements may include sliding scale volume, ALOS by type, volume of ancillary per patient, contribution margin, etc.; *see also* bundled case rate.

**Closed panel**—A managed care plan that contracts with physicians on an exclusive basis for services and does not allow those physicians to see patients for another managed care organization; examples include staff and group model HMOs, or a large private medical group that contracts with an HMO; a physician must normally meet narrow criteria to join the closed panel of a plan's providers.

**Coinsurance**—The portion of covered health care cost for which the person insured has the responsibility to pay, usually based on a fixed percentage; a percentage of cost to be paid by the insured, having already paid the maximum deductible for the year; *see also* co-payment and deductible.

**Complication**—Disease or condition arising during the course of, or as a result of, another disease, that modifies medical care requirements; for DRGs, a condition that arises during the hospital stay that prolongs the length of stay by at least one day in approximately 75 percent of cases.

**Comprehensive health services**—Health care that includes at a minimum the following: physician services, outpatient services and inpatient hospital services, medically necessary emergency health services, and diagnostic laboratory and therapeutic radiology services (may be limited regarding duration and cost); defined in Subpart A, 417.1 of the General Provisions portion of HCFA's federal regulation.

**Co-payment**—The portion of a medical claim that a member must pay out of pocket; usually a small dollar amount, i.e., $5.00.

**Cost containment**—A method or strategy to reduce health care costs.

**Cost sharing**—A method of reimbursement for health care services that holds the patient responsible for a portion or percentage of the charge, a strategy that serves to reduce utilization; normally includes an annual deductible amount; *see also* coinsurance.

**Cost shifting**—Practice whereby a health care provider charges certain patients or third-party payers more for services to subsidize service provided below cost or free to the poor or uninsured.

**Covered lives**—Refers to the number of persons who are enrolled within a particular health plan, or enrolled for coverage by a provider network; includes covered dependents.

**Covered services**—Services specified in a managed care contract; specific services and supplies for which Medicaid will provide reimbursement; these consist of a combination of mandatory and optional services within each state.

**Credentialing**—The review process by a hospital or insurer to approve a provider; a careful review of documents, medical license, evidence of malpractice insurance (in cases where the insurance is needed or not provided by the supporting hospital or HMO by agreement), history involving actual or alleged malpractice, and educational background of professional providers; may apply to seeking candidacy on care panels.

## D

**Death spiral**—Refers to a sequential spiral of high premium rates and adverse selection that causes financial losses for an insurer, because underwriting losses increase faster than the premiums can recover; an economic reference for medical practices that do not modify provider behavior toward managed care efficiencies in time to remain competitive.

**Deductible**—The portion of a member's health care expenses that must be paid out of pocket before any insurance coverage applies, usually $100–300.

**Dependent**—An enrolled health plan member who is the spouse or an unmarried child of an enrollee, or a stepchild or legally adopted child of either the employee or the employee's spouse, and whose primary domicile is with the employee, except for other arrangements as approved by the plan; dependent children status may include those under the age of 18, or children attending college full-time under a specified age de-selection of providers; *see also* exclusivity.

**DFFS**—Discounted fee-for-service; a payment method that is calculated as a certain percentage of discount from fee-for-service charges; among the least risky contracting approach, second only to billed charges; may include a sliding scale tied to volume, with varying discounts by product line; similar to full fee-for-service (FFS) except that the HMO agrees to pay billed hospital charges, or outpatient services, minus a fixed percentage, which is based on the efficiencies of guaranteed payments (usage protocols used by the HMO); *see also* FFS and global capitation.

**DME**—Durable medical equipment; equipment that can endure repeated use, without being subject to disposal after one-time use (such as insulin pumps, wheelchairs, home hospital beds, walkers, glaucometers, motor-driven wheelchairs, or oxygen equipment); generally, DME is not useful or needed by a person without illness or injury.

**Downstream costs**—Typically used to describe all costs that are incurred directly or indirectly by a primary care physician, and normally involve notions about how to reduce or control utilization of those costs as a solution for better efficiency in managing care for populations; includes inpatient services, referrals to specialists, diagnostic procedures, mental health services, pharmacy services, and all other costs that occur subordinate to the PCP; *see also* PCP and full personal capitation.

**Drug utilization review**—A review to establish the medical appropriateness of medications given by providers to patients for particular medical conditions; performed by peers with feedback and education given to the providers, as appropriate.

# E

**Emergency**—Life-endangering bodily injury or sudden and unexpected illness that requires a member to seek immediate medical attention under circumstances that effectively preclude seeking care through a plan physician or a plan medical center; immediate care needed to preserve life, limb, eyesight, bodily tissue, or to preclude unnecessary pain and suffering.

**Emergency services**—Covered inpatient or outpatient services that are furnished by an appropriate source other than the HMO or CMP for care needed immediately because of injury or sudden illness, when such care cannot be delayed for the time required to reach the HMO or CMP provider or authorized alternative without risk of permanent damage to the patient's health, and when transfer to an HMO or CMP source is also precluded because of risk or unreasonable distance, given the nature of the medical condition.

**Employer mandate**—The mandate for an employer to provide a dual choice option for employees to have access to health care; or to provide specific health care benefits to its employees, such as mental health services.

**Encounter**—A health care visit of any type that warrants payment of services by an enrollee to a provider of care or services.

**Enrollee**—A covered member of a health care contract who is eligible to receive contract services; *see also* insured.

**Enrollment**—The number of patients who have contracted with a carrier; the process or activity of recruiting and signing up individuals and groups for membership in a plan; a description of the covered lives in a plan.

**EPO**—Exclusive provider organization; the patient must remain in the network to receive benefits (out-of-network care results in payment by the patient); a plan regulated under state insurance statute that provides coverage only for contracted providers and does not extend to non-preferred provider services.

**ERISA**—Employee Retirement Income Security Act; a 1974 federal law that mandates reporting and disclosure requirements for group life and health plans, with relevant guidance on the sponsorship, administration, and servicing of plans, some claims processing, and appeals regulations.

**Exclusion**—The practice of keeping an entity out of a network for the purpose of eliminating poor health care; may be conducted by an insurer regarding hospitals, or by a physician-hospital organization (PHO), or preferred provider organization (PPO) regarding individual physicians or group practices; *see also* exclusivity.

**Exclusions**—Conditions specified in the contract or employee benefit plan for which the plan will not provide payment.

**Exclusivity**—Limitation of an HMO network to one hospital or provider or to an extremely small number of providers; the hospitals normally concede discounts in exchange for exclusivity in hopes of increased volume in return.

**Experience rating**—The method by which rates are derived from previous data for the actual costs of care and services for a group of enrollees versus the alternative of the community rating system mandated by HCFA for federally qualified HMOs; HMOs look to entities such as the American Medical Association (AMA), the Food and Drug Administration (FDA), Department of Health and Human Services (DHHS), National Institutes of Health, or the Council of Medical Specialty Societies to confirm the ultimate value of health care procedures, services, medical supplies and equipment, or drug interventions.

# F

**Fee maximum**—The most that a PCP may be reimbursed for any particular health care service, contractually agreed upon as terms for participation in a plan; normally tied to a regional assessment of those fees that are usual, reasonable, or customary; *see also* reasonable and customary charge.

**Fee schedule**—The document, under an FFS arrangement, or discounted FFS, that outlines all fee maximums that the participating provider will be paid by the health plan within the period of the contract.

**FFS**—Fee-for-service; the full rate of charge for a private patient without any type of insurance arrangement or discounted prospective health plan; *see also* FFS reimbursement.

**FFS reimbursement**—Patient's direct payment to a health care provider in response to billed charges for a unit of service versus a capitated payment; for relevant problems of cost containment under this traditional setting.

**Flat-rate pricing models**—Three types of pricing models currently used by hospitals are capitation (fixed annual fee per enrollee); per case or case rate (flat rate per admission); and per diem (flat rate per day of hospital stay).

**Foundation model**—A nonprofit physician-hospital entity for markets that do not allow physicians to be directly employed by a hospital; involves more advanced managed care integration than the group practice without walls (GPWW), open PHO, or closed PHO; contains management services organization (MSO) centralized support and physician practice procurement features, but MSO costs are paid by the foundation, not physicians; may allow physicians to share in revenue; *see also* GPWW, MSO, and PHO.

**Freedom of choice**—A law within some states that allows an enrollee the right to select a non-network provider and pay no added cost within a PPO arrangement, assuming the provider accepts the PPO payment rate; *see also* PPO.

**FTC**—Federal Trade Commission; reviews mergers and acquisitions of HMOs, hospitals, medical groups, or various levels of health networks and combinations thereof to ensure no infringements of antitrust laws.

**Full personal capitation**—Considered perhaps the ideal method of advanced capitation at the level of the individual PCP, who receives a PMPM to cover specialist expenses; the method can allow a PCP to become more efficient while ensuring quality of care, which in turn allows more enrollees per PCP; early use of full personal capitation may favor either the protection of the PCP from specialist risk or catastrophic costs (that is, more than $3,750 per member per year), or may include 6- to 12-month moving average payments; does not include global risk for facility costs; *see also* global capitation, downstream costs, and PMPM.

# G

**Gatekeeper model**—A managed care design in which a PCP serves as gatekeeper for the patient's initial contact for medical care and referrals; used within closed access or closed panel structures; precludes the patient from obtaining care from multiple sources and from gaining unnecessary direct access for specialty care.

**Generic equivalents**—Drug products not protected by a trademark that have the same active chemical ingredients as those sold under proprietary brand names.

**Global budget**—A government technique of setting a total expenditure ceiling or cap for all of the nation's health care expenditures versus regulating the price of individual fee elements.

**Global capitation**—A reimbursement mechanism that pays for all of the care needs for a population of patients, including physicians and hospitals; may involve payment from an HMO to each PCP at risk for a contractually determined PMPM amount that is to pay for the costs of all physician services; may involve payment to a provider network or IDN for all physician and hospital care, with other stated commitments or limitations for pharmacy, mental health, or other carve outs; a portion of the global cap may be withheld in a reserve fund to pay for specialist care referred by the PCP (excess remaining each year is paid out, or shortages are carried forward against future global capitation payments to the PCP); *see also* capitation rate, carve out, and risk.

**Global fee**—A reimbursement mechanism used by a provider for a given episode of care; the single fee for the entire charge of all aspects and services surrounding the episode, such as $1,600 for a normal vaginal delivery to include a stated amount of prenatal and postnatal care in addition to the delivery; best used with a large number of covered lives to spread risk.

**GPWW**—Group practice without walls; an early managed care market structure that allows physicians to retain their separate offices, combining centralized business operations with decentralized delivery of care to preserve traditional autonomy; comprises a group of physicians with varying interests and geographic locations, who may or may not have hospital affiliations as primary care or specialty orientations; GPWWs fail to attract meaningful covered lives.

**Group contract**—A managed care contract with a medical group rather than individual physicians; the document that includes an application for coverage, together with any additional contract clauses signed by both the health plan and the enrolling entity, which constitutes the agreement between the health plan and the enrolling unit regarding benefits, exclusions, and other conditions.

**Group model HMO**—An HMO model in which the physicians, employed by the HMO, are typically paid on a salary basis or fee schedule and may receive incentive payments based on their performance; *see also* network model HMO, staff model HMO, and individual practice association (IPA)–HMO model.

**Group practice**—A combined practice of three or more physicians or dentists who may share office personnel, expenses, equipment, space, records, and income.

# H

**HCFA**—Health Care Financing Administration; the federal agency that administers Medicare and oversees states' administration of Medicaid; also reviews Medicare HMO applications and publishes reports on plan performance.

**Health coverage**—Insurance to protect against the risk of sickness or injury; provides payment of benefits for medical services and supplies, dental, disability, and various other options or included benefits as listed within the contract.

**Health plan**—An HMO, CMP, PPO, insured plan, self-funded plan, or other legal entity that covers health care services.

**Health professionals**—Physicians (doctors of medicine and doctors of osteopathy), dentists, nurses, podiatrists, optometrists, physicians' assistants, clinical psychologists, social workers, pharmacists, nutritionists, occupational therapists, physical therapists, and other professionals engaged in the delivery of health services who are licensed, practice under an institutional license, are certified, or practice under authority of the HMO, a medical group, IPA, or other authority consistent with state law.

**Health promotion**—Activities by MCOs, IDSs, provider groups, physicians, and others to encourage healthy lifestyles on the part of patients and their beneficiaries through educational materials, seminars, health risk assessments, incentives, or disincentives; may include selfcare and proper use of PCP.

**HMO**—Health maintenance organization; an entity that provides and manages the coverage of health services provided to plan members in return for a fixed, paid premium; the four types of HMO models are the group model, IPA, network, and staff model; under the federal HMO act, an entity must have the following three characteristics: an organized system for providing health care or otherwise ensuring health care delivery in a geographic area, an agreed upon set of basic and supplemental health maintenance and treatment services, and a voluntarily enrolled group of patients; *see also* group model HMO, IPA–HMO model, network model HMO, and staff model HMO.

**Hold-harmless clause**—A clause in some PPO contracts that designates who is and is not held responsible for any contractual liability; often written to give the provider sole responsibility; some states require provisions to hold patients harmless from claims by providers, even if the insurer becomes insolvent.

**Home care**—Provision of medical care by a health care professional at the patient's home, traditionally administered in either a more costly hospital inpatient setting or an outpatient setting (for example, IV therapy or physical therapy); preferred method of care for patients not needing hospital care or for patients not able to ambulate to office visits.

**Hospital affiliation**—The contract between a plan and one or more hospitals whereby the hospital supports the inpatient requirements that the plan has agreed to provide enrollees.

**Hospital-based physician**—A physician who provides services in a hospital setting and who has a contractual relationship with the hospital, such as being a salaried employee; contractual relationships vary widely and include paying a physician an agreed amount or an agreed portion of the collections from patients, or the hospital may collect the funds from patients either in its own right or as an agent for the physician.

# I

**IDS**—Integrated delivery system; a single organization or a group of affiliated organizations that provide the full range of health care services to a population of enrollees within a market area that consists of PCPs, specialists, hospitals, home health care providers, and other ancillary care providers; an IDS may obtain an HMO license and market directly to employers or may seek global risk agreements with HMOs; *see also* global capitation.

**Individual specialist capitation**—A method of capitated payment to specialists, consisting of the selection of specific physicians for each specialty area and payment of a capitated amount times the number of enrollees in the plan; individual capitation can create geographic problems of referral distance for patients and patient unfamiliarity of specialists, and the plan has limited flexibility in channeling to "special expertise" specialists; also, a large number of lives are needed to sustain a specialist, yet actuarial risk may be excessive.

**Information systems**—Managed care information systems track, measure, analyze, and improve performance of managed care; including systems processing and payment; membership enrollment; benefit management by plan, product, and level; utilization review (UR) and utilization management (UM); billing and accounts receivable; and administrative support.

**Insured**—Any person or organization under a contract or policy for benefits that are received in return for payment.

**Integration**—The construction or reorganization of a health care entity by connecting previously independent segments of the care continuum to emphasize economic interactions between segments for the most appropriate care, services, and use of resources (for example, subacute versus traditional care).

**IP**—An enrollee who has been admitted to an acute hospital or other non-ambulatory setting and placed under the care of a physician for at least twenty-four hours.

**IPA-HMO model**—Individual practice association; an HMO model in which physicians form an association (as a separate legal entity) that contracts with the HMO to arrange care through individual contracts with physicians; physicians remain individual practitioners who see non-HMO patients and maintain their own offices, records, and staff; the individual practice association may compensate the physicians on a per capita, fee schedule, or FFS basis.

# J

**JV**—Joint venture arrangement involving risk and benefit sharing between one or more entities for a specific purpose, with rights and obligations specified in contractual terms; examples include a hospital JV with a provider group for 50 percent of the group profits or "downside" risk, a hospital JV with an HMO for 50 percent exposure to the mutual patient business, or a hospital buying a certain percent of common shares of an HMO to broaden sharing of business.

# L

**Least restrictive level of care**—The managed care standard calls for care at the level of least cost and intensity that will offer sufficient safety and effective treatment.

# M

**Malpractice insurance**—Insurance that protects providers against loss incurred as the result of litigation expenses.

**Managed care**—Any method of health care delivery designed to reduce unnecessary utilization of services, contain costs, and measure performance, while providing accessible, quality, effective health care; *see also* risk sharing and UM.

**MCO**—Managed care organization; a generic term applied to a managed care plan; may be in the form of an HMO, PHO, PPO, EPO, or other structure.

**Medicaid**—A medical program of aid provided by the federal government and administered at the state level to provide benefits according to established criteria for the poor, aged, blind and disabled, and dependent children; current legislative proposals would provide block grants to the states, or other strategies to make them responsible for the program with less dependence on the federal level.

**Medical director**—Physician, usually employed by a hospital or health plan, who provides leadership and decision making for an organized medical staff, authorizing referral and hospitalization decisions, while subordinate staff perform case management, utilization management, or quality-of-care disciplines.

**Medical group**—Any partnership, association, or group of physicians, dentists, psychologists, podiatrists, or other licensed health care providers working together in medical practice; group practices that pool their income may use a portion of it to employ staff, to distribute among members, or to retain profits to build group net worth; the effect of managed care upon managed care groups' profitability has been mostly bipolar—the groups that fear managed care may be left behind in gaining the new efficiency skills, only to see the value of their groups decline, while the other groups that become successful in adapting to managed care will remain profitable and may remain independent while adding and training other physicians to the group or pod-level formations.

**Medical loss ratio**—A ratio of how much it costs to provide health benefits versus how much revenue is made from premiums (or total medical expenses of paid claims plus the incurred but not reported [IBNR] claims component, divided by premium revenue); a common way to describe efficiency of an HMO plan, medical loss ratios are being reduced during the decade of the 1990s from the low-90 percent to mid-70 percent range.

**Medical protocols**—Guidelines that emerge from clinical trials to prevent, detect, or treat a medical condition and that insurance plans or MCOs may require physicians to follow; specific treatment options or steps to follow when a provider sees a patient with a particular set of clinical symptoms or lab data; also called best practices, critical and clinical pathways, clinical algorithms, practice guidelines, or practice parameters.

**Medically necessary treatment**—Treatment that is warranted; judged by the diagnosis, medical documentation, and the likelihood that peers within the medical community accept the treatment as necessary for the patient.

**Messenger model**—The nickname for an early model of physician integration, normally fostered by a supporting hospital entity to help local physicians move toward more sophisticated managed care; this formation signals non-affiliated physicians and insurers that capabilities are being enhanced to manage care and accept risk; typically, the membership is easy to obtain and inexpensive.

**Midlevel practitioner or provider**—Physician's assistants, clinical nurse practitioners, nurse midwives, nutritionists, aides, medical technicians, physical therapists, etc., who deliver medical care as nonphysicians, generally under the supervision of a physician, but at less cost.

**Mixed model**—A managed care plan that mixes two or more types of delivery systems, such as an HMO with a closed and open panel system; also called hybrid model modified FFS—a reimbursement mechanism that pays providers on a fee-for-service, but with certain fee maximums established by procedure; distinct from a discounted FFS in that it may not always be the same percentage discount from the prevailing FFS; this unit-of-service type arrangement is actually a typical reimbursement mechanism for many arrangements that are considered to involve managed care, but have not yet evolved to global risk; may involve a PCR withhold; *see also* DFFS, FFS, and global capitation.

**MFN**—Most favored nations; contracts between insurers or managed care organizations and providers grant this status to the insurer by stating that any time the provider gives a better price to a second or subsequent insurer or patient, it will notify the first insurer and give the same price reductions.

**MSO**—Management services organization; a legal entity that offers practice management and administrative support to physicians, or that purchases physician practices and obtains payer contracts as a PHO; can be a wholly owned, for-profit subsidiary of a hospital, a hospital-physician joint venture, or a private joint venture with physicians or hospitals and physicians; offers a menu of services through shared practice management (group purchasing discounts, practice management, consulting, information newsletters and educational seminars, computer and information systems, marketing, employee leasing for office coverage, claims processing), creates economies and allows physicians to delegate management and administration, but yields some profit for these functions; corporate examples include Coastal, InPhyNet, MedPartners, and PhyCor; also called physician practice management or physician management corporations; *see also* PHO.

**Multispecialty group practice**—A group of providers in which at least one physician is a family practitioner, internist, or general medical officer whereas the others practice other specialties.

# N

**NAIC**—National Association of Insurance Commissioners; national trade association with no official policy authority that serves as the representative organization of state insurance officials, who regulate the insurance industry and provide uniformity for approval and policy of HMOs within their respective states.

**NCQA**—National Committee for Quality Assurance; an independent, private-sector group that was formed in 1979 to review care quality and other procedures of HMOs and similar types of plans and to render an accreditation; a team of surveyors reviews everything from the credentialing process to record keeping; NCQA is becoming the hallmark of quality for an HMO (working cooperatively with leading American corporations), and it is estimated that nearly half of all HMOs have now submitted their operations for review.

**NCQA standards**—Standards addressed by NCQA review include the following: written credentialing and renewal policies; the conduct of initial and periodic review and approval of those procedures, credentials committee, or peer review organization (PRO) designation; the actual credentialing for all practitioners; Drug Enforcement Agency (DEA) compliance for controlled substances; verification of malpractice coverage, liability claims history, board certification or graduate medical school verification, work history, status of good standing at any admitting facility, personal statements of competency, National Practitioner Data Bank (NPDB) checks, any appraisal documentation, site reviews of practitioners, statements of delegated activities, and procedures to suspend, reduce, or terminate an NCQA practitioner with reports and appeals options; *see also* credentialing and NPDB.

**Network model HMO**—An HMO model that contracts with multiple physician groups to provide an adequate network for enrolled members; may involve large single- and multispecialty groups; *see also* group model HMO, staff model HMO, and IPA–HMO model.

**NPDB**—National Practitioner Data Bank; houses a database on physician discipline or malpractice payment experience; queried by HMOs, private and federal hospitals, and health systems; used for credentialing a provider for clinical privileges or granting status as medical director or medical staff positions; requery of NPDB is required at a two-year interval for reappointment.

# O

**Open access**—Patient access to providers of specialty care without going through a gatekeeper or primary care provider, as long as the specialist participates in the network; *see also* IPA–HMO model and open-ended HMO.

**Open-ended-HMO**—When used by HCFA, this model includes the use of a gatekeeper, although others use it to mean open access; the use of non-network providers is covered for beneficiaries, but with possible higher coinsurance; the HMO may be at full risk for in-network services and insured for out-of-network, or may propose risk sharing for out-of-network; *see also* open access.

**Out-of-network**—Refers to hospital care or other provider services that are rendered by nonparticipating providers, due to the purposeful selection of the enrollee or the occurrence of an illness or injury while on out-of-area travel; some plans call for the member to pay the fees, whereas others allow for coverage under a higher co-pay by the member.

**Outcomes measurement**—A method of systematically monitoring a patient's medical or surgical intervention or nonintervention together with the associated responses, including measures of morbidity and functional status; findings from outcomes studies enable managed care entities to outline protocols to improve health care results.

**Outpatient**—An enrollee who receives treatment or services without being admitted to a hospital.

## P

**Packaged pricing**—A reimbursement strategy used by hospitals; offer of flat fees on a limited number of case types (which may include category-base pricing) to offer employer and insurers preferred pricing on DRGs that the hospital can manage well, without setting a fixed fee for all diagnoses.

**Participating provider**—An individual provider, hospital, integrated delivery system, pharmacist, dentist, optometrist, chiropractor, podiatrist, nurse, medical group practice, home care company, behavioral or mental health entity, skilled nursing facility, long-term care facility, or other medical institution or health care professional agreeing to provide care or services to enrolled members of a particular plan, according to stated rates and conditions.

**PBM**—Pharmacy benefit management; a relatively young industry that specializes in reducing the amount of cost for pharmaceuticals, either in support of an HMO or a hospital-based system; PBM programs, connecting most of the U.S. pharmacies via computer network, provide data reporting, educational information directed toward least-cost prescribing alternatives, and software to support drug-to-drug interactions within an entire community to prevent redundant and costly patient services; some PBMs are independent organizations whereas others are subsidiaries of drug companies or insurance companies; PBMs can reduce the amount of monthly PMPM cost on pharmacy services, from an approximate savings range of $1 to $3 PMPM relative to an overall pharmacy cost of $10 to $13 for a commercial population, not including Medicare or Medicaid.

**PCP**—Primary care provider or primary care physician; a physician whose practice is devoted largely to internal medicine, family and general practice, and pediatrics; an ob/gyn may be considered a PCP, and some networks provide a focused retraining for ob/gyns so that they may enter into risk contracts for a population of female patients; *see also* gatekeeper model.

**Percent of premium**—The percent of any element measured against the price of the monthly premium that an HMO charges for a particular benefit plan; if an HMO charges $100 per month to the patient, with various PMPM amounts expended on delivery systems, hospitals, PCPs, administration, specialists, drugs, risk management, profit, and other elements, then a profit of $5 is 5 percent of premium, etc.; considered to be the greatest financial risk for reimbursement arrangements based on a percent of premium (versus a less risky continuum ranging from billed charges, DFFS, per diem, case rate, and PMPM).

**PHO**—Physician-hospital organization; an IPA associated with a hospital, often initiated by the hospital that provides management services; features a contracting mechanism for obtaining "covered lives," generally with 50:50 physician and hospital control and hospital financing; pros: physicians retain autonomy; it is a step toward full integration and basis for capitation experience; cons: strains relationships with independent physicians; hazards can come from utilization control, division of revenue, and panel selection.

**Physician services**—Services that are either personally furnished for an individual patient by a physician, contributing to the diagnosis or treatment of the individual patient; ordinarily required to be performed by a physician; or, in the case of anesthesiology, radiology, or laboratory services, additional special regulatory requirements (stated in regulations 42 CFR 405.552/.554/556) for each of these specialty areas are met; the importance of "physician services" classification comes from an October 1983 policy that said that only inpatient services not covered under Part A of the prospective payment system for hospitals will be "physician services," except for direct medical education and capital costs—as a result, physician services are paid on the basis of reasonable charges.

**PMPM**—Per member per month; the revenue or cost of a risk payment that is typically made to providers by HMOs for providing a defined amount of care for each enrolled patient each month.

**Pod-level risk pool or pod**—A group or pod of five to fifteen PCPs (many prefer four to six) given a collective risk pool based upon a budget for a distinct population that has been assigned to the pod; physicians earn money back from the physician contingency reserve or risk pool by reducing hospital and other "downstream" costs; pods are more effective with clinical protocols, advanced sharing of information (both in the didactic and automated sense), and peer pressure (which could be full personal capitation); some pods include specialists, physician leaders, and partial administrator monitoring or assistance; *see also* downstream costs and full personal capitation.

**Pool (risk pool)**—A portion of payments for services rendered are placed within a pool as a source for any subsequent claims that exceed projections, for a defined group of patients or product that is defined by size or geographic location; funds that remain in the pool after a specified term are paid out to providers, thereby creating an incentive for lower utilization; the potential for "up-side" payout from risk pools is the basis for providers to convert to a managed care style of practice versus FFS, because although the reimbursements are compressed as managed care becomes more mature within the region, the provider is capable of seeing larger populations of patients for less cost per patient.

**POS plan**—Point-of-service plan; provides flexibility for an enrollee to choose to receive a service from a participating or nonparticipating provider, with corresponding benefit or "penalty" of co-pay depending upon the level of benefit selected, with the goal of encouraging the use of network or participating provider care options; POS maintains the popularity of choice by offering the typical HMO provision, PPO, or combinations of both; in many POS plans, enrollees coordinate their care needs through the PCP; HMOs pay nonparticipating providers at an FFS rate; also called HMO swing-out plan or out-of-plan rider to an HMO.

**PPO**—Preferred provider organization; a plan or an affiliation of providers seeking contracts with a plan (by virtue of their ability to cover a broad geographic area or provide multispecialty skills); incentives for providers to participate include quick turnaround of claims payment, a valuable pool of patients, and FFS payment; payer incentive is negotiated discounts to FFS; usually, a PPO doesn't prepay physicians; a physician-sponsored PPO increasingly will bear risk when seeking arrangement with insurance companies or self-insured companies; there is great consensus that PPOs are early-stage managed care relationships that are formed in response to HMO pressure or competition, but do not result in the same savings in health care expense.

**Premium**—An amount of money that is paid to a health plan by a subscriber, or an employer group, in exchange for providing health care, claims processing, and various other administrative services.

**Prepaid health plan**—Contract between an insurer and a subscriber or group of subscribers whereby the plan provides a specified set of health benefits in return for a periodic premium.

**Prescription drug**—A medication that can be sold only by a pharmacy or dispensed after an order by an appropriately licensed physician; for medications approved by the FDA for sale under federal or state law.

**Preventive care**—Care and treatment that is given with the objective of precluding illness or hospitalization; a program that stresses education and early detection and early treatment of conditions, generally including immunizations and routine physical examinations.

**Primary care**—General medical care that is provided by family practitioners, pediatricians, general medical officers, and internal medicine physicians, and sometimes includes care to women that is provided by ob/gyns.

**Primary care capitation**—A system of payment that provides a specified amount to each PCP for each enrolled member, that is, PMPM; the amount is likely determined through the result of negotiation, but is based on the actuarial determination of primary care utilization costs for a comparable sample of patients; a portion of the capitation payment may be a withhold; some PCP capitation models group five to seven PCPs in a "pod" to share learning and risk, or involve the personal capitation of PCPs who are responsible for the "downstream" costs of specialist care and diagnostic procedures; *see also* PMPM and withhold.

**Professional health care services**—Any professional health care services immediately incident to the care of patients, including, but not limited to, the furnishing of food, beverages, medications, or appliances in connection with these services and the handling of human bodies post-mortem.

**Provider**—The generic term used to describe a physician, pharmacist, dentist, optometrist, chiropractor, podiatrist, nurse, hospital, group practice, nursing home, behavioral or mental health entity, skilled nursing facility, long-term care facility, pharmacy, other medical institution, or any individual or group of individuals that provides health care services; a distinction of the term "provider," versus "supplier," within Medicare policy, will determine payment on a charge basis for suppliers and on a prospective or retrospective cost-related basis for providers.

**Provider arrangements**—Evidence of arrangements for basic health services must be shown in an HMO's application to HCFA, in the requested area at the time the application is submitted, including either the explicit evidence of service to Medicare members or specific payment arrangements for services to Medicare members in provider contracts, or both; the application includes the listing of existing or draft contracts or letters of intent for staff (physicians, nonphysicians, or nonstaff physicians), group (member physicians, member nonphysicians, nonmember physicians, or nonmember nonphysicians), IPA (member physicians, member nonphysicians, nonmember physicians, nonmember nonphysicians), direct contract HMO physicians, laboratory services, radiographic services, hospitals, home health services, and others.

**Provider network**—A separate, non-HMO network that is capable of providing support; refers to the number of providers, the specialty mix, or the geographic distribution (any of which may attract federal or commercial payer business) not necessarily a provider-sponsored network (PSN; because PSN entities only represent a proposed formation that could enter into risk relationships in lieu of formally licensed HMOs), a group of providers supporting a particular payer; *see also* PSN.

**PSN**—Provider sponsored network; a formal affiliation of health care providers organized and operated to provide a full range of health care services; a term used in draft language of the 1996 budget discussions of House and Senate proposals that would allow Medicare to contract directly with PSNs on a full-risk capitated basis in a way that would "cut some HMOs out of the middle" depending on the ultimate language; the degree to which PSNs must be subject to the licensing, financing, and insurance considerations, as regulated by state insurance commissioners, will determine the number of providers to qualify, as compared to the more rigid HMO standards under which provider networks must currently qualify; no bill has been currently passed to grant operation to PSNs.

# Q

**Quality assurance**—Program activities that are conducted from the perspective of individual hospitals or insurers, and reviewed by internal leadership or external entities such as NCQA to ensure that medical care and service meet clinical standards of quality; includes elements of peer review and audits of care, medical protocols, credentialing, and assessment of patient satisfaction; *see also* medical protocols, NCQA, and UM.

# R

**RBRVS**—Resource-Based Relative Value Scale; a system used initially by Medicare, but with spin-off influence on other sectors, to more properly assess the skill and resource relationships to specific CPT codes, thereby dictating reimbursement levels; measurements are adjusted for regional deviations, related charges, and overhead; the resulting scale was developed to compensate for Medicare's tendency to overpay for procedural services such as surgery and diagnostic tests, while underpaying for cognitive primary care services involving examination and discussion and education with patients.

**R&C (reasonable and customary) charge**—The amount of money usually billed for individual health care services within a given region; sometimes all fees in the eightieth or ninetieth percentile are averaged to determine the R&C charge, and other times R&C charge is synonymous with fees-schedule rate ceilings, when the rates are relatively high.

**Referral**—The request for additional care, usually of a specialty nature, by a PCP or by a specialist needing additional medical information on behalf of the patient; referrals within the context of managed care are more restricted in the sense that a PCP who accepts financial risk for downstream medical care is more sensitive to the balance between medical necessity and cost; good information systems are needed to track referral costs, which aid physicians in learning more about this factor; *see also* downstream costs.

**Reinsurance**—Insurance procured by an insurance company, provider, or employer to guard against the partial or complete loss of money from medical claims; typical coverage is purchased for either individual stop loss, aggregate stop loss out-of-area care, or insolvency protection; a larger health plan typically reduces reinsurance coverage as it grows; also called stop-loss insurance.

**Reserves**—Fiscal method of providing a fund for incurred but not reported health services or other financial liabilities; also refers to deposits and/or other financial requirements that must be met by an entity as defined by various state or federal regulatory authorities.

**Revenue**—Premium proceeds paid from individual enrollees, groups, or employers to a health plan in return for health care of covered members, support, and information services; *see also* premium.

**Risk**—The loss foreseen by a provider, IDN, or insurer in providing health care services; also refers to the generic arrangements within managed care that involve a departure from FFS medicine toward prepayment, which focuses on the care of a given population by a PCP or hospital system taking full economic responsibility for that population's care needs.

**Risk contract**—A generic description of a contract involving medical claims risk on a prepayment basis between two entities, such as a provider and an HMO, HCFA and a federally qualified HMO, or an integrated delivery network and an individual PCP or medical group; the risk contract will specify the medical services to be included, together with the associated reimbursement structure, and the amount of withhold or physician contingency reserve to be set aside for potential claims above estimates, or incremental risk corridors; if claims run above projections, it is the responsibility of the party that bears risk under the contract to pay those excess costs, whereas any savings are similarly given to the party bearing risk; *see also* risk, reinsurance, and risk corridor.

**Risk corridor**—A mechanism to share risk within a stated range of performance, such as the case when providers are assessed penalties or given financial rewards if their actual claims PMPM fall outside a specific percentage above or below an established claims target (so, for a 10 percent corridor on a PCP set at $23 PMPM, the physician will be subject to rewards for amounts under $21.70 and penalties over $25.30 for PMPM claims costs).

**Risk factors**—The health factors related to disease that may be either established factors (for example, heredity, sex, race, and age) or factors that are influenced by behavior (for example, smoking, inactivity, or response to stress); with the growth of managed care, health plans and systems are learning the outpatient and inpatient costs of various diseases, and the average total monthly claims costs per covered life for hypertension, atherosclerosis, etc.; the goal of current studies or programs is to promote behavior that reduces the cost of care for populations.

**Risk sharing**—A generic term used to define any mechanism that gives financial incentive to managed care providers for rendering cost-effective, high-quality care; *see also* pool.

# S

**Self-insurance**—A risk strategy that allows the potential profit that an HMO or carrier traditionally receives from funding insurance risk to be experienced instead by an employer or other legal entity, such as a hospital-based delivery network; different from reinsurance in that an external insurance protection is not used as a general format, but certain protection may be sought for a segment such as catastrophic; essentially, the health benefits are funded from internal resources without purchasing insurance; self-insurance entities may obtain outside administrative assistance to manage requirements; *see also* reinsurance and stop loss.

**Service area**—The specific region in which health care services are conducted; outlined for approval by a state insurance regulator as of the effective date of the agreement; within an IDS context, the service area is the local area that the network considers to be their immediate market area, and also the approximate border line that may constitute agreement with nearby provider systems for non-competition according to an agreement.

**Shared risk**—An arrangement where any two entities, such as a health plan and a provider, agree to share in the risk of some contracted percentage of hospital costs that may come in over budget, as well as agree to share profits for care provided under budget; *see also* risk sharing and pool.

**Sherman Act**—(15 U.S.C., 1&2) establishes safeguards against health entities forming monopolies, restraint of trade or commerce, or against conspiracy; strategies that contain an anti-competitive outcome or market power to control prices by acquisition are problematic, which leaves the course of being better and smarter as competitors as the only safe method for growth.

**Short-stay hospital**—A category of general and special hospitals that average less than 30 days ALOS for patients.

**Site visit**—The second step of HCFA's procedures to federally qualify an HMO or CMP, in which the HCFA team visits the candidate for two days to verify information provided in the application, explore issues in depth, conduct interviews, and specifically review finances, marketing, health services delivery, and legal systems; at a closing session, the team identifies any added information needed to finalize review and issues a fourteen-day suspension.

**Specialty coverage**—Most contracts between MCOs and employers outline minimum provider network requirements for specialties as either on a specialist to members ratio or geographical driving distance for the patient.

**Staff model HMO**—An HMO model that enters into a relationship with its physicians as employees to provide health care to its members; premiums are paid to the HMO, which in turn pays providers as staff members; increasingly, the staff models are exploring new incentive pay structures versus a flat salary that may not properly provide incentive for desired behaviors; normally, PCPs within this model are not allowed to have a large portion of FFS patients; considered by some as the most efficient managed care model; *see also* group model HMO.

**Stop loss or stop-loss insurance**—Insurance that is designed to stop the loss, or limit risk-exposure beyond a stated amount, for either the catastrophic loss of individual patients or group claims; stop-loss insurance is sought by nearly any entity that accepts risk, and—true to standard insurance concepts—the more protection, the higher the insurance cost, so a point of attachment to stop loss at $75,000 might cost $2.50 PMPM, whereas an attachment at $100,000 might cost $2.00; *see also* reinsurance.

**Subcapitation**—Any capitation arrangement at a level subordinate to global capitation, such as a subcap between an IDS and PCPs, specialists, or ancillary services.

**Surplus**—A description of the funds remaining relative to a risk product or arrangement for payout as bonus or retention, either at the level of an HMO, a hospital withhold pool, an IPA, a medical group, a pod-level entity, or an individual PCP under full personal capitation; *see also* withhold pool.

# T

**Tertiary care**—Health care treatment and services within a sophisticated specialty care setting that is approved under all requirements for tertiary care, serving as a referral and support alternative to primary and secondary care settings.

**Third-party payer**—A public or private organization that pays for or underwrites coverage for health care expenses or another entity, usually an employer (such as Blue Cross and Blue Shield, Medicare,

Medicaid, or commercial insurers); also called third-party carrier; the individual enrollee generally pays a premium for coverage in all private and some public programs, then the organization pays bills on the patient's behalf, which are called third-party payments.

## U

**UM**—Utilization management; the process of evaluating the necessity, appropriateness, and efficiency of health care services; a review coordinator or medical director gathers information about the proposed hospitalization, service, or procedure from the patient and/or provider, then determines whether it meets established guidelines and criteria, which may be written or automated protocols approved by the organization; a provider or IDS that proves it is skilled in UM may negotiate more advantageous pricing, if UM is normally performed by the HMO but could be more effectively passed downward at a savings to the HMO.

**UR**—Utilization review; the evaluation of the medical necessity and the efficiency of health care services, either prospectively, concurrently, or retrospectively; contrasted with utilization management in that UR is more limited to the physician's diagnosis, treatment, and billing amount, whereas UM addresses the wider program requirements; *see also* UM.

**URAC**—Utilization Review Accreditation Commission; established in 1990 to provide accreditation and advancement of utilization review programs, while maintaining quality for patient care; a new initiative expands the URAC's role in accrediting non-capitated provider networks that pay providers on either a fee schedule, discounted FFS, or DRG basis.

**Urgent care center**—A care facility providing immediate, but nonemergent care for minor illness or injury, allowing ambulatory walk-in service that may be either extended-hour or twenty-four–hour service; these facilities had their genesis in managed care principles to provide timely access to care that is less costly than that found in emergency room settings.

**Utilization**—The use of health care services and supplies by an enrolled member or a group, a major focus of the managed care industry to ensure the medical necessity and appropriateness of all expenses; *see also* UM.

# W

**Wellness program**—Any of a growing number of health education programs that promote healthier employees, thereby reducing health care costs, which may include in-house or outside source expertise to assist with education, or activities to encourage exercise; data are important to form wellness policies that best impact health status; *see also* health promotion.

**Withhold**—A portion of a provider's reimbursement from an MCO that is withheld to protect the MCO from financial losses if the provider does not manage its capitation or budget adequately or inducement for the provider to manage care and costs appropriately.

# Index

## A

Access, 23
Acquisition, 1–2
Actuarial consultant, contract
  negotiation, 47–48, 58–59
Actuary, defined, 313
Adverse selection, defined, 313
Affiliated health care provider,
  defined, 313
Affiliation, provider group, 33
Age/sex factor, defined, 313
Aggregate reinsurance, 117
Ambulatory care, defined, 313
Ambulatory care contracting, 209–227
  contract terms and conditions, 227
  cooperative operational
    commitment, 227
  field comments, 224–227
  provider panel nature, 225–226
  reimbursement, 226
Ambulatory surgical services, 209–213
  capitation, 212–213
  case rate, 211–212
  contractual arrangements, 210–213
  fee-for-service, 211
  shift to outpatient care, 209–210
American Society of Anesthesiologists,
  relative value unit system, 95–97
Ancillary, defined, 314
Ancillary care contracting, 221–222
  contract terms and conditions, 227
  cooperative operational

commitment, 227
field comments, 224–227
provider panel nature, 225–226
reimbursement, 226
Ancillary care provider, managed care
  contracting, 10–11
Anti-gag rule legislation, 275–277
Antitrust, 285–303, 308–309
  agreements that lessen competition,
    289–296
  boycott, 288–289
  consolidation, 293
  current environment, 306–309
  division of markets, 289
  field comments, 306–309
  integrated delivery system, 300–301
  joint conduct, 286–288
  market monopoly, 293–296
  merger and acquisition, 293
  messenger model network, 298–300
  price fixing, 288
  provider group
    financial risk, 308–309
    market definition, 308
    operational integration, 309
    organizational structure, 308
    protective measures, 309
    provider organization development,
      307–309
  provider network, 296–298
  size of parties, 291–293
  tying, 289
  unlawful agreement, 286–289

341

# About the Author

**Wendy Knight** is President of Knight Communications and Consulting, a consulting firm specializing in health care delivery issues with a particular focus on managed care. The firm develops communication and market strategies; analyzes, establishes, and manages provider networks; conducts product and market assessments; and prepares advocacy, educational, and marketing materials for clients.

Ms. Knight has worked in the business and policy arenas of managed care. She was previously the Assistant Director of Managed Care for the Health Insurance Association of America and most recently served as the Acting Executive Director of CIGNA Managed Care Network of Northern New England. She has held contracting positions with Prudential Health Care Group, Aetna, Inc., and NYLCare.

Her extensive experience in contract negotiations and network development includes negotiating full-risk and specialty capitation contracts; establishing networks for commercial and government programs; implementing HMOs, PPOs, POS plans, and other managed care products, converting networks from fee-for-service to capitation; and developing networks in both urban and rural markets.

Ms. Knight has written extensively on managed care and other health care issues. Her work has appeared in *Group Practice Journal, Healthplan, Managing Employee Benefits*, and *Newsweek*.

# About the Contributors

**Michael J. Alper** is President of Meridian Health Care Management, LP, a company that develops and manages IPAs across the country and provides consulting services to physicians, IPAs, medical groups, and managed health care systems. He was previously Vice President of Medical Management Associates, Inc., President and CEO of Health Source Management Group (formerly, Cedars-Sinai Physicians Association), and Senior Consultant at Fred Rothenberg & Associates, Inc., a managed care consulting firm specializing in IPA management and operations. Mr. Alper received his Bachelor of Arts degree in Sociology with a health care emphasis from the University of California, Los Angeles and completed the Graduate Certificate Program in Management and Administration of Health Care Facilities at the UCLA School of Public Health and the University of Southern California Management Development in Health Care program. He has had numerous articles on managed care operations and related issues published in national journals, and is coauthor of a chapter on health insurance in a reference book for physicians. Mr. Alper holds a membership in the Healthcare Finance Managers Association, Medical Group Management Association, American College of Healthcare Executives, and other professional organizations and was a founding Board member and Vice President of the National IPA Coalition (formerly the IPA Association of California), a developing trade association for IPAs.

**Kim Bellard** is responsible for the Prudential HealthCares's Southwest Ohio, Northern Kentucky, and Southeast Indiana operations, which covers over 50,000 members in HMO, POS, and PPO plans. Prudential's managed care network in the Tri-State area consists of

2,500 physicians and 29 hospitals. Mr. Bellard previously served as Director of Health Care Policy in Prudential's corporate office, where he was responsible for staffing Prudential's executive office on the development and communication of Prudential's health care policy and in other positions at the company. He served for nine months on the minority staff of the U.S. Senate Special Committee on Aging, working on a variety of health care issues and assisted the late Senator John Heinz, the Committee's ranking minority member, on the Pepper Commission. Mr. Bellard is a summa cum laude graduate of Bowling Green State University, Bowling Green, Ohio.

**Michael J. Benenson** founded Benenson & Associates, a health care consulting firm specializing in strategic and market planning, product and service development, and the mergers, acquisitions, and valuation of health care companies. He directs the company's wide-ranging consulting activities. His current work focuses on providing these services for cardiology and oncology programs, imaging and surgery centers, and physician networks and organizations. Mr. Benenson has been a management facilitator and trainer to a variety of senior health care executives and has served as an advisor to many groups, including The Advisory Board, The Cardiology Round Table, the Association of University Programs in Health Administration, and the Advisory Council on Aging. He has published numerous articles, chapters, and studies in key industry journals from American Hospital Publishing, Aspen Publishers, Inc., Infoline, UCLA School of Medicine, and others.

**Dolores M. Blanco** is the Executive Vice President of Meridian Health Care Management, LP, where she is responsible for directing the activities of the company's network management and business development. Her consulting client work focuses on organizational structures, contracting, operations, and administration. Ms. Blanco previously served as Vice President of Managed Care Business Development with Tenet Healthcare Corporation, Manager of Network Development and Contract Services for Aetna Health Plans of Southern California, Inc., and Manager of Healthcare Delivery Systems at MetLife Healthcare Network of California. Ms. Blanco received a Bachelor of Arts degree in Microbiology and a Master of Public Health degree in Epidemiology from the University of California, Los Angeles. She is a member of the American College of Healthcare Executives,

Health Care Executives of Southern California, Women in Health Administration, and other professional organizations.

**Raymond R. Girouard, MHA, FACMPE**, is the Managed Care Director for MedPartners, Virginia Region. His experience and duties encompass a multitude of contracting venues including capitation, sub-capitation, and fee-for-service for both primary care and specialty practices. In addition to his work in contracting, Mr. Girouard has been a frequent presenter in the area of information management systems as they relate to managed care administration and capitation management. Mr. Girouard is a member of the Medical Group Management Association, a Fellow of the American College of Medical Practice Executives, and serves as the current President of the Managed Care Assembly. In addition, he is a member of the MGMA Electronic Information Standards Committee.

**Alan M. Gnessin, Esq.** entered the field of health law in 1981 as a trial attorney with the General Counsel's Office of the Health Care Financing Administration (U.S. Department of Health and Human Services). After leaving the government, he developed a specialty in managed health care law and founded Alan M. Gnessin, P.C., the predecessor to Gnessin & Waldman, P.C., in 1986. He graduated magna cum laude from Union College with a B.A. in Political Science and received his J.D. with honors at the National Law Center, The George Washington University. Mr. Gnessin lectures throughout the year and has written extensively on topics ranging from provider contracts to liability in the managed care setting.

**Richard A. Gold** is a consultant in the San Francisco office of Towers Perrin's Integrated HealthSystems Consulting. He has 16 years of health care experience with hospitals, hospital systems, and HMOs. His broad HMO management experience includes network development and contracting, new product development, and staff development. His hospital operations experience includes managing clinics, emergency services, and group practices at teaching and community hospitals. In addition, Mr. Gold has worked extensively with hospitals and physicians in diverse markets to develop integration strategies geared to strengthen the managed care position of the participants. His provider group experience with IPAs, medical groups, MSOs, and PHOs includes development, strategic planning, implementation, and ongoing operational support. Mr. Gold received his Bachelor of

Science degree from Syracuse University and his Master's degree in health administration from Tulane University.

**Steve Gutman** is a managed health care consultant with 15 years experience in the formation, operation, and marketing of nonhospital, health care provider organizations. As a Senior Consultant for Advanced Health Corporation, he has established statewide and regional physician-owned cardiology and orthopedic provider networks in New York, New Jersey, and Pennsylvania. He currently provides marketing representation for these networks. Mr. Gutman previously established and managed the Colorado Health Care Network, a statewide integrated delivery system that introduced several innovations to the market, including the first PPO for the auto insurance industry and an integrated management information system. He was a founding partner and Executive Director of The Eye Health Network, a multistate integrated eye care provider organization, and for many years provided management consulting, marketing representation, and contract negotiation services to multispecialty IPAs in the Rocky Mountain region. Mr. Gutman enjoys speaking and writing about the implications of managed health care for physicians.

**John S. Hoff, Esq.** practices law in Washington, D.C. He specializes in health care law and policy and represents clients across the range of the health care field on a variety of matters, including regulation of managed care organizations and proposals to reform health care financing and delivery systems. Mr. Hoff received his AB and LLB degrees from Harvard University.

**Donald H. Hutton, FACHE** has 26 years experience in health care management, with 15 years experience as Chief Executive Officer of large hospitals and 4 years experience as Chief Executive Officer of a large physician group. He was founder, Chairman, and Chief Executive Officer of The Morgan Health Group, an alliance of 350 independent primary care physicians. He previously served as President and Chief Executive Officer of Northside Hospital in Atlanta. Mr. Hutton is the founder of the Morgan Consulting Group, an independent consulting firm that works with hospitals and physician groups to build provider-sponsored networks and organizations. Mr. Hutton is an acknowledged expert in national health policy and has been cited as a visionary in health reform.

**John L. McDonald, MS, MPH** is the founder and a principal of McDonald & Company, a consulting firm specializing in helping physicians, hospitals, and managed care organizations meet the challenges and opportunities of the rapidly changing managed care marketplace. His two decades of health care experience include the design, reengineering, and implementation of PHOs, single and multi-specialty IPAs, and MSOs. Mr McDonald received his Master of Science degree from the University of Connecticut and his Master of Public Health degree from Boston University.

**Kathi S. Patterson, FSA, MAAA** is an Actuary with the Seattle office of Milliman & Robertson, Inc. She has been with the firm since 1995. Her area of expertise is group insurance, including medical (commercial and Medicaid), stop loss, dental, disability, and life. She focuses on health care–related issues and assists clients with benefit design, pricing, health care cost projections, rate filings, provider reimbursement and risk sharing arrangements, reinsurance, reserve adequacy analysis, experience analysis, and risk adjusters. Her clients include insurance companies, hospitals, Blue Cross/Blue Shield organizations, governments, the Veteran's Administration, physician groups, provider-owned health plans, HMOs, and PPOs. Ms. Patterson is a Fellow of the Society of Actuaries and a member of the American Academy of Actuaries. She has a Bachelor of Arts degree in mathematics from Whitman College. Before joining Milliman & Robertson, she worked for SAFECO Life Insurance Company for 10 years.

**Edward P. Potanka, Esq.** is an Assistant General Counsel of CIGNA Corporation. He is a cum laude graduate of Amherst College, where he received a Bachelor of Arts degree, and the Cornell Law School, where he received a Juris Doctor degree. He joined Connecticut General Life Insurance Company's Legal Department in 1974 and has served in a variety of capacities with Connecticut General and its successor, CIGNA Corporation. He currently counsels CIGNA HealthCare's Managed Care Operations. Mr. Potanka has authored numerous articles on insurance and managed care.

**Nancy L. Reaven** is principal and founder of Reaven Consulting Group, a health care consulting firm specializing in managed health care. Prior to founding Reaven Consulting Group, Ms. Reaven was Chief Executive Officer of a provider-sponsored organization (PSO), Managed Care Providers, Inc. Previously, she held positions as Director of Operations for Prudential Insurance Company of America and Director of Development for Maxicare Health Plans. Ms. Reaven's consulting work focuses on strategic business and market development, managed care product development, and provider system development. Her firm also develops advanced analytical financial management and sales tools. Consulting clients have included hospitals and hospital networks, MSOs, physician organizations, national home care companies, ancillary care provider networks, and health care equipment manufacturers. Ms. Reaven received her Bachelor's degree from the University of California at Berkeley and completed graduate studies in medical sociology at the University of Chicago. She is a frequent speaker at national health care conferences, and has written for several health care publications.

**Richard B. Ryan** is widely recognized as one of this nation's foremost authorities in the dental managed care industry. He began his career working for Blue Cross of California's dental program. Mr. Ryan founded Dental Management Decisions (DMD) in 1986 and became a national resource to dentists struggling with the new health care delivery system. DMD quickly gained national recognition as the only managed care consulting firm dedicated to the needs and financial interests of private dental practitioners. Mr. Ryan has become an international spokesperson for the dental profession, educating dentists about managed care programs, plan compensation, and administration. In the past 11 years, DMD has assisted more than 5,000 practitioners with practice evaluations, provider contract review and negotiations, administrative staff training, and videos and manuals. Mr. Ryan authors the *DMD News Release*, a monthly publication that discusses today's changes and challenges in the health care environment, and is a regular contributor to numerous national dental journals.

**Lisa A. Sansone** is a successful consultant in the managed care industry, with 15 years of in-depth managed care and health insurance experience. Her expertise is in managing all aspects of national network development and evaluating market potential for HMOs, PPOs, and other managed care networks. Ms. Sansone was employed by CIGNA Corporation for 13 years, most recently as a Director for CIGNA HealthCare. She is the owner and President of Nutmeg Consulting, Inc. and a senior consultant with Knight Communications and Consulting.

**Kenneth W. Schafermeyer, PhD** earned a Ph.D in Pharmacy Administration from Purdue University in 1990. Before that he served 9 years as executive director and lobbyist for 2 state pharmacy associations and served as consultant for several managed care Medicaid agencies. Currently he is Associate Professor of Pharmacy Administration and Director of Graduate Studies at the St. Louis College of Pharmacy. Dr. Schafermeyer is a coauthor of 6 books. He has conducted research and written extensively about health economics, public policy issues related to medication usage, managed care coverage of pharmaceuticals, and the outcomes of prescription drug therapy. He was the 1996 Outstanding Educator of the year for the St. Louis College of Pharmacy and also received the Emerson Electric Excellence in Teaching Award in 1996.

**Philip A. Shelton, MD, JD, FACS, FCLM** is a graduate of Columbia College, the New York University College of Medicine, and the University of Connecticut School of Law. He has been practicing medicine in Connecticut since 1964, and was admitted to the Connecticut Bar in 1979. Dr. Shelton is the senior partner of Shelton & Shelton, a law and consulting firm in West Hartford, Connecticut whose clients are predominantly managed care organizations and medical practices. Dr. Shelton is also a founding director of ConnectiCare, Inc., the largest not-for-profit HMO in Connecticut with over 195,000 members and over 3,000 participating physicians. He served as Chairman of its Board of Directors for more than 9 years, and as its President and Chief Executive Officer. Dr. Shelton has lectured and published extensively on the interface between law and medicine. He has served as President of the Connecticut Society of Eye Physicians and as Chairman of the Connecticut State Medical Society Committees on State and National Legislation. Dr. Shelton practices both medicine and law, consults nationally in the areas of practice management, managed care and physician integration, and currently serves on the Board of Governors of the American College of Legal Medicine.

**Eric Sorkin, RPh** is currently Vice President of Provider Relations for Express Scripts. Mr. Sorkin also plays an active role in the areas of corporate strategic planning, sales and marketing, and the international businesses of Express Scripts. He has over 20 years of diverse health care experience including negotiating managed care contracts, evaluating pharmacy performance, and developing pharmacy cognitive service and quality assurance programs. Mr. Sorkin was previously Vice President of both the Rite-Aid Corporation and Pathmark, Senior

Vice President of Thrifty and Pharmacy Direct Network, and President of Sorkin Consulting. His retail pharmaceutical experience includes operations, personnel, pharmaceutical purchasing, and managed health care. Mr. Sorkin has been successfully involved in the start-up and growth of health care companies. He has consulted for pharmacy benefit management companies, health care software companies, health care financial institutions, legal firms, and large retail pharmacy chains. Mr. Sorkin has served on PBM and HMO advisory panels, state and national health care committees, government affairs committees, and a health care software company board of directors. He has also lectured at many regional and national events and taught courses at numerous universities. Mr. Sorkin received his Bachelor of Science degree in pharmacy from Brooklyn College of Pharmacy, Long Island University.

**C. Joël Van Over, Esq.** is a tenured counsel with Swidler & Berlin, Chartered, in Washington, D.C. She graduated magna cum laude from Boston College Law School in 1983. A former health care consultant, Ms. Van Over specializes in antitrust; in particular, health care antitrust counseling, litigation, and confidential internal compliance reviews.

**Peggy M. Vargas** is the Director of Administrative Services for Dental Management Decisions (DMD), a managed care consulting firm specializing in dental practice management. She conducts administrative training programs for dental practices. Prior to joining DMD, Ms. Vargas held a variety of positions in a large group dental practice and was a provider relations representative for Blue Cross of California. Ms. Vargas has had numerous articles published in the *DMD News Release* and in a national PPO quarterly newsletter. She is the author and presenter of a series of training videos for the dental practitioner participating in managed care.

**M. Toni Waldman, Esq.** began her law career in health care law upon graduation from Syracuse University Law School where she was a member of the Law Review. A partner in her firm since 1993, Ms. Waldman also graduated from Smith College with a Bachelor of Arts degree in American Studies and did graduate work at the Maxwell School of Citizenship in the Master of Public Administration program. At her firm, Ms. Waldman has concentrated on preparing provider contracts and counseling clients on a wide array of regulatory matters. She has also presented papers on a variety of managed health care law topics.

**Vance J. Weber, MD, FACC** obtained his medical degree at S.U.N.Y. Upstate Medical Center in Syracuse, New York and trained in internal medicine and cardiovascular diseases at Boston University Medical Center. During his fellowship training he performed basic science research in the then-emerging area of interventional cardiology. His experimentation was centered on mechanisms of angioplasty and restenosis in animal models and resulted in publications and presentations at national meetings, including the American College of Cardiology and the American Heart Association. He obtained a post-fellowship academic position as a staff cardiologist at Long Island Jewish Medical Center in New York and in 1985 entered private practice in New Jersey with continued practice in clinical interventional cardiology. In 1993, he began to develop interest and expertise in the economics of health care and was instrumental in fostering the development of various physician-led organizations designed to effectively cope with the rapid changes occurring in the medical delivery system. Dr. Weber is the President of Mid-Atlantic Cardiology, P.A., the largest integrated cardiology group in New Jersey, and Cardiology First of New Jersey, P.A., a statewide network of cardiologists. He also has leadership roles with Specialist Physicians MSO, L.L.C, a unique multispecialty organization composed of specialists, and a local primary care IPA.

**Richard M. Weinberg, MD** joined the executive staff at Morristown Memorial Hospital (now Atlantic Health System) and the Mountainside Hospital as the President Chief Executive Officer of Morristown Memorial Physician Hospital Organization, Inc. (MMPHO), and the Executive Director of the Mountainside Hospital PHO in 1995. He has administrative responsibilities for radiology and laboratory services at Morristown Memorial Hospital. Dr. Weinberg has 20 years of practice experience in pulmonary and critical care medicine, and in 1978 was appointed the Medical Director of Respiratory Care Services at Morristown Memorial Hospital and the head of the pulmonary and critical care medicine section in the Department of Medicine. While the medical director of MMPHO, he participated in managed care contracting and oversaw the PHO's quality assurance and utilization management programs. A graduate of the Albany Medical College of Union University, Dr. Weinberg completed his postgraduate training at Georgetown

University Medical Center. He is a member of the American College of Physician Executives.

**Ross Wetsel, DDS** is President and CEO of Grant/Moana Dental Offices, a group practice in Reno, Nevada. He is also co-owner of a forty-operatory dental facility. He graduated from Baylor Dental College in 1963. Dr. Wetsel has practiced general dentistry in the U.S. Air Force and is currently in private practice. He is a member of the American Dental Association, Nevada Dental Association, Northern Nevada Dental Society, and American Academy of Dental Group Practice.

**Beth Winter** is currently Senior Director, Provider Relations for NYLCare Health Plans of the Mid-Atlantic, Inc., a 400,000 member, multi-product health plan that extends from Baltimore to Tidewater, Virginia. Her extensive managed care background includes leadership positions with Kaiser Permanente's southern California region, UCLA Medical Center and Medical Group, and an integrated delivery system associated with Inova Health System in northern Virginia.

**Ruth Zachary, MSW, CSW** is a health care manager with more than 13 years of provider-side managed care experience. She currently serves as the Executive Director of the West Park Medical Group, PC, a private group practice in New York City. Ms. Zachary has responsibility for the group's business planning and for the management of its global risk arrangements including contracting, network development, and utilization and cost management. In addition, Ms. Zachary is the founder of Private Practice Managed Care, Inc., a consulting firm offering practice management and managed care expertise and education to physician groups, PHOs, faculty practices, and individual physicians.